MORE THAN COINCIDENCE

More Than Coincidence

MALCOLM G. MACKAY

THE SAINT ANDREW PRESS
EDINBURGH

First published in 1979 by
THE SAINT ANDREW PRESS
121 George Street, Edinburgh EH2 4YN

ISBN 0 7152 0416 5 (CASED)
ISBN 0 7152 0445 9 (LIMP)

Printed in Great Britain by
Robert MacLehose and Co. Ltd.
Printers to the University of Glasgow

Contents

Thanks To William Barclay . . .

In April 1973, after a delay of nearly six months, I finally decided to post a letter to Professor Barclay. It had been written while I was Minister for the Navy in the Australian Government, after being captivated by some telecast lectures by that matchless old teacher. Like millions of others, I had seen what I had thought to be dry subjects come alive as he presented them simply and authoritatively.

There was one lecture dealing with situation ethics in which several things had troubled me. Many of the points under discussion had meant a great deal to me for I was by training and background a Christian minister, then serving in national defence. It was after seeing that lecture that I dictated my letter to Dr Barclay, but later felt that it was far too presumptuous of me to send it. My personal secretary, however, had become more than a little interested in the discussion and had frequently pressed me to post it. I did so, together with a note explaining the delay.

Almost by return mail came a long and gracious reply, readily admitting that one of my criticisms was perfectly correct and on another point detailed discussion commenced which we continued by correspondence. That was the beginning of a friendship which grew more significant for me in the following five years until his death.

In July 1973 I wrote to let him know that my wife and I would be visiting Britain later that year. At once came a letter inviting me to contact him on arrival to make arrangements to meet. Thus began several hours-long lunches in the University of Glasgow Staff Club, where I sat at his side – always on the left so that I had access to his hearing aid. In those times we talked intimately, sharing our deepest convictions and experiences on many themes, such as our children, war, the Christian's death, life after death, and much more.

During this time I passed on to him many of the stories which make up this book, and each time, as he rejoiced in new evidence of faith rewarded, of God's power at work in his world, Willie would say, 'Now that must go into a book'. When I returned to Australia I wrote to thank him for his kindness and included these words:

> Since our talks I have felt increasingly strongly that I want to work on a book in which I would tell, somewhat autobiographically, the way in which I have come to a new and virile faith, and the great hope I now have for the future . . .

Thereafter by correspondence, and later by two visits to Scotland, the shape of this book grew under Barclay's generous encouragement. I recall one luncheon when I raised the topic of the way I believed we Christians had shrunk the global significance of Jesus of Nazareth to make him just one more of the religious leaders of the world, the patron of one of the many religious sects of mankind. I put it this way:

> It seems to me that when Jesus said 'No man comes to the Father but by me', he could be interpreted in two ways. One way would be to argue that, unless a man became a Christian in the technical sense, subscribing to the basic Christian creed, then he could not truly know God. The other way would be to assert that no man can have a true and valid experience of God, whether he yet sees and understands it or not, except through Christ, for Christ is the Word by which the one and only God enters his created world.

Barclay said instantly:

> Of course it is the second, but remember, Jesus did not say 'No man can come to GOD but by me', but 'No man can come to the FATHER but by me.' There is the difference. It is only through Jesus that we can know God as the one whom Jesus could call Father.'

During the next two years we had many such meetings, and to my sorrow I saw this gallant old man with his giant library of a brain getting weaker and weaker physically while his mind and spirit were as strong as ever. We talked deeply, and at times he told marvellous stories, for he had a roguish sense of humour. He persistently urged me to complete my writing, counselling against what he felt to be a fatal error of mulling over and over what had been written. He seemed to think that all writers could commend the flow of knowledge and skill to plunge straight ahead with their subject, as he could.

Finally, there came the day when I slipped into his home in Glasgow with a loose-leaf binder filled with typescript, some three-quarters of which is now this book. He came to the door himself, in pyjamas, explaining that he had not had a good day. But he took me into his study and after ten minutes or so I left, hoping that he would find time to read what I had written. A fortnight later I was invited to return, which I did. Before Mrs Barclay could come in with the tea he made my spirits dance with his pronouncement: 'I've read your book. It's a real thriller. Do get on and finish it without delay.'

We had long before discussed his writing a foreword for it, but I could now see that this was not to be. Less than a month after that he died. I happened to call to see how he was on the day that he was leaving for the hospital. Mrs Barclay didn't say much, but I knew that I would never see my friend again. Then came the announcement which went across the globe – the great Willie Barclay was with his Lord whom he loved so deeply and had served so magnificently.

Many knew him longer and more deeply than I, but I can only say how profoundly he has affected my life. Without his unhesitating and robust encouragement I would never have dared to uproot my family and home and come to Scotland to write. Even now it seems presumptuous, but that is how I have come to write this book.

Malcolm Mackay
Dumfries,
Scotland

Introduction

This is a book about experiments across the frontiers of the mind. It begins with the story of a search which I have been carrying out over the past few years, ever since I spent five days in the company of a man whose confidence and gaiety challenged my own widening penumbra of cynicism and gloom.

If the stories he told were true, and I was determined to sift and search them out, then it was time for a new dimension to come into my thinking.

The stirrings of hope and anticipation which he aroused were at first shattered and then moved into a higher gear by the news that he had died some five days later. I received the news with resentment because I felt that I had been cheated. This man, who had not only a first-class intellect, global experience and a vivid faith, was dead, and so, it seemed, was my own opportunity to work over some of the ploys with him which had been stirring in my mind.

Then we received two letters from him, posted on the day he had died – one to my wife and the other to my son. Both were delightful and Ruth's letter concluded 'merry days ahead'. Somehow that clicked into place in my mind. So did another and compelling thought: 'What if those five days you had with Roger, at the end of his sixty-seven rich and productive years, were for the express purpose of passing over to you some of the unfinished business of which he spoke?'

That thought felt rather like a challenge if not a commission. I went to his funeral service in Sydney, and found it unlike any I'd experienced before. A bishop spoke of what this man had meant in stirring his faith; a top civil servant in the foreign affairs field did likewise; and a bearded, long-haired, hippy-type youth confided in me his sorrow that he had not spent more time with him, adding 'That man was a flippin' prophet!' The atmosphere was triumphant.

In the five years which have followed I have come into direct contact with people in many countries who have not only confirmed the extraordinary events Roger had described, but added a wealth of new facts, which, I believe, are highly relevant to the future of mankind.

Then too there have been my personal discoveries which have increasingly changed the course of my life, united my family, and given us a real sense of purpose in a world where, to be frank, I once felt it had been a mistake to have children at all.

The story which is told in this book is not in the form of a journal from that day to this, but rather is an attempt to put together a large number of stories, a wealth of evidence, into some semblance of order. To pass on to others, as accurately as possible, not only a lot of almost incredible happenings and 'coincidences', but to put them into a developmental framework, to point to a way they can become real for everyone.

Man is distinguished from the lower animals in that the major thrust of his existence is an endless search for a surer way, a superior wisdom and a better life. We have lived into an age where science and technology have appeared to answer most of these urges, only to find ourselves in dire distress. We are being forced to go on and on along roads which we fear will increasingly lead to disaster.

Perhaps it is high time to look in other directions for that surer way, superior wisdom, and hope of a better life!

Rather than begin with stories from our highly developed western world, I invite you first to consider two incidents described to me by one of the most hard-headed businessmen I have ever met, about a race considered to be the most primitive people on earth – the Australian Aborigines.

The Aborigine is the least 'developed' man on earth in terms of our modern technologies and standards. He never learnt to built a hut or sow seed, to plant anything or develop a machine more complicated than a boomerang. Yet his skills in other fields are tremendous. He can exist in deserts where you and I would perish; he can see signs and trails which are impossible for us to discern; he can sit immobile for hours where our restlessness would drive us to distraction. But he has also developed another faculty – one which western man may have lost to the very peril of his existence – a capacity to reach out beyond the physical and material world in the extension of his mind and psyche into the 'numinous', the mist-shrouded dreamtime world of a transcendent reality which we try to describe by calling it intuition.

It is in order to pass on some of the evidence I have discovered which relates to this bigger world of what we can only call 'the spirit' that this book is written. We go first to the wide, silent horizons of the trackless bush of Central Australia, and from there follow through what I am convinced is a proper and orderly progression or voyage of discovery into this new world – actually the oldest of all, but startlingly new for most modern men facing the consequences of a narrow, materialist specialisation. Specialisation, says the ancient law, leads to extinction.

To make matters more complicated and very much more urgent, the twentieth century has also seen the emergence of reactionary philosophies, of deliberate reversion to the jungle, with the destruction of all the rules and standards which mankind has so painfully discerned as essential for his growth out of the trees and the brutishness and misery of sub-animal behaviour. Combative materialism holds up the barrel of the gun, the appeal to hate and the law of the sharpest tooth and claw, as the great 'discoveries' for the future! The choice before mankind is literally one of following this death-wish of 'back to the jungle', or of a rediscovery of the basic propulsive power behind our common humanity and our growth into a life which reaches out from the clay towards a reality which transcends the physical senses.

This book is primarily a look at some of the evidence for that reality. In the course of my search, however, fresh insights have emerged in my personal 'theology' and new certainty has developed around some of the great doctrines of the Christian faith. More than this, I believe that these experiences have pointed out new paths ahead, insights into ways whereby the one God who made us all and is the Father of us all, may bring increasing unity to his large and divided human family.

CHAPTER 1

The greatest need of mankind today – socially and individually – is a true sense of direction. Our world is like an Atlantic liner deprived of rudder, compass, sextant, charts and wireless tackle, yet compelled to go full steam ahead. There is magnificence, comfort, pulsating power; but whither are we going? Does that depend solely on the accident of circumstance and the ever-changing balance of conflicting interests and ambitions? Or is there available for man, if he so will, guidance on his dark and dangerous course from some Wisdom higher than his own?

B H Streeter, *The God Who Speaks*

We moderns are faced with the necessity of re-discovering the life of the spirit . . . it is the only way in which we can break the spell that binds us to the cycle of biological events . . . There is nothing that can free us from this bond except that opposite urge of life – the spirit.

C G Jung, *Modern Man in Search of a Soul*

Obviously, many primitive intuitions have been corrupted and blunted by civilization and speculation; but I still believe that both these have collected, and continue to collect the elements of an intuition far superior to that of primitive men (or, if you prefer, I believe that they are collecting the elements of a much better practical application of primitive intuitions). However, mysticism remains the great science and the great art, the only power capable of synthesizing the riches accumulated by other forms of human activity.

Teilhard de Chardin, *Letters from a Traveller*, pp 86–7

CHAPTER ONE

Out of Silence

The plane carrying the Flying Doctor touched down at a remote Northern Territory cattle station and my friend got out to exchange greetings with the manager. While they were talking he noticed an aged Aboriginal sitting on a rock staring into space. The bearded figure, half naked, was completely immobile.

'What's the trouble with Jackie?' he asked the manager.

'Well, it looks as if he's getting a message of some kind – best not disturb him', was the reply.

A full half-hour later, just before take-off, Jackie stirred from his place, slid down the side of the boulder and slowly walked across to the group.

'Well Jackie, what's the news?' the manager greeted him.

'Boss, I must go.'

'What for Jackie?'

'My brother, him die', was the laconic reply.

The manager had experienced this kind of thing before and he accepted it without further comment. Turning to the pilot he said 'Are you going anywhere near Numminbah?' mentioning a place some three hundred miles distant. It so happened that the pilot was scheduled to pass in that direction, so the manager asked if he could give the old man a lift to save him days of walking.

My friend, with the Aborigine, the pilot and the patient went aboard the little plane, and nearly two hours later they circled and touched down at an airstrip near the old man's tribal home. There, waiting for him on the strip, was a group of his own people! There had been no communication, other than the same kind of primal intelligence that had flowed to the old man as he sat immobile on the rock.

Coincidence? Those who have had experience with the Australian Aborigines know that the statistics are against such an explanation.

This friend of mine himself owns a large cattle station in the Northern Territory, carrying more than ten thousand head of cattle. Most of the work on his station is carried out by Aborigines belonging to the local tribe.

During the hottest part of summer, in January and February, it is usual for the tribe to go walkabout. They take themselves off to live by hunting, reverting back to the age-old primitive lifestyle which is so near to their hearts. During this time the station is almost deserted.

On one such occasion a heatwave more severe than usual was causing great distress to the cattle. Pregnant cows were prematurely dropping their calves and the earth was so hot that the calves were dying as a result. The very few people on the station tried in vain to cope with the enormous task, but there was no way at all of getting in touch with their Aboriginal workmen. Then, almost as if there had been a radio broadcast received by the tribesmen, they began to drift back into camp. When asked the reason for coming back weeks ahead of schedule the reply was generally the same. One of their number actually spent fifty-three dollars of his own money in taking a taxi back from Tennant Creek because of his inner sense of urgency. He put it simply:

'Boss, I just knew the station was in trouble.'

Coincidence? It is impossible to believe that this is an adequate explanation. ESP, thought-transference, call it what you will, such words are only to give a name not an explanation. Here is one of those phenomena beyond the fringe of everyday experience which are on occasions available to the human mind and spirit. Indeed, many people have come to believe that, having crossed the frontiers into space, mankind has still one last and ultimate territory to explore, namely the world of the spirit. Perhaps this is mankind's ultimate birthright.

This is not to suggest, of course, that there is a continually mounting curve of progression from primitive man through modern technology into such spiritual awareness. There could even be quite a strong argument to the contrary. For example, it would appear to be among the less 'developed' countries, in the western sense, that intuitive rather than reasoning processes dominate decision-making.

In late 1977 I was invited to participate in a fascinating house party in the home of a leading official in the EEC to which Members of the European Parliament and Ambassadors from African, Caribbean and Pacific (ACP) developing countries were invited, together with their wives. The purpose of the gathering was to develop the theme of an earlier meeting at Scy-Chazelles, former residence of Robert Schuman, which was described as 'a plea for intuition in a technological world'. The official EEC Journal *The Courier*,[1] reported:

> In the peace of Scy-Chazelles, it was the EEC delegates who listened, perhaps for the first time, to what the ACP countries had to offer them – if there is material poverty on the one side, there is spiritual poverty on the other, and in the latter respect Europe received a timely warning.
>
> One top official of the ACP–EEC Council of Ministers said at the end of the first day that she had heard words at Scy-Chazelles she had never heard before in all the days and nights they had worked together. These were the words

> that led the current Vice-President of the European Parliament to conclude: 'I never imagined that such profound thought could emerge from so few hours of work. There is material inequality between us, inevitably, but how should we determine the level? Criteria based on wealth will disappear, but we have much to learn about the real ways of measuring things. We must change the established, or apparently established, order. We have seen it held up to question. Our ignorance of your soul, your heart and your state of mind is frightening. We must come together. We will never do things in the same way again.'
>
> The message from these 'underdeveloped' continents was an appeal to a Europe in danger of losing its soul. 'Perhaps we are the deviants', the head of the European Institute of Ecology in Metz suggested; 'we have developed the powers of analysis of the human brain and this has provided us with our technological development, but we have allowed our intuitive faculties to lie dormant. We know where power will lead us if it is not wisely used, and this is why we must be ready to listen to what traditional societies have to say. We need their help to find our lost soul and to ensure that there is a future for life on Earth.'

Having passed through an age in which the wide horizons and seemingly limitless opportunities of science and technology have provided the major incentives for the young, we are now seeing a marked reaction, if not a direct reversal of such values. Materialism is becoming a dirty word among significant groups of youth in the 'developed countries' also.

After completing his year as Moderator of the Church of Scotland, the Very Rev Dr T F Torrance recently reported that, in conversations with the heads of universities and colleges throughout the nation, the one word most frequently used to describe the modern student was the word 'religious'. This by no means implies churches full to overflowing on university campuses, but it does mean that modern students are increasingly aware of capacities within their own nature which clamour for fulfilment and which exceed those of the purely material. From the occult to the charismatic movement there is an increasing probing of things relating to the 'spiritual' nature of man.

It has been contended that man is distinguished from the animal kingdom in that he is a 'religious' animal, that he has within him not only the capacity to reason and the compulsions of 'ought' and 'ought not' – primitive incentives and sanctions which lead to developed personal and social behaviour patterns – but also a yearning after things which transcend his five senses, which are unseen, mysteriously powerful and link him with the eternal.

If the great religions have a basic validity then all must begin with the hypothesis that man has within him a capacity to know and come into his own personal relationship with this mysterious world of the spirit. It is this objective which has been so greatly neglected or even rejected in recent centuries of frenzied struggle for material development, for scientific and technological achievement, when success has been measured in terms of the number of things a man possesses or the salary he commands. There has until recently been little room for the entirely different set of values which characterise man's spiritual development.

But now the golden road which once seemed unending appears to be leading to the edge of a chasm which could spell global disaster. The values and incentives of materialism and the results of the technological 'achievements' of mankind appear to threaten his very existence.

The Club of Rome in its third report outlines eight major areas where disaster looms ahead if mankind pursues his present policies:

The arms race is depriving mankind of enormous financial and human resources as 'almost half the world's scientific and technological manpower devote their skills to military research and development'.[2] Military expenditures are almost three hundred thousand million dollars a year, and by the 1980's the world's nuclear reactors will have produced about a million pounds of plutonium, enough to manufacture fifty thousand bombs. The Club of Rome gave a solemn warning on the situation when they said:

> The problem is not to shift from a war to a peace economy, but from a war to a peace mentality. Whether mankind is able to achieve this will largely determine its chances of surviving the twentieth century.[3]

World population problems mount, but not just in terms of numbers. The rate of shifts of population to the cities from the country is an even greater problem, and slums are growing much faster still. Many demographers consider that the world population will increase to three or four times its present size by the middle of the twenty-first century, before reaching a reasonably stable or stationary position. The resulting pressures on social and economic systems, especially in the poorer countries, is barely imaginable.

Food at once comes to mind as a major problem. Despite all our agricultural know-how, and the global publicity directed to the problem, over three hundred million children today suffer from grossly retarded physical growth and development, while many more are undernourished. Northern America with Australia and New Zealand are the exporters of cereals to the rest of mankind, whose production is inadequate, and getting more so. Eighty-five percent of the world's fertiliser production is controlled by the industrialised countries, and is dictated by market forces which militate against the most needy underdeveloped and poorer countries. The small farmer everywhere carries increasing burdens, and the countryside gets less and less economically attractive in terms of residence and employment. The United States Secretary for Agriculture may have had a CIA report indicating that their food surplus gave them 'a virtual life and death power over the fate of the multitudes of needy' when he stated:

> Food is a weapon. It is one of the principal tools in our negotiating kit.[4]

From a largely rural population at the beginning of the twentieth century the earth is becoming largely urbanised. The Highland Clearances of the eighteenth century in Scotland, whereby peasants and small farmers were driven off their land by the aristocracy who were turning to large-scale sheep farming, are now being re-enacted on a global scale. Especially in the less developed countries this shift of population to the cities is accelerating. By the end of this century possibly half the world's population will inhabit some three hundred to four hundred huge cities.

The life-support systems of our human environment are belatedly becoming the object of global concern. This is a little-known area of science and most major questions are unanswered. The very habitability of our planet is at stake, and as populations and cities grow, as industries produce more and more sophisticated by-products and waste, it is not inconceivable that we could pass the limits set by nature in order to preserve the living environment.

As the various areas of mounting problems are considered, and one could go on to discuss water and energy resources, the use of the oceans and of outer space, as well as the rapidly mounting crisis in monetary and trading systems, a common denominator clearly emerges. The Club of Rome report puts it succinctly:

> Few of mankind's pressing problems have purely national solutions, they call for co-operative solutions: actions multilaterally and globally . . . without concern for a common interest, the agenda of 'high politics' is in danger of becoming hopelessly overloaded . . .[5]

'The idea of brotherhood is not new', Leon Eisenberg said in 1974, 'but what is special to our times is that brotherhood has become the precondition for survival.'[6]

Many years ago the famous Oxford theologian Canon B H Streeter foresaw this when he warned 'a race which has grown up intellectually must grow up morally and spiritually or perish'.

It may well prove, however, that developing interest in the realm of the spirit may yet point to the salvation of the human race by establishing other values, standards and objectives than the increasingly destructive ones bred of competition, and the insatiable clamour for more and more, both for oneself or one's group.

The Club of Rome looks toward some form of world government as a solution, while choosing to assume that, at least in theory, all nations wish for these problems to be solved in a way which ensures peace and freedom. But surely not everyone is thinking in these terms. The followers and successors of Marx and Engels have opted for a retaliatory form of massive collective materialism on the part of the underdog, using the same dangerous values as dominant motives for the masses as have already proved disastrous in the ruling minority.

Yet as the years pass, it becomes more and more apparent that Marxism is being no more successful than capitalism, nor what has loosely been called democratic socialism, in producing the 'new man', the man who is basically brotherly and unselfish and prepared to live by the idealist creed of contributing to society according to his ability and only demanding those things which he actually needs. More and more the centralist states turn to the constraints of force, censorship and iron curtains, backed by the massive retaliation of the state against any divergence from orthodoxy to ensure adherence to their creed. Their ideology has failed. Thus in both East and West today freedom is being destroyed. Even the limited freedom still known in western competitive society steadily diminishes as the concept degenerates into mere demand for licence for each individual or group to seek its own advantage.

Yet despite all this a near miracle, which a few years ago would have seemed to be utterly impossible, seems to be emerging – that a generation could yet arise which sets little store by material possessions and the enticements of affluence and luxury. Such people are looking elsewhere for the values, ends and goals of living. Universities and colleges, and indeed most of the places where younger people meet today, are thronged with those who wear the simplest of clothing and who have seriously challenged, and in many cases rejected what were sacrosanct standards, authorities and objectives for living, unquestioned until a generation ago.

A great deal of this has been naive in the extreme and in some cases deliberately provocative and destructive, but the exciting and challenging fact is that there is so much readiness and eagerness for fundamental change. Large numbers are apparently no longer predisposed to that individualist drive for affluence which had become a basic characteristic of western man. The facts of the situation are making themselves felt.

The question which emerges however is what will be the source of authority and the basis of decision-making in the lives of those seeking radical change.

Seated in the lounge of the European Parliament in Luxembourg recently I was interested to see a group including some Scottish trawlermen come and sit nearby. They were joined by some United Kingdom members of the Parliament and then another man who was introduced as the then President of the Assembly. He listened to the case put on behalf of the Scottish fishermen, and finally made his reply. His first words were: 'Well, as you know, I am first and foremost a ——' (giving the name of his country, of which he was Foreign Minister). I thought then how far we were from a global body of world statesmen who could think and act above national or sectional advantage, when after two world wars and a decade of determined effort the spirit of even the European experiment is so volatile.

If not a global law-enforcement agency, then what?

Global dictatorship by the finally victorious super-power? Such a possibility is fraught with the ultimate in terms of danger, and certain only to be achieved over the corpses and ashes of most of the civilised world.

Is there any other way?

The only alternative is in the movement towards a radically new concept of man, his value and values, his destiny and his inter-relatedness. The growing accent on 'human rights' is a response to this new note in international affairs. There is only one choice – for either it is true that man is no more than a materialist animal, incurably selfish and resentful of others, or he is in embryo a child of God, however that expression may yet be interpreted. There are few things more powerful than an idea when its time has come, and especially if it is presented to waiting mankind as a living reality. The demonstration of a way of life which satisfies deeper desires, fulfils more imperative demands, opens new and exciting areas of growth and adventure. Such a force could set ablaze the tinder-dry desert of human and international affairs and turn the course of history.

There is an immediate and reasonable suspicion which arises when such revolutionary changes are envisaged and that is whether we are not simply looking for some way of escape, of putting the ugly facts of the mess we have created on planet earth into the 'too hard' basket, and opting for pie in the sky. Are we really on the track of a comprehensive and adequate answer, or of a Shangri-La? How relevant is the search for the fifth dimension of the spirit to the other four of the natural world? Can this possibly prove to be the missing part of the jigsaw which will help rearrange the pieces to make a new and viable pattern?

If our enquiry is to be relevant, if we are to begin to hope that there is a way which can bring an answer to the massive and global problems of our day, then there are at least five criteria which must be satisfied:

First the method must be universally valid and available everywhere, even to the simplest people on earth.

Then such a way must have deep and compelling appeal, able to lay hold of the hearts and minds of countless people, to offer them hope and inspire their loyalty and enthusiasm.

Again, there must be a latent source of power available which has the capacity to effect the most fundamental and radical changes in the lives of individuals and in the systems and structures of nations.

Directing and guiding it all there must be a source of intelligent and purposeful initiative which is able to comprehend the entire global course of events and transcend the inadequate capacities of the past and even the current dictates of the superpowers or of international organisations.

Finally there must be a basic freedom which characterises this way, which means not that everyone does as he likes but everyone can like what he does; where the inner sense of 'ought' and 'ought not' in every man is fully compatible with the ethos, values and constraints of the new society; where the individual is free to be and to grow and reproduce in kind in a hospitable environment.

This may seem to be a long way from those simple stories of the Australian Aborigines, and yet the implications of such examples of primal communication are deserving of study. For example, it is worth pondering the kind of character which is able to apprehend and respond positively to those two different instances of inspired action, the kind of man who can conclude:

'I must go back to the station homestead.'

'I must be willing to spend my own money to take a taxi.'

'I must be prepared to walk three hundred miles.'

'People need my help – so I must drop my own plans and go . . .'

Behind and within these simple examples lies a developed and developing concern to honour kinsfolk, the tribe and its laws; to have care and responsibility for friends and employers, even of another race; to act selflessly in terms of money, personal possessions etc. Indeed as one ponders such incidents one begins to ask much more fundamental questions still, such as 'who are the more civilised in today's world: simple people with such values or the highly developed pressure and power-exploiting groupings of capital and labour in the western world?'

Quite apart from personal and ethical considerations there is also the disturbing possibility that so-called 'civilised' man in such situations would be frustrated by the narrow confines of his own constructions. He would be out of touch by telephone or radio, he would therefore have no facts to go on about conditions in remote places, so part of his mind would be closed. His day would be filled with talk and activity so that the possibility of the expansion of his area of responsibility and activity into wider realms than those controlled by his own known capacities would be very remote. The adventure of stepping off on an unknown path for an inexplicable reason, responding to an 'inner voice', the prompting from an uncontrolled and uncontrollable extension of his own being, and there finding purpose and fulfilment – such experience is all too often denied modern man. The very ways by which this inner source of direction and initiative can be at first detected and then encouraged, enhanced and developed are well-nigh unknown to western civilisation. The 'guidelines' of intuition, the ground rules for the sensitising of one's mind and spirit to new dimensions of consciousness which are healthy and sound is therefore one of the prime objectives of our search.

CHAPTER 2

The way to a knowledge of God will be through a re-orientation of purpose and desire, and a constant re-dedication of the self to the highest that it knows. If that be so, we should expect to find that, at a certain point of spiritual development, the personality will become sufficiently sensitive to the influence of the Divine to reach an awareness of God's will which may find expression through a voice within.

It is a historical fact that the hearing of such a voice on certain occasions by certain individuals, for example the prophets of the Old Testament, has made epochs in human history. With more ordinary men and women, on more ordinary occasions, a similar awareness may express itself in the urge of conscience or the conviction of divine guidance in the affairs of daily life.

B H Streeter, *The God Who Speaks*

Even as light and colour and sound come into our minds at the prompting of a world beyond, so these other stirrings of consciousness come from something which, whether we describe it as beyond or deep within ourselves, is greater than our own personality . . . The man who commonly spoke of his ordinary surroundings in scientific language would be insufferable. If God means anything in our daily lives, I do not think we should feel any disloyalty to truth in speaking and thinking of Him unscientifically, any more than in speaking and thinking unscientifically of our human companions.

Sir Arthur Eddington, *New Pathways in Science*

CHAPTER TWO

Just Conscience

When the matter of an 'inner voice' is raised many people respond by saying, 'Oh, you mean the conscience!' This description cannot be rejected, at least out of hand, even though it does precious little to supply any worthwhile explanation. I suppose when I myself use the word conscience I do generally mean an inner voice, but one which has certain limitations. I think of it as the voice of one's better self, of a developed capacity to compare and criticise one's own action, or inaction, in accordance with one's own standards of right and wrong. It is essentially a matter of conforming to previously established guidelines. When it transcends this and breaks new ground, when it ventures into new and untrod paths of behaviour, of determining new criteria of right and wrong, then I tend to call it something else, something more than conscience.

One of the very early stories about this larger-than-conscience process at work is the biblical incident when the patriarch Abraham at first felt obliged, by his conscience if you like, to demonstrate his complete submission to his God by conforming to the barbaric practice of his day and offering his own son as a burnt offering. Abraham is at first seen as obeying this inner urge, right to the point of slaying Isaac; but when the knife was about to descend and complete just one more ritual killing, in that moment when he was totally prepared and ready to complete the act dictated by his conscience, then another more powerful voice spoke to him. This was not the voice of his paternal love or of reluctance to kill his son, nor of rejecting his religious obligations, but a positive and clear sense that his God did not wish the lad to be harmed – that the place of the human being should be taken by an animal. This was new and revolutionary thinking. It altered the course of history.

In that moment of enhanced obedience to that larger inner voice the religious life of mankind took a giant stride into the future. Human sacrifice became now and forever a wrongful and outmoded practice in the eyes of Abraham and his people. This remarkable man had once more listened, obeyed, and found fulfilment of his being in a new and deeply satisfying way. All this was possible because he had already developed his touch with this inner voice, trusting it so deeply and completely that he could pack his belongings and move with his family out into an unknown country. He left behind his own land, with its mystical relationship to his God, obeying the imperious voice which made the then incredible proposition that his God would go too, no longer confined by territory and geography. Two thousand years later an unknown writer to the Hebrews put it succinctly, 'by faith Abraham obeyed and went out . . . not knowing where he was to go.' Islam, Judaism and Christianity all look back to that moment as one of the great formative acts of implicit obedience which laid the foundations of their faith.

This is far more than conscience at work, for here is evidence of a guiding, directing force which builds on the willingness of man to listen and obey. New criteria of right and wrong emerge, and conscience, the developing repository or guardian of such new truth, itself thereby moves forward.

The stories from the *Book of Genesis*, stretching back thousands of years into antiquity, are however open to some question. Are they exact records of the actual events as they occurred or are they interpretations, the developed versions of religious lore, later shaped to make the point of a faith rewarded? With the stories of Abraham we have much archeological support but we cannot give a conclusive reply except by intuition or faith itself, yet these stories are far from unique. It makes all the difference when one can talk with people actually involved personally in such events, and having come to know them well and intimately to know one can trust their detailed evidence. Such a series of stories come from Papua New Guinea and those involved are or have been my close friends. In them these old records come to life with new authority.

I relate these stories, told me by Russell Abel during the Second World War, for several reasons. First they are modern, and many of the witnesses are still very much alive and willing to corroborate for the sceptical. Then too they relate to people who hadn't the slightest contact with the social and ethical concepts of white men or Christianity: any such thoughts and imperatives which came to them were completely 'out of the blue', untaught and unprompted. Finally they were a people who, at that stage, were so far removed from such values and concepts as to have no words for '(brotherly) love', 'apology', 'forgive', or even for 'honesty' or 'unselfishness', and certainly no word for or developed idea of God.

The story begins back in the pre-war years in the area around Milne Bay at the eastern tip of Papua New Guinea. On a small island called Kwato a unique family had lived for many years, ever since the Rev Charles Abel established a London Missionary Society outpost there in 1891. Abel of Kwato, as he became known, was a man of far horizons who refused to be bound by existing conventions and establishments. He saw ahead to the day when this primitive land would become a responsible and proud nation in its own right. He set to work to train young Papuans in the trades and skills most needed in their national growth. Boat-building, carpentry and nursing were some of the projects developed to a very high level of competence. His children, who journeyed to Britain for education, returned to build further the influence of the Mission, and began to train young men and women who would one day hold the first ministerial offices of the young nation.

His two sons Cecil and Russell were involved in the fascinating adventures which are the setting of our story, when they felt led by this same inner voice to take up the challenge of the Kunika peoples who inhabited the inaccessible ridges of the uppermost crags of the Owen Stanley Ranges. It is hard to realize that it was only during the years immediately before World War II that many people in Papua New Guinea were to see their first white man. Indeed, in the Western Highlands area of New Guinea it took the war itself to open up many areas with dense population. What little was known of the mountain-dwellers of the Eastern Highlands prior to 1930 was frightening and gruesome.

The life of these people was rooted and grounded in murder, head-hunting, cannibalism and sorcery. They could enjoy good sport after a victory and prepare for the major feast by arranging hors d'oeuvres. This could and did on occasion consist of gouging holes through the hands of their prisoners, threading them on a long cane line between trees, placing brushwood between them, setting it alight and gathering in delighted groups to watch the last desperate attempts to escape as their victims slowly burnt while struggling to find a less fiery place. The women scorned any man who did not wear the feather of the hornbill in his regalia to signify that he was a murderer.

The instantaneous reaction of a Kunika when meeting a stranger in the jungle was to kill him. No reason existed for any other course. Food was not plentiful, for gardening was highly restricted in the little plots perched on the crests of mountain ridges, sometimes overlooking precipitous slopes to rivers and valleys thousands of feet below. Each village was an entity with its own fortifications, and when food was needed the common practice was to mount a raiding expedition, especially directed at the more peaceful and industrious inhabitants of the plains and coastal villages.

Towards the Eastern tip of Papua New Guinea the mountain-dwellers or Kunikas belonged to the Dorevaidi tribe. They were so cruel and fierce that their very name was a curse. As far back as 1900 the government administration had tried to make some headway towards civilisation with these people but without success. In 1900 an official Papuan report states that 'Dorevaidi natives have overwhelmed with their power and terror the tribes not only on their side of the main range (the Owen Stanleys) but also the Okandi and probably other tribes . . .'

In the early 1930's however the government decided to try a new approach. Patrols with power to arrest murderers and to try to enforce law and order had been a dismal failure. The new idea was to host a mammoth 'sing-sing', the feast, sing-song, dance and general merry-making of a major Papua New Guinea festival. Here, it was hoped, the Dorevaidi and all others would see that the intention of the administration was to ensure their own best interests. To the delight of the hosts large numbers came, including many Dorevaidi and other Kunikas. So too did Cecil, elder son of Charles Abel, together with some of his friends from Kwato.

Cecil is a tall, very lively and outgoing man who is at his best with Papuans. Any thoughts of racial or other discrimination rapidly evaporate when Cecil is so obviously interested in people as people, and in prising open closed personalities with his fun, trust and complete lack of self-consciousness. So it proved at the sing-sing at Abau. He even brought the leaders of the Kunikas to unbend, and this in itself was a near miracle, for they thought of him as one more of the mangrove mudflat-dwellers of the coast.

When they parted the Kunikas were at least moved to genial but sceptical laughter when Cecil promised to visit them in their fortress villages. 'Namo heria Taubada' (very good, big man), they responded, adding a sly dig about their steep hills soon discouraging white amateurs. But Cecil was serious, and he waited and planned until, some months later when the monsoon season had passed, he led a party of his brown and white friends from Kwato on a trek into the hinterland which towered over their horizon, the craggy sawtooth outline of the Owen Stanleys.

That an unarmed party should travel this area from village to village, without molestation, was a major miracle. Part of the reason could have been the sheer shock to these fear-ridden, violence-orientated peoples of seeing the laughing, happy, mixed-race expedition who greeted them as friends, who came to learn and repay a visit.

One result of this expedition was the decision of three of the fiercest chiefs to visit Kwato to try to find for themselves the secret of the new way of life so evident among the strangers.

I met Russell Abel during the war and remember well his description of one incident which proved to be formative in the life of these people.

On their way back Cecil had the strong conviction that he should try to convey to the chiefs the secret at the heart of life on Kwato. One morning he sat in a circle with the three men, each wearing the emblems of homicide and ritual murder, noses and ears perforated and decorated.

Cecil opened the conversation.

'Do you believe there are bad spirits?' he asked.

There was a rather incredulous exchange of glances and a quick reply.

'Oh yes, Taubada, yes indeed.'

Then Cecil asked, 'Do you believe there is a good spirit?' This time there was no reaction to be seen. Silence dragged on and on until finally one of them, Sibodu, said 'Well, perhaps there is, in fact there must be.' Then a quick and paternal piece of advice, 'But don't worry about him, Taubada, he won't hurt you!'

Cecil went on to explain to the chiefs that, in the existence of this good spirit lay the secret of their lives. They had found that the good spirit was more powerful than all the evil ones put together, that indeed his power could be discovered and become available to any man who was prepared to obey the simple rules.

'We have found that if we turn to the good spirit and tell him we will do what he asks, and really mean it, then he will talk to us and give us his commands. When we act in this way the power of the good spirit begins to work', Cecil told them.

Then he made a daring suggestion, so daring that Russell told me that Cecil felt inclined to panic in case he had overstepped the bounds of possibility.

'Let us see right now if the good spirit has anything to say to us', Cecil proposed.

There and then, on the beach, the little group became absolutely silent, immobile except for one of the chiefs who began to make patterns in the sand with his toes. Time passed, and Cecil felt that this was really too much. What on earth could occur to the minds of these men without any instruction in ways other than the voices they had obeyed since birth?

After what seemed an age Cecil looked up. The three brown faces were deadly serious.

'Well, has the good spirit spoken to anyone?' he asked.

Three heads nodded gravely.

'Yes, Taubada', they all said.

One by one they spoke of the thoughts which had come. One of them was very direct.

'Fighting must finish', he said.

Then he confessed to a feud which had been dominating his life and how he had been planning to kill another man. The new thought in his mind was to go unarmed to see this man and to go alone; he must try to win him too to this new way.

Later he carried out his directions and, despite a hostile reception when his arm was slashed, he finally won his man.

Almost as revolutionary, and certainly the prelude to great advances in the social and family life of these people, was the simple thought which came to the feared chief Sibodu of Kuroudi.

'This way is right', he said, 'the good spirit tells me I must talk of this with my wife when I return.'

To a westerner this may not sound very unusual, at least as to informing his wife. But in Papau New Guinea, with its widespread polygamy, where the woman is of value mainly for manual labour and procreation, the idea itself was novel to put it mildly. When one knows more of the wife to whom Sibodu referred, the fact of such a conviction becomes well-nigh incredible. Sibodu's wife, Mui, was a cruel, moody shrew, a woman whose foul temper had brought about the death by baby-bashing of the five children she had borne. Sibodu hated her, and yet her power was such that he had taken no other woman as a second wife.

Nevertheless Sibodu carried out his new-found instructions and in time won his wife. Mui became a transformed person, a leader among the women in turning to the new source of power and direction. Each morning now the conch shell would call the sleeping villagers to meet for prayer and quiet together.

Then came larger and more significant plans for the future. The good spirit, now known by the name of Dirava, was leading the mountaineers to plan to establish new villages on more fertile and flatter ground nearer the coast and this was also a conviction shared by tribes in whose area the new villages would grow. A conference was planned to complete plans, and folk from Kwato would also be present.

Swollen streams delayed the arrival of the whites, and the gathered villagers waited several days. During this time Sibodu's eye fell on a most attractive and unattached young woman from a visiting tribe. He felt desire both for her and for the heir which was now an impossibility from Mui. Without consulting any other authority than his own lust, he abruptly announced to Mui that he would be taking a second wife. The result could hardly have been unexpected. Mui rose in fury, and in a moment she was her old self, screaming abuse and threats. Sibodu was unmoved.

Next morning Sibodu was not one of those who responded to the call of the conch shell but, amazingly enough, Mui was. Dirava spoke to her clearly. After breakfast she went to Sibodu and told him quite simply what had come to her mind in that time of quietness. She would offer no objection if he took this new woman to wife, provided he had first prayed to Dirava and believed it to be his will. Sibodu could only agree, so they sat in prayer and quiet.

Telling what happened in his splendid reconstruction of these events made from Russell Abel's journals, Dr Berkeley Vaughan comments: 'During that silence the knell of polygamy sounded in the Kunikas.' Sibodu's guidance was clear. 'It is wrong for me to take the woman', he announced. 'God's way is for a man to keep to one woman until she dies.'[1] Mui's convictions were identical. The couple later repeated their newly discovered truth to the whole company, and some of them clearly felt this was going too far. But, says Vaughan, 'Two years later there was no polygamy in the Kunikas. No arbitrary law of monogamy was laid down, no law imposed. One by one, from their own convictions, the people settled this matter for themselves. There had been no upset to the social system . . .'[2]

The task was no doubt made easier because there had been great imbalance between the strong and wealthy older men who had several wives and the younger bachelors who could afford none at all.

In days when land and its ownership play such a vital role in international relations, whether in Palestine, Pakistan, Ulster or Namibia, some of the events surrounding the move of the Kunikas to the plains hold special significance. When violence and murder are increasing in so many areas, lessons may well be learned from these primitive people, once steeped in the practices of homicide and pitiless cruelty. 'Murder and sorcery had been the chief cornerstones of their culture. Most ceremonies were closely concerned with the production or prevention of magic, or the glorification of murder, as was the case with certain ornaments and head-dresses,' Vaughan reported. 'The leaders were determined to wage war on all that pertained to the cult of killing. These ex-murderers were determined that old tendencies should not break out again. They feared that killing would recur, and undo the firm stand their tribes had taken.'

'They were not the only ones who were afraid,' Russell Abel wrote in his journal. 'They were being keenly watched by many observers who had the best welfare of the country at heart, including the Lieutenant-Governor of Papua, Sir Hubert Murray, with whom they had an audience in Port Moresby . . . Kunika leaders knew how deeply rooted was the homicidal tradition, and debarred many picturesque effects because of their grim association. They feared that bright feathers and drum-beats and dancing, even indulged in for its own sake and without the magico-religious significance that underlies primitive ceremonies, could stir the blood and bring back the old lusts. It was too risky. "If we do these things we shall want to kill", they declared, as they banned some seemingly harmless social pursuits'.[3]

Dr F E Williams, the government anthropologist, made a thorough investigation of the results of the movement among the Keveri and the

B

Dorevaidi. He deplored the disappearance of many old rites, and was intrigued because he could find no evidence of any personal compulsion to account for this. These people seemed to have dropped their customs by common consent. He observed the new life of the mountaineers, keenly attended their meetings (when they would switch from their own unknown tongues into pidgin Motu out of courtesy to their guest), and paid tribute to their sincerity:

> 'I never hear a Keveri pray', he wrote, 'in any manner that could not be called reverent, dignified, and seemly.'
>
> He was struck with the universal habit he found of natural, spontaneous prayer:
>
> 'They appeal to Dirava to guide and protect; to lead them from the evil ways of the past; to make them peaceful minded, forgiving, etc.; as well as a servant of the various practical rules of living . . .
>
> 'The Keveri are seized of a new idea, viz, that they should be friendly, and demonstrate their friendliness, to all and everyone. That idea, I am prepared to think, lies at the very centre of the Kwato teaching; and, in so far as it had been realised among the Keveri, it represents a very great advance . . .
>
> 'They are opposed not only to the old habit of murder for the sake of murder, but strife of all kinds. Quarrelling, vengeance, violence, are all denounced; the people are to be friendly to all. They should neither offer violence nor fear it.'[4]

Abel discerned that these changes left many a vacuum to be filled.

Tribal activity, that formerly had found its highest pitch in murders and reprisals and in effecting the appeasement of the spirits by magic, had to find new scope. Now the people could concentrate their energies on the future. The Kunikas were looking ahead, thinking on new levels. There was really no purpose now for isolated units hidden away in mountain pockets. Inaccessibility, once an asset, now became a liability, a hindrance to the fellowship of other people, and to the new stimulation.

The first new community effort of the Dorevaidi, therefore, was the carving of a better road to their mountain eyrie. At this time, Ina, the pass over Mount Clarence, was alleged to grow more and more vertical as one gained the cloud-hung summit. Dripping mosses and shrouded trees covered the mountain top. Through rifts in the clouds appeared breath-taking vistas of heavily-timbered mountains and valleys, magnificently indicative of Papua's enormous economic potential.

The Dorevaidi worked with a will and achieved great results, using only primitive digging-sticks, native mattocks, and their bare hands. When one of them, visiting Kwato, was asked what tools they had used, he replied, 'Our chief tool was lalotamona (unity)'.

The lessons learned in this joint enterprise were valuable, but Ofekule, chief of the Dorevaidi, was not satisfied. In his opinion, the people were temporising. His conviction was that Dorevaidi and kindred villages should move down to the plain and combine with other communities. Coexistence with the people of the plain would mean further growth through co-operation, as they had learnt through the making of the Ina Pass. Fighting would be less likely to recur if they lived together as good neighbours, and became absorbed in new activities. Schools for the children, out of the question in their present scattered mode of living, would be possible in the new community.

This revolutionary step was not popular. Ofekule felt that he should not press for it: that the rest would come round to his point of view, if it was right.

On one occasion Ofekule had gone down to Amau, on the plain, and was visiting a party from Kwato, camped near-by on the river bank. It was customary for them to meet very early in the morning for prayer and Bible study, and those from round about who had picked up enough English or Suau often joined in. The group sat around on the floor with Bibles on their laps, studying the life of Abraham.

'And the Lord had said unto Abraham, get thee out of thy country, and from thy kindred, and from thy father's house, unto a land that I will show thee.'

Ofekule interrupted. 'Read that again', he said, 'Who was this man?'

'One who lived a great many years ago – mumuga eai – in the very past, before the times of the white man, long, long before Christ.'

'Why, that is what God said to me! That is my own conviction that there is no future for us in the mountains; that we must leave the lands of our fathers and go to new country that He will show us.'[5]

Meanwhile the people of the plain had not been idle. To them too the Great Spirit had spoken, and all were moving towards a single objective. To village after village came the conviction that they should develop a wider community teamwork and build a larger life together. In a country where more than seven hundred entirely different languages express the divisions among the people, such thinking was novel and valuable.

There remained however the final and vital question, that of ownership of the land. In the Amau district the old cannibal chief Belei, who had greeted the first expedition in 1934, had handed over his power to his son Maiau, one of the first group to visit Kwato. Maiau was therefore personally the legal owner of rich forest land where ample water made gardens and agriculture easy and profitable. He was intensely proud of his heritage and the prestige associated with it.

Now a new concept of land tenure began to develop in the young chief's mind as he spent his morning time of meditation seeking God's will. Gradually he came to a firm conclusion: 'The land is not mine; it is not just for the people of Amau', he said, 'it is God's land, and he is the Chief over all.' So the way was clear for the new and greater Amau to grow: a model in social reconstruction. Tribal limitations were vanishing and a new step towards nationhood had begun.

The voice of the good spirit was the cornerstone of the new construction. Every morning the leadership of the several tribes met to compare notes and share convictions and plans. The government anthropologist, Dr Williams, reported:

> The natives are a clean, healthy looking lot, while the village itself is charming. The various sections of the community have their rows or clusters of dwellings; the houses are well built and in good repair; ornamental shrubs are making good progress; the grounds are neatly drained, and careful householders tend their borders of crimson balsam. Some of the houses show quite an amount of ingenious carpentry. More important members of the community occupy two-storeyed dwellings, with wooden shingles. And things are kept clean and in good order. I came on one man systematically scrubbing out his house (which had a number of separate compartments) with broom and bucket of water. The people themselves look comparatively tidy and there is a good deal of bathing – though no doubt for pleasure as much as for cleanliness – in the stream that flows through the village.[6]

The whole story of this remarkable development, completed within a decade, should be studied for its relevance to some of the most pressing problems facing mankind today. It might help to enumerate some of them:

1. Land tenure and the use of natural resources for the good of all.
2. Unity above the barriers of ancient hatreds and resentments.
3. The eradication of violence and warfare and their replacement by strenuous programmes of development and reconstruction.
4. The answer to marriage breakdown and child-beating.
5. The development of new pride in communal property and the answer to vandalism and untidiness.
6. The discovery of a source of leadership and direction greater than the voice of the most powerful or even of the majority – the authority of the source of 'what is right' rather than 'who is right'.

These and a host of other problems facing modern society found practical and viable answers in the simple willingness of these people to seek the way of the spirit.

'Except you become like a little child you cannot enter the kingdom of Heaven.' Somehow these words have a new dimension as one ponders the events which followed the simple act of faith by which these primitive people asked for the directions of the good spirit. 'We have allowed our intuitive faculties to lie dormant', says the European scientist, 'we know where power will lead us if it is not wisely used, and this is why we must be ready to listen to what traditional societies have to say.'[7]

The point is, however, that it is not so much what existing traditional or long-established societies have to say which is so important. True, there are many wise, continuingly valid and even indispensable customs and conventions derived by bitter experience over the centuries which traditional societies can contribute to our modern dilemma, but the more important factors are by no means merely a willingness to transpose past structures to the present.

The road for which we are searching may well have passed through that way, but we must join it at another point in time. Rather than listening to what these more traditional societies have to say we need to study and learn from them what it was that spoke to them, how that voice was heard, and how it is to be distinguished from the multitude of voices which clamour for our attention in our modern world.

In the case of the Papuan experiment, the five criteria[8] applying to the search for a new method or way of living are well satisfied. There is no apparent limit to the universal availability of the method, and it is certainly available to the simplest people on earth.

The new way has a deep and compelling appeal, and its power is such as to sweep aside the strongest and deepest fears, conventions, beliefs and hatreds of tribal life. The existence of a source of intelligent and purposeful initiative transcending all the constrictions of the status quo is certainly demonstrated, and all this without the rule-making and law enforcing of contemporary administration. A superior form of freedom emerged which enabled individuals and tribes to be and grow, in obedience to their own innate sense of right and wrong, in a hospitable environment.

There is one great area of reservation or at least of query about all this activity, however, which must now be faced quite squarely. How can these people, who on their own admission believed in the existence of evil spirits, and who had previously carried out cruel and bestial acts in obedience to such promptings, how could they discern the differences between the various voices in their minds and hearts?

In one way the Bible both in the Old and New Testaments is a study of this very question. In its pages one sees the ways in which the basic ground rules for living under the sovereignty of the Spirit emerged as this unique race continued the empirical method of their forefather Abraham. Viewed through the eyes of a later stage of development many of the conclusions reached in the early days of the experiment were far from perfect and in some cases one would call them savage and barbaric. The grave error of many historians however, and those who today deliberately distort history to produce emotive reactions among their audience, is to view the past through modern eyes. The treatment of slaves by Britons and Americans, for example, or the callous actions of the early settlers in Australia towards the Aborigines, can be rehearsed and made the source of much bitterness and hatred today among present-day blacks who have never suffered personally and who fail to see that such inhumanity was not uncommon in that society. It was due not so much to racial exploitation and arrogance as to prevailing and common attitudes and practices of that day, for few slaves from Africa can have been treated much worse than the coal miners and their wives and children were treated in Scottish mines in the eighteenth century.

At the beginning of the eighteenth century collier serfs in Britain wore the iron collar, and their children were sold into similar slavery at their baptism. Women carried the coal up steep ladders in creels weighing as much as 170 lbs and requiring two men to lift them on their backs. These women developed peculiar bone formations of the jaws, as much of the weight was taken by a strap around their foreheads, and one scientist observed that they had mouths which were 'wide, open, thick-lipped, projecting equally above and below, accompanied by traits of almost infantile weakness.'[9] Many such women had worked in the mines since their infancy and in 1780 in the still productive Alloa colliery there were once one hundred and three boys and girls under seven years of age at work. Punishment for disobedience often meant being tied facing backwards to the shaft by which a horse worked the winding gear and being forced to run backwards all day.[10]

The murder of Aborigines, appalling though it was, was hardly much worse than the prevailing practice of murder at the gallows for simple acts of theft to feed one's starving children.

So too for Africa. It is a moving and deeply humbling experience to sit around the fireside of an African home in a troubled city like Soweto or in the simple homes of Africans in Lebowa or Gazankulu or others of the homelands, and listen to the best and most honest thinking of the dehumanised black Christians today. They speak with sorrow, not bitterness. They tell of shattered hopes as the black man, eyes and ears at first eager for the white man with his message of God and Jesus, his culture and his wealth, came to realise that the newcomers brought not peace, love, prosperity and development as of older brothers, but only bitter and callous subjugations and exploitation; with deadly, soul-destroying paternalism and emasculating condescension.

But these men have, in so many cases, seen beyond the facile identification of the white man's creed with the white man's greed. They have found their own reality in religious experience, and in many cases they have grown to a stature which is well able to come to the aid of the moral cripples and the deformed minds and hearts of white men suffering from grievous spiritual malnutrition.

The reason is that they have discerned the truths and standards which the white man betrayed, the rules of religious reality which he broke or ignored. They have learned for themselves from the history of man's search that there are moral and spiritual criteria by which the right and wrong way can be differentiated and that they, with the white man and all the rest of humanity, are part of the pilgrimage of the human race towards its spiritual heritage.

In the case of the Papuans they were able to grow spiritually because of the new human environment rather than instruction in their new relationships. Indeed the people of Kwato had a clear sense of its being wrong for them to 'rush in with ideas, doctrines or ethical teaching or to lay down new sets of rules' but rather, in their own words, to let the Holy Spirit lead them. Nevertheless, while there were no words for them to speak of love, honesty, selflessness, they could and did speak of friendship and unity and more importantly demonstrated this in their own lives. Vaughan comments 'For those people, their first conception of God was of a Supreme One, who willed brotherhood and friendship. Elementary as this was, and incomplete, it was a far cry from the old animism with its fear and placations and it vastly changed their whole outlook.'[11]

Overarching it all was a lively sense of expectancy and of discovery. New convictions were eagerly passed on to the whole community. 'A new life was inaugurated; not because the white man said this was right or that was wrong but because individuals were able to say, "This was the word of the Great Spirit to me this morning." Day by day faces grew brighter, clearer, happier. The impulse was from within, and the conviction was their own, not the acceptance of someone else's philosophy.'[12]

Such were the stories told me more than thirty years ago by Russell Abel. At that time, barely out of my teens, I was eager and enthusiastic about my faith and trying to fit together all the many-sided objectives and appetites of youth. As the years had gone on they had rather slipped into the limbo of memory, and their significance only came alive for me once again by the arrival in our home of an unexpected visitor. That should be the next story to be told.

CHAPTER 3

You bring me news of a door that opens at the end of the corridor. Sunlight and singing: when I had felt sure that every corridor only led to another, or to a blank wall.

T S Eliot, *The Family Reunion*

CHAPTER THREE

The Visitor

When the telephone rang at my home in the Blue Mountains on that day in December 1972 I little thought that it was the beginning of a new and even more exciting and satisfying chapter of my life. My first reaction was one of annoyance. It was 9.30 on Christmas night. The telephone number was not listed, and I was not in the best of moods. A few weeks before I had been a Minister of State, and very few people other than the senior officers of my department or my immediate colleagues would have disturbed me at such a time. Now here was this almost unknown Englishman with his Oxford accent, asking to meet me.

There was another reason for my hesitation. It went even deeper, to old hurts and resentments. For eighteen years my wife and I had avoided any contact with the activity variously known as the Oxford Group and Moral Re-Armament, and I gathered that this man was one of them. Not that he had raised such things at our one and only meeting. That had been at a luncheon at Parliament House in Canberra when a senior public servant, the adviser to the Prime Minister on Foreign Affairs, had suggested that I might care to meet him to hear some background stories about India. Roger Hicks, for that was his name, had lived in India for many years, at one time being a trusted confidant of both Mahatma Gandhi and the Viceroy, and so he had been able to act as a go-between when tensions were running high before independence was granted.

'If Hicks is still connected with Moral Re-Armament, then I don't want to see him', I told my wife as we discussed his call. On the other hand I must admit to being intrigued by what he had told me. He was alone, staying in a not-inexpensive motel in Katoomba, at the height of the tourist season, and it was Christmas Day! That sounded very unlike the thing you would expect from a full-time evangelist living on faith and prayer, unless something had gone radically wrong, or he was acting under a strong sense of direction.

Ruth was, as always, less precipitate. Like me, she was more than a little curious about the reason for the call. We had been talking only shortly before about the necessity to remake our future, as defeat in the elections a few weeks earlier had brought my parliamentary career at least temporarily to an end. I was in my early fifties and looked back on all the way that I had come since serving during World War II as a lieutenant in the navy. There had been the long grind to complete three degrees, ending in ordination to the Presbyterian ministry. Then the invitation to become General Secretary of what is now the Australian Council of Churches. The next move had been a call to become the first Australian Minister of the Scots Church in Sydney, Australia's oldest Presbyterian Charge, founded in 1823 by politician-preacher and pioneer, John Dunmore Lang. From Scots I had accepted the challenge to be the foundation Master of the first residential college in the new University of New South Wales, and for five years had enjoyed working both with students and my colleagues on the Professorial Board.

For almost five years too I had been producing and chairing my own weekly current-affairs TV programme, at first on commercial and later on the national channels. Finally I had felt the urge to have a direct voice in the important and varied themes with which I was dealing week after week so, after talking things over with the Prime Minister, the late Sir Robert Menzies, and one or two senior persons who had become friends, I decided to throw my hat into the political ring.

At first my wife was horrified at the prospect, and so were many of my colleagues and friends. But in November 1963 I managed to take an inner suburban seat named after Evans the explorer, defeating the Labour Party candidate by a respectable margin. I knew that Evans was getting more and more precarious as a Liberal seat however, and looking back on it I was very lucky to have held it through three successive elections until the great Whitlam bandwagon rolled into power in 1972 on the catch-cry 'It's time'.

The decision to enter political life had been a particularly hard one for me, a child of the great depression years, for not only did it bring a substantial drop in salary but it meant surrendering the security of the government superannuation scheme to which I subscribed. Then too Evans was a swing seat, which meant that I was virtually certain to lose my place in any substantial movement against the government, so I looked for some additional form of security.

I found this by entering into business and commercial life as a director and later as chairman of an old-established oil exploration company, using some of my earlier training as an engineer as a starting point. Over the years this association grew until it was demanding far too much time from my increasingly exacting parliamentary duties, so I relinquished my commitments and finally all such associations when I was appointed to the Ministry early in 1971.

The defeat of the Liberal Government however now meant that I was without any business associations from which to derive an income, and without a job. What was even more serious, I was also pretty well without a faith. I had become increasingly cynical and sceptical about religion. I had

had many differences with churchmen and with the pronouncements of ecumenical bodies and my personal faith was tattered and threadbare. I still used the words, but my performance often did not match my profession.

Well, here I was out of office, and there are few persons so 'ex' as an ex-politician. There were no longer queues of people waiting to see me to get my support for a whole spectrum of matters, so I was additionally surprised at the arrival in Katoomba of Roger Hicks.

'Let's have him up for a meal, and see what goes', I suggested to my wife, adding facetiously, 'perhaps he's been kicked out of MRA and that's why he is all alone at Christmas!' Ruth had the last word before I took my hand from the mouthpiece and suggested a dinner date next night: 'After all we have been trying to find the right plan for the next phase of our lives', she said, 'so maybe this will give us a clue.' I met this with a most unenthusiastic silence.

But he did come to dinner next night. There were no attempts at propaganda, no more than a friendly interest in how things were going with us since the elections. He got on famously with the children, with whom he played guessing games while I was busy just before dinner. He talked a little about India and other issues close to Australian politics at the time, but just as any other well-informed guest would do. We did discover a little more about how he came to be in the mountains at that time. He was expecting to stay with an Anglican clergyman who was in charge of youth work in the huge Sydney diocese, and he had also been seeing something of a group of youth connected with the Jesus Movement. He obviously had a wide-open mind when it came to religious matters; quite unlike what I had expected.

Yes, I was intrigued, but very, very wary.

Roger rose to go back to the motel quite early, and I drove him down to the village. When I arrived home Ruth was as impressed with his visit as I had been. It was extremely hot at the time. Our house was a good deal higher than the village, and we had a cool guestroom available, so I asked Ruth what she would feel about offering him a bed for a few nights to save his cash from motel bills! A couple of days later he accepted, and during the five days which followed I experienced some of the most memorable friendship I have ever known. Part of the time was taken up by his telling us story after story from a very full and eventful life. He had lived much of his time in India. Being a friend of Mahatma Gandhi he had lived with him in his *ashram* on a number of occasions, and he told some fascinating stories of those days.

There was one story however which went right back to the early days of his Christian life and had to do with a communist community, and I realised that, if he was telling the unvarnished truth, then here was a factor of vital importance to the whole future of mankind. If right and wrong are simply expediency (whatever is in the interests of the 'revolution', as the Marxists declare); if conscience is just a residual carryover from the past; and in particular if morality based on religious values is simply a system to keep people in order in the interests of the exploiting classes; then almost any behaviour can be acceptable according to the situation of the moment. On the other hand, if there is in every man on earth an innate and inalienable factor which speaks to him of right and wrong, not as a construction of his environment or the creation of his society or class, but as an eternal and absolute imperative, then the whole process of ideological motivation and strategy must inevitably yield to this fact.

Because Hicks had become a Christian through meeting the Oxford Group in its early formative years while at the University, there were two basic facets of his religious approach which were important in a story he told of Bulgaria. The first was his belief in absolute moral standards as revealed by Jesus Christ as being the index of all human behaviour; and second the belief that God, in Canon Streeter's words, is a 'God who speaks', communicating with all and any men who will hear his voice.

Many Christians and those of other faiths too have criticised this as an inadequate base for beginning on the religious life, and I confess that I had long been among them. However, on reflection, those two requirements are not a bad summary of the starting point of the Old Testament journey of discovery which led out from Abraham and Moses to Isaiah and John the Baptist.

So let me tell the story exactly as Roger Hicks told it as we drove up to Katoomba from Sydney along the splendid new expressway from the suburbs to the foothills of the Blue Mountains on New Year's Day 1973.

Not long before the Second World War Hicks had gone to Sofia with Dr Buchman and others of the Oxford Group. After leaving the country he felt a strong and continuing urge to return. He said it was almost as though he heard a voice repeating to him, 'Go back to Bulgaria. Go back to Bulgaria.' There was only one person whom he could call a friend in that nation, so he wrote to tell him of his plan to retrace his steps. A few days later he was met at the airport by this man Cyril, a government clerk. Cyril was pleased enough to see him, but plainly worried about the implications of it all.

He knew of Roger's convictions, and he was anxious about any attempt to enlist people in a religious approach inside a largely atheist country. On no account whatever should the name of God be mentioned, he cautioned Roger.

Not having any other basis to meet people, Hicks asked Cyril to invite a dozen or so of the students who were studying English at the University to visit him in his hotel. They had a pleasant chat until, in telling one of his experiences, the Englishman forgot his warning and mentioned the name of God. As predicted, there were indignant and angry scenes and the visitors left abruptly.

Hicks had a second chance however because of the habit in Sofia of people, especially the students, of walking slowly up and down the main street during the evening. There he again met this student group and they agreed to a second meeting, on condition that the same mistake would not be repeated. This time Hicks was better prepared.

'I hear that you are all keen scientists in Bulgaria', he said. 'Now tell me about your approach as scientists. Do you know all that there is to be known, or do you make experiments and seek to learn new truth?'

They all assured him that the latter was the right answer: they were very open-minded, very fair, and ready to experiment.

Roger then went on to tell them story after story of the things he had personally seen taking place, such as seeing fear, hatred, frustration and defeat taken out of the lives of people and communities. They listened intently, and as there was no mention of anything remotely like religious language or concepts, they became more and more relaxed.

After more than an hour, Hicks felt that the time had come to speak more plainly about the basis of it all.

'I have given you a lot of evidence', he began. 'From your attitudes I gather you agree that what I've been saying could be important. I may be lying, of course, and then on the other hand I could be telling the truth. Don't you think that the time may have come for an experiment?'

One or two of them soon took the opportunity to leave, but quite a lot remained as Roger explained the experiment to which he challenged them. Every day for a month they were to take adequate time to be alone and listen to the deepest thing they knew inside them. Then, provided that the resulting thoughts squared with certain standards of morality, they would then obey those thoughts implicitly. They would receive no outside suggestions or instructions, the voice they were seeking would be heard in their own hearts and minds. As long as actions which eventuated did not cut across the standards of absolute honesty, purity, unselfishness or love, then they were to be followed, no matter how difficult they might appear at first. Not all of them agreed to experiment, but about a dozen did so.

Thus began a month of fascinating development which, even to Hicks who was expecting something to happen, was a revelation of an 'outside power' at work. It was almost as though a virus had begun to germinate in the group and Hicks was able to study the development of its symptoms. Their first attempt at contacting this inner voice in their own lives had brought one or two casualties to the experiment. Having been encouraged to be definite enough about their thoughts to write them down, one student stood up and announced, 'I stop'. 'This is too prickling', he said as he stalked out of the room. After ten or so minutes Hicks closed the gathering with the injunction that they move out to put into effect any practical steps they might have envisaged, adding that they were free to talk over anything with him if they felt it would help.

Soon only one lad was left, and he was known to be the most revolutionary of them all. He seldom went anywhere without a gun, and was Macedonian by background. He had come to the University not so much to study as to create a secret revolutionary cell. Now he looked hesitant and bewildered. He explained that he had had a thought which he could not possibly carry through. Asked what it was, he told how he and his brother had had a bitter quarrel and had not spoken to each other for some years. The thought had come to him that he ought to go to his brother and apologise.

'That would not be absolutely honest', he complained. 'Why should I make the move and the apology when my brother is clearly the one who is to blame?'

Hicks realised that here was a new factor at work in this lad's life and he must not let him down. 'Was your brother totally to blame, or could it be that as much as five per cent of the fault was yours?' he asked.

'Well, maybe five per cent, but certainly no more', was the defensive reply.

'Then perhaps all that is intended is that you go to your brother and put right that five per cent', Hicks commented.

Silence.

At last Pirin, for that was the lad's name, went off obviously still troubled. But a day or so later he was back with his face open with pleasure. 'It was wonderful', he said. 'We are again good friends.' Then he added rather shyly, 'On the way to see him I reviewed the whole thing and saw that I was probably as much to blame as he was. Anyway', and now he began to get a defiant note in his voice, 'it was only a small quarrel, and it didn't need any God to come into it.'

Hicks would not be drawn. 'We are conducting a scientific experiment', he commented. 'We will not draw conclusions until we have all the evidence at the end of the period.'

So, over the course of the month, more and more things happened which gradually amassed a whole pile of evidence. Most of it was simple enough, but the interesting thing was that the thoughts for restoring broken relationships and behaving according to new standards came to young men and women who had no background at all in the theory or philosophy of reconciliation and forgiveness.

Not only were relationships mended which had broken, but quite startling changes came about in the thinking of this group in terms of their behaviour. Pirin had gone ahead with his experiment to repay money to an insurance company which he had cheated, and now came the thought that he ought to discontinue the common enough practice of sleeping around with the girls. He had told some of his friends of this thought and they came to Hicks with the plea that he try to make Pirin see sense and start to behave 'normally' once more.

Hicks, who had never remotely touched on such a topic, as evidenced by their coming to him to deal with Pirin, once more realised that there was something very powerful at work in this situation which he must not hinder in any way.

'This is most interesting', he said to them. 'We all agreed at the beginning of this experiment that each would be completely free to decide, in accordance with his own deepest sense of values, what for him would be right and wrong. Let us go ahead on the basis of this experiment and carry out honestly all these thoughts which arise.'

A few days later the hotel manager came to see Hicks, obviously worried. 'There is a young woman student asking to see you, and she looks very angry', he said. Hicks went out to see her. He was met with a storm of protest that he had come into their city and was upsetting friendships and causing the men to act unnaturally in not behaving towards the girls as before.

Hicks explained to her about the experiment, adding that he was in no way the instigator of this particular development. He gave her a couple of books which he felt would help her to see more clearly what it was all about, and she went away convinced that he was mad, but nonetheless admitting that he was also very sincere, as he had given her the books without even getting her name and address!

Later, as she read the books and pondered their conversation, she decided to try the experiment for herself. As she sat quietly just one thought emerged as an insistent imperative in her mind, that she should go upstairs and apologise to her younger sister for a quarrel in which she knew she was mainly at fault. To apologise to a younger sister was unthinkable, but the thought would not leave her, so with great trepidation she obeyed. The result was so overwhelming and she felt so thrilled with the new and deeper relationship, that she decided to continue the experiment.

This time the thought was quite different. 'Go to the church', was the word which came to her. Now that was absurd, for that was a thing she never did. However she was now prepared to obey, and for a time she sat there in quietness. Two further things began to clarify in her mind. The first was the implication of her experiment in her own life and, beyond that, the effect it could have on their nation. If only others across Bulgaria could find the same joy she had experienced in reconciliation! Then the other aspect of it, that she had a personal responsibility to see this happen. She felt impelled to get down on her knees and commit herself to the God who had spoken and was speaking to her. Then as thoughts began to flood into her mind and she had nothing on which to capture them she raced off home and grabbed the first thing available which happened to be her father's huge ledger book.

Hours later she came back to see Hicks, and he was startled to see the weighty tome under her arm, but no less startled to hear as she read from it what he recognised to be a God-given strategy for the development of a new approach in Bulgaria.

So, in these and other young lives, the experiment proceeded apace until the month was up. They met at last and sat down to assess what they had found. Story after story was told and finally Hicks tried to sum up.

'Do you all agree that we have found evidence of a power at work in these last days?' he asked. They readily agreed. Some commented that it had even changed the habits of a lifetime.

'Would you also agree that it is personal?'

'Well, it certainly knows more about us than we seem to know ourselves', one student answered. 'A damn sight too much', commented another.

'Would you also think that there was evidence of there being a strategy, a plan behind all this?' Hicks asked. Once more, as the girl student and others had indicated, they could not deny this aspect of their experiment.

Finally, with a sense that this was now time to call a spade a spade, Hicks told them, 'Well, you call this thing anything you like, call it rheumatism if you wish, but for myself, if it is personal, powerful and has a plan, I call it God.'

Once more a long silence. This time Hicks had had a further thought which, try as he would, he could not set aside. 'Teach them the Bible.' Of course when he asked if they had ever read it he was greeted with a set-piece reaction, much as he had expected, 'What, that pile of superstitious rubbish!' This time the answer was easier.

'If you have never read a book, is it scientific to dismiss it as a load of rubbish?'

They were caught, and finally one of them, whose mother had a Bible, agreed to get copies made of *St Mark's Gospel*, and they would all read it before their next meeting.

A week later they discussed what they had read. 'What is your opinion about this Jesus?', Hicks asked.

There was a long silence, broken by someone who commented, 'Well, he did very well indeed – much better than I could have done.' The others nodded concurrence.

Then Hicks read them from the *Book of Acts* the story of the way the apostle Peter had a compelling daydream in which he was commanded to break his life-long rule of never eating 'unclean' animals, and how this was followed by a visitor who asked him to come to the home of a Roman soldier, a thing he would never have done before because of the danger of being ceremonially contaminated.

'When was all that written?' one of the students asked.

When he was told that it was almost two thousand years ago he commented that it seemed to be the very same thing which had been at work among them in the past two months. Hicks then asked a further question.

'In the story I've just read, Peter felt that he was getting his orders from someone whom he called Lord. Who could that be?'

Once more there was a long silence, as though some did not answer because they did not want to do so rather than because they could not guess.

'Perhaps it was this Jesus', one replied at last.

So Hicks was able to suggest that they might like to read more about what Jesus had said about himself, and they went away to study *St John's Gospel.* At this same time it became necessary for Hicks to leave Sofia, which he did with the strong sense that the seed sown during his stay would continue to germinate. Months later he was thrilled to get a postcard signed by them all under the subscription, 'Your brothers and sisters in Christ'.

Hicks told me that day in 1972 that only during recent months he had heard from members of that group, Iron Curtain notwithstanding, and he was overjoyed to know that they were continuing what they had begun so many years before.

Well, by this time Hicks had certainly captured my imagination. If there was indeed the possibility that lifelong counter-indoctrination could be ineffective against a deeper and more fundamental moral and spiritual sense, especially among eager young Marxist intellectuals, then here was a factor of which the whole world must eventually take cognisance.

'How much of this inspiration which came to your young communist friends could have been derived from residual Christian values still to be found in their homes or community?' I asked him. 'Was it really a voice from without or may it have been a remnant from the past, welling up from deep in their own personalities?'

Hicks answered with yet another story. The setting was in Burma, in days soon after the Second World War. At this time a great deal of friendship and spiritual fellowship had been encouraged between Christian and Buddhist leaders by the then Bishop of Rangoon the Rt Rev George West. The Christians had adopted the approach of encouraging the Buddhists to experiment with the spiritual sixth sense or inner voice by which Jesus declared God could speak to men. As there is no place for such a personal deity in Buddhist orthodoxy, a beginning was made with the proposition that, in a time of meditation, each person should seek to hear the deepest tones in his own innermost self.

If the thoughts and initiatives which came to mind at such a time squared with the highest moral standards one knew, then one should treat them as imperatives to be heeded and obeyed. Some of the Buddhists had happily engaged in this practice and deepening relationships resulted.

On one occasion the Christian fellowship was arranging a weekend conference-cum-house-party in a distant village in the mountains and they issued an invitation to one of the leading Buddhist abbots of the nation, an intellectual leader with a world-wide reputation, who had begun sharing their fellowship.* To their delight this dignitary wrote to say that he was planning to be present and named the train by which he would arrive on the Saturday morning.

When the villagers heard the news they were excited and overjoyed, and great preparations were made in their Buddhist shrines and monastery for the reception of such an important priest. All was in readiness for an almost regal reception at the railway station.

On the Friday morning the host group were sitting together planning the final preparations for the following day when, to their amazement the abbot walked in, twenty-four hours ahead of schedule. When the courtesies of receiving their guest were over, one of them ventured to enquire how it was that he had arrived a day ahead of the time mentioned in his letter. Without any vestige of a smile, indeed treating it as elementary, the priest explained:

'Well, you have been teaching me to listen to the inner voice and obey the thoughts which come. I had a strong sense that it was right for me to come today, so here I am!'

There could be no argument after that, and soon all were engaged in an amended schedule of visits and consultations, and little more was said of the matter until the next morning, when they listened together to the news broadcast at breakfast. The first item of news told how the train their

* As he is alive and living in Burma today I do not use his name here.

visitor had originally planned to take had been derailed by bandits and the passengers machine-gunned and robbed.

'Great awe fell on the whole company', said Roger, describing their reaction to the news.

Some time later the Buddhist abbot was invited to Britain and he gave a lecture to Buddhists in Oxford. Time and time again, he referred to 'God' and in such a personal way as to bring remonstrances from some of the orthodox present. In reply he said, 'I know what you say, very well. But I also know that when in my meditation I listen for a voice to speak to me I find there is *someone* there!'

No amount of theological argument or doctrinal proselytism could have produced such a result. There had been a power at work in that man's life which could not possibly have derived from his home or community attitudes, but which made me think of the promise of Jesus regarding the Holy Spirit that 'in the last days God will pour out his Spirit upon all flesh', and again that the Spirit will lead men into the full truth.

As we are discussing coincidences, let me add a singular instance of this regarding this story from Burma. Just before leaving Australia for Britain at the end of 1976 my wife and I were invited out to dinner at the home of life-long friends in Melbourne, whose son was a secretary in our Australian High Commission in Malaysia. They had recently visited him and had gone on to visit Rangoon. There in a hospital they had 'chanced' to meet this same Buddhist abbot – now very frail and unwell. He had given them a book which he had written telling of the spiritual pilgrimage he had pursued through a long life, and containing many other instances of this voice in his heart that he had come to love and trust. The book was written in Burmese, of course, so I have not yet been able to read it, but when my friends heard of my intention to tell this story they insisted on my keeping it.

Coincidence? Maybe.

But in a scientific laboratory 'coincidences' which are repeated and reproducible demand serious attention as possible evidence of new laws and truths to be discerned.

All this time, however, I was nursing grave reservations. I had been down this path once before, at least in part. I had seen and heard things done in the name of the guidance of God which had revolted me and I had even got to the point of preparing to write a book to be entitled *I Have Seen God Made*.

Indeed on that New Year's Day in 1973 I had deliberately tried to find out what really lay behind Roger Hicks' visit by proposing that we play a kind of game of making New Year resolutions not just for ourselves but for each other as well. I thought that I would be able to smell out any predatory purposes Hicks might have regarding the Mackays in what he would produce for us then. I'm glad that I did make the proposal, for it produced evidence of insight and real caring for each of the family, but nothing of any plot or plan to inveigle us back into a movement.

Looking back on this period there were two or three things which held me about Hicks. First there was his obvious freshness and openness, his personal dynamism and very evident commitment to his faith. When he said on one occasion 'Jesus is my best friend', it was said so undramatically but with his whole face alight that I knew it to be absolute fact.

Then there was his astonishing capacity to include us in with him, treating us in every way as his colleagues and comrades-in-arms in the greatest battle of all. Finally there was his refusal to be drawn into any kind of 'advice giving' or other roles of influencing our decisions or objectives. 'I've learnt the hard way', he would say. 'One of the biggest lessons in my life is not to try to play the role of Deputy God.'

With such a man I felt I could at last begin to build a free yet close friendship. I wanted to know more about him and I felt that I might even be able to discuss with him some of those areas of bitter experience in my own life where hurts and disillusionment had destroyed faith, not only in activities like Moral Re-Armament, but in the Church itself and even to some degree in parliamentary democracy.

I invited Hicks to tell me more of his own life story first. Later it was possible for me to get a tape recording of an occasion when he did so in even more detail to a lunch-hour gathering in La Trobe University in Victoria, so he can tell that part of the story for himself. He spoke in a terse, crystalline way, first of all about what he called the 'blind alleys' down which he felt his life had led him:

> I was born in the upper middle class in Britain: father, mother and three brothers, and eight servants to look after us. I never learnt to make a bed or shine my own shoes or to do anything for myself, I expected everything to be done for me. My great personal friend and the person upon whom I depended most of all was my father. He was a religious man and he took us to church every Sunday. I had to write out the collect and learn it by heart. In a sense father was my god.
>
> Then one day, just after my eleventh birthday, I was brought back from school and told that he had committed suicide. Mother stopped us going to church, took down every portrait of father, and his name was never mentioned again at home. I was sent back to boarding school with a great black band around my arm and a black tie, and every time anyone was kind to me I burst into tears. So I decided I would harden myself

and on no account would I be hurt again like I had been hurt. That was my first blind alley, hardening myself, keeping myself to myself.

I think I went through the whole of my schooldays, including my entry into the Royal Navy at thirteen and my 'honourable retirement' at the age of seventeen at the end of the First World War, without making any friend who was close enough to hurt me, whatever happened.

Then I went out to Heidelberg University in Germany, because I was still too young to go to Oxford. I was the first Englishman (I think) to go back there after the First World War and I saw the most deplorable conditions. I got a passport, I still keep it, for which I paid thirteen billion marks to have renewed. Such inflation had a terrible effect. For example I lived with a doctor and his wife and on £2 a week I fed the whole family as well as myself. He had been a highly respected doctor and had become a coal-heaver. When I said goodbye to him and added I would be back before very long he said that it must be before January 1st. 'I am going to shoot my wife and then myself on that day', he said. I asked 'Why?' He said because fifty of them were getting sacked and there was no other provision. 'My wife is a tender woman and I can't put her on the streets, so I think that is the best thing to do', he added. My host and hostess confirmed that thirty of their close friends had already done that.

So I lost all faith in God. I said, 'How can there be a God who let that happen to my father, who let that happen to a country?' I opted out. Then I went up to Oxford University and found freedom for the first time in getting gloriously drunk. I graduated from that to being the very important person, the President of the Wine Club. I hired a fellow to put me to bed every Saturday night (he eventually became the Prime Minister of Thailand), and it was a very good time. I enjoyed myself very much. Anyone who says I was depressed by it, well, it's not true. I had my moments of depression, such as when sex got on top of me, but by and large I had a good time. I did quite a bit of athletics, but I saw that this life wouldn't last. I didn't know what to do.

I was offered a job in business, but I said 'Look, father was a highly successful businessman, uncle was the President of Lloyds in London. He offered me a job too, but I said that if that is the end of a successful business career it's not the kind of rat-race I want to go into.'

Then I was offered a job as a lecturer in South India in Madras University. I arrived there and found that I was expected to be a Christian. I hadn't got a Bible with me. I had my pipe; in fact I always had two pipes with me, one in my mouth and one in my pocket ready to put in my mouth. I claimed at Oxford to be the only undergraduate who could wash his hair in his bath without his pipe going out.

But this college was surrounded by the poorest of the poor, what were then called the untouchables and outcasts. Do you realise that ten thousand people in India die every day of starvation? We saw this poverty all around us but not one student in the University ever went out to them. So some friends and I began organising students who cared enough to visit these huts and homes. We started night schools for them, made hens lay bigger eggs, carried earth on our heads, levelling fields and did all that kind of thing.

The first home I went into they were all huddling in a corner as the rain was coming through the roof, as only monsoon rain can come in India. They said 'Please help us.' I said 'Yes, I've come to help you, but why don't you begin by helping yourselves and mending the roof?' They said, 'But our house would be dry.' I said 'Well, that would be a good thing.' They looked at me as if I were an imbecile. I said 'Why wouldn't it be a good thing?' They explained that if it was dry the landlord would come and keep his cattle there, and it was better to have the rain than the cattle.

Well, we did this for two and a half to three years. Then the Viceroy of India came down and saw it and said that it was the finest such work he'd seen in India. I was invited by two State Governments to do it on behalf of their whole states. But I was doing it off a shoestring, I really knew nothing about it; so I went up to Cambridge University to do a post-graduate course.

There I met Frank Buchman and what is now called Moral Re-Armament. They rather pestered me. Fifteen times I was asked to go to their meetings and fifteen times I refused. The sixteenth time I was not invited, so I went along to see what they were doing. I was slightly contrary. I was, in spite of myself, tremendously impressed. I saw couples about to get divorced going away radiantly happy and willing to make a new start. I saw labour and management talking as man to man and not as boss to employee, and finding the right solution rather than the conventional one. I saw people speaking with a tremendous authority of what had happened to them, and not about what they had read in books.

They all used to whip out little books and write down their thoughts and say that this was 'guidance'. We thought that this was very funny indeed – Almighty God sitting up there and guiding all these people to write down in their little books. And we picked on all kinds of silly things people had said and used their jargon. For example, at table I would say, 'Are you guided to share the salt with me, would you mind checking it with your team and let me know your decision as soon as possible?'

We were just about as rude as we could be, but nobody seemed to be irritated.

One day I went off to a quiet place where no one would find me, which was the College Chapel, and said 'God, if you are really there and want to talk to me, then I am willing to do what you want. Now is your chance.' There were no angels' flapping wings, no holy thoughts from the Bible came. I had a clear thought to go and ask a friend of mine we'll call Guy to come to the evening meeting. Well Guy was one of my pagan friends and I knew he would laugh at my being at a meeting of Moral Re-Armament at all and tell all my friends, 'Oh! Roger's getting changed. Ha, ha, ha!', and spread all the kinds of stories I'd spread about other people beforehand. So I dismissed the thought. But I couldn't get any other thought, so I wondered 'Is this what they mean by being guided?' I was told to test it, that it is honest, pure, unselfish and loving. Yes, it passed all those tests. I said, 'Then why did I reject it?' I said three things to myself: 'Well, it's a very trivial thing for an important person like myself to have to do; then, it means getting out my car, missing my dinner, and going out and getting him; and again he would tell all my friends Roger is trying to get me to a Moral Re-Armament meeting. Ha, ha, ha! So I'm being guided now by being the important person, by comfort, and by what other people will say.'

Now this was an extremely trivial incident, and I did it very cowardly. I got out my car, didn't tell anyone about it, but I went and called on him and said, 'Guy, you know these extraordinary people the Buchmanites, I believe it's one of their odd meetings tonight. Wouldn't it be rather fun to go and see what they're doing. Ha, ha, ha!' Well, it was very simple.

The next thought I got was about having cheated at a Derby horse race. You see I had some very innocent friends, and I was asked to put some money on for them with some bookmakers. I won't tell you the story in case you're tempted, but the result was that I kept money which belonged to them. This was years before, and I had the thought to write and tell them about it, and tell them how I was experimenting with living a life based on absolute standards of honesty, purity, unselfishness and love, and taking time to listen to find out what they were. And I thought, 'Oh no, that will only embarrass them, that's not absolute love.' But every time I thought about it I thought 'that's the honest thing to do.'

So I wrote and told them. And they were enthusiastic. They said, 'This is so much more interesting than all the drivel you've been writing to us before. Please come and tell us about it.'

Eventually, to cut a long story short, the time came when the thought came very clearly to me, 'You have not yet given your life to me, get down on your knees and do so now.' It had a ring of authority about it, of a power which could direct me. So I did that. From that moment a directing force came into my life. A new power came. Lots of old habits fell off. I knew I was in touch with the force which makes the universe work.

I have a lot of intellectual difficulties. I find it extremely difficult at times to believe in a God who allows cyclones to happen, monsoons to fail and the innocent to suffer. I can't explain God and I can't prove God, but by being obedient and following the thoughts that have come, I have come to the conclusion over the years that there is a power there which guides, which is intelligent, which is personal, and powerful and with a plan. For lack of a better word I call it God. So now Christ has really become my best friend.

Well I could tell you stories from here until you went to sleep of how I've seen that work out over the world. My first assignment really, after a bit of training, was to live with the Foreign Minister in Holland, which was quite an experience. I asked him what he saw as the most difficult question he faced, and he said, 'Well, for sixty years we've had trouble with Belgium over the waters of the River Scheldt, three foreign ministers have been dismissed, correspondence is sixteen metres high in the Foreign Office and there is one man whose full-time job is to keep it going. That is our biggest problem.' In six months' time I was up in the gallery of the Parliament and heard him announce how that problem had been solved to the satisfaction of both peoples.

I spent most of my time however in India, living quite a bit with Mahatma Gandhi, the apostle of peace and non-violence, running messages during the war between him and the Viceroy, backwards and forwards. What impressed him was the change in Englishmen. I once said to him, 'What would happen if the English ever said they were sorry, they were wrong and needed help?' He threw back his head and he laughed for about half a minute and he said, 'I can't even imagine it, but if it ever happened it would make all the difference.'

I told him of a very senior British official who had intended to retire because he was angry at the promotion of Indians over his head but who had then decided to spend his life listening to God's voice, obeying, and deciding everything on the basis of 'what was right' instead of 'who was right'. As a result, instead of giving orders in his Province, he used to call in prominent men – Hindu, Moslem, Parsee, Christian – and say, 'This is our problem; this is how I propose to go about it: what suggestions have you got to make?' And Mahatma Gandhi said to me, 'That is the only part of India where there is not trouble.'

When I told him he should enquire further about the change in this man (he was a very sceptical fellow, the Mahatma), he said, 'I'm sure it's very interesting, I'm sure it's very interesting', and seemed to dismiss the matter. However I went and stayed with him three months afterwards and he said, 'You know those stories you were telling me last time; well, I had the Chief Minister investigate them, and they were all *true*!' He said, 'This is a completely new factor in politics. We play politics against each other. It's like chess: we know the value of the pieces, we know the possible moves, but this upsets the whole chess-board. Go and tell the Viceroy from me that, remembering all his difficulties, if we both had this spirit we would agree within half an hour.'

But the Viceroy was six foot six of aristocratic Presbyterian Scot, who was not of the opinion that the British had been wrong at all, about anything, at any time. So I tried what I hoped was a little humour. I said, 'Your Excellency, if we couldn't begin by admitting we'd been wrong, do you think we could start by admitting we'd erred?' All he did was to take a pencil and write 'erred' on a piece of paper and draw circles around it. But there *was* a time then when the leaders of Pakistan, whom I also knew intimately, and the Mahatma were willing to settle things on this basis of not 'who was right' but 'what was right'.

Well, I've been doing that kind of thing for forty years now. After the blind alley of shutting myself off; the blind alley of opting out, by drink and so forth; the blind alley of just doing condescending good work and keeping the system vitally the same; all three are totally different from the revolution I found forty years ago, much more challenging, of changing people so they are fellow workers in a revolution that really works.

The night before last I was with a leading industrialist in this country and I was rather blunt. I said to him, 'The trouble I find here in Australia, in your very comfortable, lucky country, is to get well contented and well-padded Australians out of their comfortable chairs to do something for a world that is needy and hungry.' He said, 'This is too hot for me', and walked off.

But that is the battle! Ten thousand people die a day from starvation in India. What are we concerned with?

I'm concerned with bringing about a Christ-centred revolution, such as the one which Rajmohan Gandhi the grandson of the Mahatma, has undertaken. He has got many of the students of India behind him now, including Naxalites, who were so fed up with the inequalities of society that they all carried knives, but have now found a better way than violence and are enlisted in it. And I believe that this University and the other universities of this country could give the kind of leadership to a desperate world which is far more interesting than internal squabbles.

Two hours ago a window cleaner came into my room. I was thinking about what I was going to say to you today and I said, 'I am going to talk at La Trobe University. What shall I talk about?' He said, 'Well, tell the students to play their part.' An interesting reply wasn't it? He thought that you were people of privilege, people of responsibility.

The world's in need.

'Tell them to play their part.'

Then Roger invited questions and the discussion continued for more than an hour. This then was the man who had come so precipitately and so opportunely into my life. A man with whom I felt increasingly that I could be completely frank about my own adventures, and misadventures, in the faith, and the areas of my own cynicism.

CHAPTER 4

There are two basic ways to learn, understand and possess the Divine Word.

The first could be defined as external listening, scholastic, catechistic or cultural. It means learning what the Lord has said.

There is another way of listening, to listen to our inmost self. This gives a predominant place to the relationship between God and man . . . Do you hear the voice of the Lord which calls, inspires, orders, counsels, directs and consoles – the true promise and hope of the destiny that awaits us?

It is not an easy matter . . . there are a thousand other voices around us. We are in the midst of a deafening noise. Newspapers, television . . . how can we distinguish . . . the voice of the Lord which is not more resonant than the rest? The Lord in fact does speak in grave and solemn tones, but His Voice is mild and gentle. He speaks to those who want to listen.

He who goes after what he likes, that is temptation, instinct, gain and self-interest, is treading a false path. We must, on the contrary, listen to the voice of the Lord not because we like it . . . but because it is the voice of God with its authority, its mysterious preponderance of all human voices, even the inner ones . . . the desires of the heart come after the absolute primacy of the conversation with God.

Pope Paul VI, *L'Osservatore Romano*, Palm Sunday, 1968

We have stopped listening, and our spiritual life has died on us, although we keep up appearances and go through the motions.

Archbishop Coggan of Canterbury, Lambeth Sermon, 1978

CHAPTER FOUR

Making an Experiment

I realised, as I listened to my visitor, that the time was getting near when I had to be prepared to make a completely honest experiment. There were many hurdles to be surmounted, and perhaps the greatest obstacle of all lay in my deep suspicion, amounting virtually to a fear, of the phoney or the fallacious in the question of the guidance of God. That was why, years before, fresh from painful and costly experiences with friends who placed great emphasis on this aspect of faith, I had even contemplated writing that book of warning to others entitled *I Have Seen God Made.*

I had seen much which was not deliberately, but patently, synthetic. In a more extreme form one sees similar excesses amounting virtually to brainwashing in some of the lunatic fringe sects today.

Quite clearly God has not given us a religious sense, a capacity for communion and even communication with him, in order to bypass his own gift of intelligence, our primal decision-making freedom, or our capacity to make mistakes. He would be a poor kind of father who brought up extremely obedient children who came running to him at every turn to ask for direction. One of the hallmarks of good parenthood is surely the evidence of the growing maturity and proper self-reliance of the child.

On the other hand there is the opposite danger: that of the precocious and arrogant youngster who rejects all parental guidance, standards, and advice out-of-hand, so complete is his self-assurance and indifference to experience and its wisdom.

If the analogy of the family applies, and it has obvious limitations because parents do not have divine wisdom, then the ideal situation would be one where real freedom meant each member of the family was free to express ideas and suggestions, but increasingly the developing child came to feel responsible for making his own final decisions. In the flux of merely mortal affairs as the child matures the role of the parent becomes more and more quiescent, less necessary in everyday living. On the other hand the divine 'parent' is never irrelevant or unnecessary: he is the absolute, the one always 'in front' and in such a way as to be always essential in terms of each event and experience in life.

Life is always a matter of growth and development. The story of man's religious pilgimage is by and large the history of his development of criteria, standards, principles and guidelines which are eternally valid and intended to be so used that there need be no re-learning or return to first principles, no waiting for special directions, no hesitation or uncertainty in essential areas.

The Ten Commandments are a major step towards the crystallisation in history of the immutable laws of God for all men for all time, pointing forward to the Sermon on the Mount and the absolute ethic of Jesus Christ. Here the Old Law is not diminished but raised to its ultimate expression; not, as did the Pharisees, in a comprehensive series of rules and regulations, but in clearer concepts of the Way, the Truth and the Life in one who is both truly human and truly divine. Mere men make rules and constitutions and conventions, regulations which can be attained and kept, and so sects or 'religions' are born. God has finally given us no such easy way out, for he has shown us what absolute love means, explicated in a life tempted in all points just as ours are, but without sin. Absolute forgiveness, absolute selflessness, absolute purity, absolute humility, absolute honesty, these and other eternal principles or standards are set up before us in Christ, but they are never within our grasp, never attainable but always imperative and relevant in our lives. They burst through all the rule-making of priests and pharisees, all the conventions of the sects, all the little rituals which can be so readily accommodated in daily living, and are always there . . . the word of God himself, out in front all the way of our pilgrimage. But it is our pilgrimage, and for each one of us there is our own unique situation, our own *milieu* where we hear and obey the living word.

The eternal word of God, impinging on our practical everyday living in ethical terms and standards, is thus not a set of laws but a living, dynamic person. Truth is spelt with a capital letter. So is the Way. So is the Life at its fullest. Hence Hicks moved on from mere standards of morality to the point where he could say, with his face alight, 'Jesus is my best friend'.

Much of this was firmly in my thinking long before Roger Hicks came into our home. The major problem for me centred around the ways by which man can distinguish and determine the voice of God, the word of God in everyday living. I was dissatisfied with the prevailing attitude of many churchmen with regard to this aspect of the faith, for it seemed so often to be one of tacitly accepting the view that direct guidance and inspiration do happen but are characteristics of a past age. Thus in our own day we simply revert to the analysis, exegesis, and the application of derived principles from scripture and tradition to modern problems. We begin our assemblies and synods with prayers for guidance, and then everyone sets to work to argue for his own view, to demolish other points of view and generally to look for the endorsement of numbers.

The early Church was faced with precisely this challenge in the second century with the rise of Montanism. Montanus was the forerunner of many claimants for special divine roles in Christendom; he believed he was the promised Paraclete of *St John's Gospel.* Leaving aside the individual however, thousands of devout Christians were attracted to the ensuing movement which looked, among other things, for a much stricter moral life and a return to expectation of continuing revelation through prophecy. There was much sympathy in the wider Church for some of their aims, but as they became more intransigent and demanding in their attitudes, and seemed to be setting up their prophets as rival authorities to the hierarchy of the Church, they were eventually branded heretical.

Unfortunately the Church itself went to the other extreme in opposing them, and virtually insisted that the age of prophecy had closed with the apostles, and so denied credence to any claims of direct inspiration by the Spirit. Humanly speaking this may have been a safer course, but it can destroy the soul of religion and reduce it to a manageable and negotiable code instead of a living relationship with God himself. The dangers are that decision-making can revert to merely human choice on the one hand, or to an irresponsible and irrational individualism on the other.

Accepting the fact of a God who speaks, who is the divine word ever available to all who have ears to hear, there are nevertheless many areas where danger lurks.

Perhaps the greatest area of danger, and certainly one which requires enormous sensitivity and purity of purpose on the part of religious leaders and counsellors, relates to the hypersensitive area of decision-making when feelings of guilt, self-criticism and desire for forgiveness are running high. These deep feelings may be scientifically deplored but can never be eradicated by psychology or mere rationalisation. When personal crises come they emerge once more, self-accusing, hoping for cleansing, for renewal, for forgiveness.

If, on the one hand, it is possible to break away the crust of one's defence against such feelings of guilt, a crust which is progressively developed by us all as we see, but fail to take measures to mend, our failures and misdeeds, then the self lies exposed and vulnerable. Religious movements large and small have cultivated this self-exposure by an untold number of techniques. These have varied from the wholly legitimate to the utterly unscrupulous. In particular there are those especially active times, such as at adolescence, in bereavement, at the time of marriage or on the birth of one's child, when the self stands aside from the protective paraphernalia of everyday life and exposed to new thoughts and criteria. Such periods of enhanced sensitivity are not to be deplored, but on the contrary they can and often do prove to be times of great positive importance in reshaping lives and enhancing values and objectives.

However it is dealing with this area of increased insight, of aroused guilt, or of longing for love to fill the void of one's divine loneliness that some of the most vital factors of religion emerge. From the primitive and barbaric compulsions to offer sacrifice to please and appease angry and offended deities down to attempts to dispel guilt in the permissive practices of some modern sects, who call every abomination sacred, the search for absolution, renewal and spiritual freedom has been pursued.

To take a long hard look at oneself alongside the life and ethic of Jesus Christ is to arouse many of these feelings. Religious tyranny can intrude at this point and offer acceptance and fellowship in return for conformity and submission. Instead of bringing a man to his knees to accept forgiveness, cleansing and renewal as a free gift of God, the temptation is always there to set conditions on salvation. In the main stream of the Church the confessions of the seeker are held to be sacrosanct and entirely private, even anonymous. In many sects and movements this has not been so, and what is virtually a species of blackmail can emerge whereby the repentant individual can be held to the plans and purposes of the leadership or group.

This was one of the areas of concern which remained in my mind at this stage of my relationship with Roger. When I raised the matter and spoke with great frankness of things I had seen and experienced, I found him to be in complete agreement. I felt I was talking to one who had suffered in this way himself, and who was well aware of the blind alley it finally represented. To discuss such things with him was a joy.

It was like an eager comparing of notes with someone who had experienced many dangers and difficulties which proved to be remarkably like one's own, enough to constitute the foundations of a firm friendship and further pilgrimage together in the future.

After six days Roger left us for a brief stay with his Anglican friends and family, planning to return for a much longer stay in about a fortnight. While he was away I felt that I really must make a wholly new attempt to overcome my mistrust of committing thoughts from times of quiet meditation to paper. It did not help greatly to remind myself that I could tear it all up or tell nobody else of any part of it unless I wished. The thing I most feared was a 'foreign' source of influence within my innermost citadel of self; usurping my own primal responsibilities and self-determination. I had no desire to play the puppet.

When I finally brought myself to an honest attempt at 'listening', I was more than a little surprised by the result. There were certainly some clear thoughts about things which I might do or not do, but the overwhelming sense which replaced my fears and misgivings was one which I summed up as follows: True communication with God will not be foreign transmissions on my passive receiver but a coming into resonance between my truest self and my Creator. If this is right, I will be more truly 'me' than at any other time. I can only report that this has continued to be the case. Gone are those days of old when I felt some kind of constraint to get thoughts to impress others in my circle, or to match the lines of leadership in one direction or another. As I have continued essays in 'guidance' one of the most astonishing things which has happened has been the way new and even radical thoughts have come (for example, about money and security generally), which earlier I would have regarded with great distrust and even fear, and yet now they have been seen to be quite definitely not only my own deepest convictions but even areas of new adventure and expectancy. I have felt quite at peace with them.

Then came a shattering blow. At 9.30 one morning, less than a week later, I had a telephone call to tell me that Roger had died. He had had a massive heart attack. Only then did I discover that for some years, especially since his sixty-fifth birthday, he had known that he was living on borrowed time with a heart that could give up an unequal fight at any moment.

My first reaction was not just one of grief. I felt utterly shattered by the loss of one who, in an amazingly short time, had become the nearest to a brother I have ever had, but I also felt a sense of rebellious indignation. If there *was* a God, and I had come to a fairly strong belief in him again by now, then why had he removed Roger just when I was looking forward not only to a fine friendship but to some important teamwork with him in the interests of the kingdom of God? Why send him and then take him away so suddenly?

Almost at that moment the postman called, and there were two letters from Roger, one for my son Andrew – then eleven years of age, and the other for my wife. Roger and Andrew had played a good deal of chess in the time he was with us in the mountains, and he had also been interested in Andrew's stamp collection. It was at the time the young American champion Fischer was playing Spassky in the World Chess Championship in Reykjavik. Roger's letter to Andrew read:

> Dear Andrew,
> Here are stamps from my Christmas cards as promised. All the best.
> Brush up on your chess and be ready for
>
> Your Uncle Roger Fischer.

Ruth's letter not only concluded with the assertion 'Merry Days ahead', which did not sound as unreal as may have been expected in my first great sense of loss and grief, but it also cleared up a misunderstanding. I had been very critical of some people who, I felt, had let Roger down, and I had not known certain important facts which explained their behaviour. This Roger put right in his letter.

A few days later I found more of how those letters came to be written. Roger was staying with friends who, like himself, were very keen on the word-game 'Scrabble'. This night they had invited him to join them in a game. However, after a moment's hesitation, he had replied that he felt there were some letters he ought to write before going to bed, so he retired to his room, wrote and posted the letters, and then went peacefully to sleep. He died during his sleep. Later still I found how he came to be in the mountains that Christmas, staying in a motel and having a 'holiday'. A lifelong friend in England, knowing his heart problem and his nature had sent him a gift of a hundred pounds on the express condition that he used it for himself in having a holiday. He had been given my telephone number by my brother-in-law, whom he had met in Adelaide; and for the rest there can be no question that it was more than coincidental that he was in Katoomba at that time. Roger had been too long on the road to make such a move without feeling convinced that it accorded with the deepest sense of direction in his life.

After reading these letters I went off alone, and now there was no hesitation in the stream of thoughts which came pouring in upon me. I wrote them down as they flowed in, and it was as though I were receiving a commission. The principal conviction, after feeling deep gratitude for the depth of fellowship and intimacy of conversation I had been privileged to share with this remarkable man in the last days of his life, was one of a mantle falling on my shoulders. Roger had had so much on his mind and heart which remained as 'unfinished business'. I was sure that many of these tasks were now mine. Some of these related to care for individuals and others were more general. One or two major decisions also resulted. I would go abroad and see for myself some of the things Roger had told me. I would commit myself for the rest of my life to seeking and following the leading of 'the still small voice' in my innermost mind and heart. I would seek help to trust God with my financial security and the needs of the future. I would regard everyone on earth who was genuinely seeking God's will and way as a brother or sister to be cherished as such. Roger was wide open to this fellowship of the spirit, and one of his frequent sayings was 'we who have faith must pull together'.

The decision to follow the guidance of God meant, for me, the commitment to an earlier rise than normal to have an unhurried time alone before the bustle of the day begins. A wit once described it as 'a matter of mind over mattress'. I have friends who value their time of quiet but who find it better to have some other period, but for me there are now the conclusions of experience which point to the earlier time.

What do I do? Well the first thing for me is usually a cup of tea for myself, my wife and others of the household who join in this practice. Then comes the daily reading and study of a portion of the Bible, often helped by one of the great modern commentaries such as those by William Barclay. Then I let my mind turn from what has been read to whatever direction it will, and there is always a piece of paper or a notebook to capture particulars as needed. There is no magic about pen and paper, but they certainly aid the memory. For example, I am more than grateful that I can look back at this very moment to notes taken at the point of Roger's death and refresh my memory of the feelings and convictions of that time.

The thoughts which arise are mainly my own best thinking on all kinds of current themes, on occasion a 'shopping list' of chores to be done, letters to write and so forth. In addition however there is very often the possibility of capturing my waking thoughts, wherein at times there is a new way of approach or a solution to a problem from the subconscious mind, the product of the night. There are still other 'pluses' however, thoughts which come 'out of the blue' and sometimes ones which seem to have no logical basis, but which, when pursued, lead to some of those 'coincidences' which are the results of a life of prayer.

Let me describe some of these additional experiences which have given me fixed points in my pilgrimage towards a robust faith. The danger here, as in selecting any set of coincidences, is that they are exaggerated or accorded a larger place in the scheme of things than in real life. In telling these stories I do not wish, in any way, to suggest that they are a daily or regular occurrence. I'm not even sure if I would welcome it if they were. What I do assert however is my profound gratitude for experiences which, to my mind anyway, constitute clear instances of a hand higher than mine at work in my life. It is like navigating a ship in foul weather. Occasionally the mist clears or the clouds part to enable a swift and accurate 'fix' to be obtained, and then the routine tasks of following dead-reckoning continue. The sight of the star or the shore however has given the navigator an unassailable sense of security in his general navigation which makes all the difference. So it has been with a number of these strange and faith-giving experiences in my life over the past five years.

When the conviction came to me, at the time of Roger's death, that I should trust God with my financial and material security it was something which went very deep in me indeed. I was a child of the Depression, or more accurately I was a child of the First World War, and was at my most sensitive and formative stage when the great Depression of the 1930's struck. My parents had met at Gallipoli in 1915, during the Dardanelles Campaign. Mother was a staff nurse with the AIF, and was posted to a British transport ship converted into a temporary hospital ship, HMT *Ionian.* The ship had not been fully prepared for her first patients and was lying off Gallipoli not far from the British battleship HMS *Queen Elizabeth.* An invitation came from the navy to the Australian nurses and ship's officers to attend a dance on board the battleship and all the nurses accepted; leaving one solitary girl on duty back on the *Ionian,* my mother. Then, in the darkness and confusion, four hundred badly wounded soldiers were brought to the ship. Mother was the only medically trained person on board and signals were difficult in the presence of enemy gunners. So she got hold of the senior officer still on board and had him turn out all hands. Under her supervision they scrubbed their hands and put on clean clothes and then, under the watchful eye of the Engineer Officer, they were set to work to wash and assist in dressing the wounds of the pitiful spectres of men from the trenches. By the time the party returned from the *Queen Elizabeth* all four hundred were bathed, wounds dressed, temperatures and pulses charted, and they were bedded down in the wards of the ship. For this my mother was decorated and later married the Engineer Officer, George Mackay, my father: a Scot who had trained first on the Clyde.

After the war, when they had settled in Australia, my father found it hard to get suitable work, but eventually joined the South Australian Harbours' Board. For a time all went well until the Depression deepened and finally the activities of the Board were reduced almost to nil. My father was retrenched. So mother turned our house into a private hospital for terminal patients, my father and grandfather building outbuildings for the family. Then my father started a tiny grocery shop, arguing that he might not get many customers but at least he would get our groceries wholesale. So we existed during the Depression years. It was a grim battle and income was never able to meet all our needs. Many a time I woke at night to hear my parents, close by in a galvanised iron lean-to room, talking and talking about debts, mortgages, necessities and the grim state of our resources. Yet mother especially always seemed to be able to help others in worse plight. My dad told me later how he would turn a blind eye as she secreted away some of his small stock of foodstuffs to give to a desperately needy old couple or a family with sickness.

Nevertheless I grew up with a boy's deep resolve that if ever I had the chance I would become financially secure. We had to drop plans for me to study medicine, but it was just possible that I could get to the University if I could win a place with the Adelaide Electricity Supply Company in their drawing office. They had a practice of selecting three or four lads with good academic records from the Adelaide Technical High School and employing them as trainee draftsmen while allowing them time off each day for lectures in engineering at the University of Adelaide. I was lucky in getting such an appointment, and from 1937–1940 I pursued these part-time studies while earning a small wage.

Then came the war of 1939 and the bombing of Pearl Harbour. The Navy wanted men with my training, so in 1941 I was fortunate to be selected as a sub-lieutenant RANVR in the Anti-Submarine Service. Here I served throughout the war, becoming all the more certain, however, that my real calling was not to machinery but to people and especially in terms of tackling the causes of war as they were germinated in human nature. The postwar Reconstruction Training Scheme of the Australian Government enabled me to change to training for the Christian ministry, so I completed degrees in Arts and Divinity soon after discharge – eventually working my passage to Britain in order to continue my studies at Edinburgh University where I took the further degree of PhD.

I never lost my apprehension of financial insecurity though, for even now it was a hard struggle to pay my way, and my parents had retired and become old-age pensioners. Gradually my academic background carried me into more and more responsible posts however, and all the time I tried to keep some savings for a 'rainy day'. By the time I left the Federal Parliament I had what I felt to be enough resources to enable me, together with my Parliamentary Retiring Allowance, to live in modest comfort and security.

Then came this thought about trusting God and not investments and property. What did it mean? My wife and I talked it over again and again, and in matters of faith she far exceeded my own tentative ventures. She too had been a victim of the Depression when her father, a Methodist minister with four children, had often had to go without stipend and rely on gifts of produce from his country congregation to keep body and soul together. Eventually however there came the day when I felt absolutely clear about the fact that 'no man can serve two masters . . . you cannot serve God and money'. I knew I had to be prepared for God to give the orders in terms of use of my money, even to the point of using what I had once considered essential reserves if he so directed. My wife and I made that commitment together, and on our knees. The only reaction I felt was one of relief. I no longer felt that the family's security depended on me alone and on my ability to manage our affairs. So far so good.

Then, a few weeks later, quite out of the blue, there came the thought one morning that I should send a thousand dollars to a group of young people in India who had been working to produce a musical show called *Song of Asia* – telling in song, dance and sketch the ways in which hatred could be broken and peace come to former enemies. They wanted to take this essentially

Christian message of forgiveness and reconciliation into some of the hottest spots in India and Asia.

It was one thing to have such a noble, if costly, thought but a man surely had to be businesslike as well, I argued! At that time I had been trying unsuccessfully to get what I believed to be a fair minimum price for the house in which I had lived while in Parliament to enable me to purchase land and build in Katoomba – where we all felt we should live and get to know each other as a family after the demands of parliamentary life. As a result of the failure to sell the house and the need to set up home in Katoomba, so the children could begin their school year there, I had incurred a very substantial overdraft. What was more natural then, when this thought of a gift to *Song of Asia* surfaced, than to add my own rider '. . . as soon as I sell the house in the city'.

It seemed very logical, but it didn't work. The conviction about the gift grew in my mind. I was on business in Melbourne some days later when the voice in my mind could be denied no longer, so overdraft or no overdraft I wrote a cheque for one thousand dollars and sent off the cash to India.

Next morning I returned to Sydney and the first message I received on arrival was from the estate agents. They had sold my house. And the price? A thousand dollars more than the target figure I had set! Coincidence? Of course. But when it becomes part of a number of similar experiences it is surely logical to wonder if it is not something more. Indeed, even to suppose that someone 'up there' has got a real sense of humour!

Ten days later I received a letter from India. In it I was told that at the time the bank rang to tell of my gift the entire cast of over forty was spending the morning in prayer for the fares as they had no money to get to their first engagements. To them too it was an answer to prayer.

I began to ponder a God whose economy is so much wider than our human concepts, where all can be used here and now as needed, rather than hoarded for contingencies which may never arise.

After all, Jesus was mighty specific: 'Lay not up for yourselves treasures on earth where moth and rust corrupt and thieves break through and steal . . .'

I had begun on a new road of economics, not an easy one, not one where I've been faithful all the way by any means. When I *have* heeded and obeyed that voice in my heart however, I've had experiences very like that first one, and in some cases involving very much larger sums of money – reducing very significantly my 'nest egg' resources. I don't for a moment believe that Jesus was giving a general or universal direction when he told the rich young ruler to give away all his possessions to the poor. It is often the easiest way, simply to discard all and resort to 'faith and prayer'. For that young man it was obviously a specific need to meet a specific problem. For me anyway it is not so dramatic – but it *does* mean a daily battle to see that it is really God and not self who has the final say in my decisions, and we are frequently called to take steps which are beyond our available resources. So far we have never lacked anything we have felt to be essential; and we still manage to help others as we go.

Now let me be honest. For much of my life I hated and feared living like that. I've been very personal and autobiographical to help explain why. The Scot in me as well as my human nature as such rebels at this point perhaps more than anywhere else, even more than in the area of sex, for basic security as regards bodily needs and provision for one's family runs very deeply.

However I can only report honestly what I have found. I do *not* feel that any 'foreign' forces have been at work. No heat has been applied to make us respond financially. If we've adopted foster children through World Vision; or sent money to help refugees from Indo-China; or contributed to the fares of young leaders in the Jesus Movement to get additional training; or helped build a Christian training centre, all of which we've done, as well as personal gifts to people without resources, in every case the thought to do so has come as our own, unsolicited and often totally unexpected. Certainly it has sometimes meant making a gift when we were already budgeting the pennies for other things – but it has opened up our lives and brought others into a fellowship of common endeavour with us which has in itself been an enormous recompense. But far more than that is the sense which grows in our minds and spirits that it is part of the process of prising us loose from the disappearing world of materialism and the first faltering steps along a road where entirely new values and securities are to be found.

One of the most fascinating experiences I ever had of the sense of God intervening directly in my life concerned a visit to South Africa. While I was in Europe in 1973 I met a group of black national leaders from South Africa and in the course of two or three weeks we became very good friends. When they told of hurts and disappointments, betrayals and dehumanising methods used by whites against them, and above all when they still refused to reject their Christian convictions and principles, refused to hate or contemplate violence, and yet believed in the rightness and coming victory of a solution which would sweep aside apartheid for ever, I longed to be able to share more deeply in their situation. One morning the thought came to me, which I passed on to them and to some of the white South Africans with whom they were working, that I would indeed visit them in the days ahead, and for long enough to be able to share in their feelings and hurts.

No more came of this at the time, but reports were received of a conference for people of all races in Africa to be held in Pretoria at Easter time in 1974. I very much wished to be there, but could get no clear sense of right or wrong about it. I was very involved in several important matters in Australia and it did not seem very practicable, so I rather put any thought of it on one side.

One morning my wife and I were sitting quietly seeking God's will for the day when a clear and very definite thought came into mind quite imperiously, 'Go to South Africa. The problems here will work out in good time.' Then came a second thought. I had written down the precise wording of the first, as it was so definite, but now came an equally if not more definite assertion, yet I hesitated to write. It seemed so far removed from my normal everyday thinking that I feared it would be foolish, and probably faith-destroying to record it. The thought was, 'This will be confirmed in the mail today.'

Now mail deliveries to Katoomba are usually in the mornings, and I had always gone to the village after 8 am and cleared my box, not finding it worthwhile returning again until next day. On this occasion my wife and I were naturally very eager to see what would await us. When we eventually opened the box there was one letter there only, a bill from a local merchant! To say that we were crestfallen would be an understatement.

That afternoon Ruth was going into the village for some shopping and I asked her to get some stamps from the post office. She did not take the key of the box as no mail could be expected. When she was paying for the stamps the Postmaster came to the counter and said, 'Mrs Mackay, an overseas mail has just come in and I think I saw something for you. Just a moment and I will get it.' (We had never had that kind of experience before, nor since for that matter.) There was a letter from Johannesburg, from one of the principal figures arranging the conference. In it was not only an official invitation, but a letter and two newspaper cuttings. My name featured prominently in the press reports as one who would be present, and the letter was an earnest emphasis of the desirability of my attending together with an apology for having presumed on my acceptance, but they had all felt that it was God's plan and needed to make an early announcement so they had gone ahead in faith!

Could anyone seriously call that *only* coincidence? Or could I doubt that it was indeed God's will for me to attend?

The guidance of God then has become for me a focus of my faith, for it is so very easy for my rather philosophical and theoretical kind of mind to be carried away into words and principles without action. When commitment is required of me in black and white terms however my thoughts are more apt to issue in 'deeds', in several senses of that word. Nevertheless it is far from a clear or cut-and-dried path to follow. I am still working at discerning some of the ground rules. Most basic is the necessary sense that these thoughts and concepts are truly *me*, and any action proposed must be one for which I fully accept total responsibility as for my own personal wish. Nothing must intrude on that basic sense of integrity. Then too I have learnt to mistrust any thought or prompting to a decision which arises in a pressure situation, e g in a group where there has been much discussion, and where the desire to please or conform, or to oppose, can so easily be the source of the proposal. I have seen decisions made after a time of quiet under such circumstances which were much more the expression of a group mind and will than the mind of God.

Jesus said, 'Where two or three are gathered together in my name there am I in the midst of them.' I am quite sure the fellowship is a vital necessity in living the Christian life. 'Nobody who is truly guided by God works alone' is the conclusion of a very wise Christian. But teamwork is not group conformism, it is the robust building together of minds and spirits each of which is primarily devoted to its Lord. There is a legitimate and an illegitimate rôle for the group in the Christian fellowship. The object is to discern the voice of God, not the popular voice. The Church is not a democracy but a theocracy, and only when those who assemble in the name of Christ do so with a clear and single heart as to their primary loyalty can they best contribute to necessary decisions and procedures for common actions.

On the other hand, of course, the most idiotic and absurd individualism can emerge where each person sets aside intelligence, common sense, the lessons of experience and the common mind of his fellows in an attempt at every point to discern new and particular 'guidance'. One doesn't need special guidance from God to feed one's children or wash one's face. Yet even here I can understand the conviction that one must always 'keep an ear cocked' for the supernormal, for the 'plus' factor of the as yet unknown and unknowable. Common sense, conscience, experience – these should be there all the time, but never as a closed room. There must always be a door ever so slightly ajar for another factor to emerge. The imperious thought, 'Stop! – Do not eat that (apparently perfectly good) food', heard and obeyed, has saved more than one life. 'Don't catch the train on which you are booked, go by another!' has saved at least one life to my certain knowledge. A lady well-known to me had a similar clear sense of direction about cancelling a passage on a ship in wartime, and her life was saved by her obedience, even though such passages were enormously difficult to obtain and a reunion with her husband was the attraction for her to sail.

It is a matter of learning to discern the 'extra' or 'other' factor, the additional and finally authoritative voice, superseding the capacities of the partially developed self, which is what spiritual growth is all about. Here one finds a power, a purpose, a person, a friend who is *there*, and is to be trusted, infinitely.

None of us likes this way, especially at first. It seems to be an invasion of our essential freedom and selfdom, but this is none other than what Jesus described as 'saying no to oneself and following him', of 'taking up one's cross'. The self, with its will and protectiveness, has to die to live. It is so much easier to set aside any attempt to let God's voice become our arbiter and guide, and instead to make our own rules, guidelines which we can manage, which are then really only the basis of our own little individual 'religion'. The adventure of true and growing spiritual discernment and development stops short when we do.

CHAPTER 5

Our position in the world is different from that of antiquity. We are, so to speak, old; and we reason like old men. The world has had experience of other systems . . . and it finds them unsatisfactory. It had, if I may say so, the experience of a long life to go upon . . .

The original relationship of man to God, being a relation of love, is ethical . . . man is a moral and independent being. The relation in which he first stood to God was a moral relation; the relation in which he is to stand anew is a moral relation; the means, therefore, used to bring him into this new relation must be moral means. Thus grace, or the scheme of salvation, is the great moral agency employed by God for bringing again His moral creature, man, into the perfect moral relation of soul with Himself.

A B Davidson, *Old Testament Prophecy*

The latest lesson of the laboratory and study appears to be that, while we can go very, very far in our study of the material world, there are mysteries that our methods can, by their very nature, never touch . . . Materialism, dialectical or otherwise, is a form of faith founded on predilection and belief which has an appeal for certain minds, but it certainly has no support from the findings or the founders of modern science.

E N deC Andrade, *An Approach to Modern Physics*

CHAPTER FIVE

What is Religion?

I have used the word 'religion' in what may appear to be a disparaging way so the time has come to be much more definite about it.

What is religion?

The definitions are plentiful – and partial. Indeed the definitions, like the universe, seem to be expanding. When Roger Hicks finished his talk at La Trobe University the first question he was asked was, 'Is religion necessary?'

He began his reply by saying, 'It depends on what you mean by religion.' He went on to make an interesting statement to the effect that the observance of any particular rite or the wearing of any particular label was not essential, but the discerning of and commitment to a power which is personal, powerful and purposeful (which he called God, for want of a better word) was.

In the way in which I used the word at the end of the previous chapter it referred to the structure built up by groups or individuals to enable them to carry out those practices and precepts which they have thus far come to see as the way and will of God for them. Religion, in this sense, is a framework to enable the individual or group to live more nearly to the best that they know of God's purpose for them. But in using the word 'God' at all one has narrowed down the field of relevance of what I believe is a universal phenomenon.

The communist, for instance, would instantly reject the word God except under great stress, as we have heard from the Kremlin on occasion! Yet the Marxist, in accepting dialectical as opposed to mechanical materialism, has admitted that, at the very base of his philosophy there is something purposeful. Atheism may be, for him, the rejection of the idea of God as developed by the world's religions, but nevertheless his faith is alive and powerful, he believes in goals and so in values, in the 'good' which is to come out of the process of clash and confrontation between opposites. The communist rejects the proposition of a personal God, but he is prepared to live and even die for his faith. It is even a messianic faith – for he will assert with his last breath that final victory will come to his cause, inevitably, no matter what happens to him as an individual.

There is something horribly splendid, and even hopeful, about the upsurge of terrorism across the world today. Increasing numbers of young men and women count life cheap compared with their commitment to a cause and its outcome in history. At least some of them are idealists. They care. They are prepared to reject the world, the flesh and God (if not the Devil, although he too would have to carry their torch to be acceptable) for their ideology. Discipline, dedication, and finally the immolation of self are all there. They are the ones we call extremists – which is really the same as saying they have done within the Marxist parameters what the great heroes, prophets and ascetics of religion have done through the centuries: they have carried their faith and philosophy to its logical and ultimate conclusion and dared to live it.

If they have been conditioned to believe that man is really expendable, a mere cog in a machine, that there is nothing sacred about human life and human relationships, that the end justifies the means; then why should any act of terror, bestiality, murder or treachery be outside the scope of available weapons to fight their war?

It is more important than ever then that we as a race have a thorough re-examination of our goals and purposes, of the objectives which provide mankind with motives for living. Perhaps it is indeed high noon, as the Club of Rome's studies would seem to indicate, in the very history of our civilisation. Not only because of terrorism but because 'respectable' western man too has taken hopelessly inadequate and at times utterly destructive values and purposes for which to strive. We have all come to the point where we are dealing in death – in violent, horrible, soul-destroying murder – whether by a bomb in an aeroplane, a knife in the dark, nuclear war, or starvation in India. Dealing out death in one way or another, or preparing to do so, preoccupies a high proportion of the brains, resources and energy of a large portion of mankind.

We are all in it. The first thing we need to face, if there is to be any future, is the fact that we *are* all in it. Communist, Christian, terrorist, tycoon, monk or housewife, whether in person or by proxy we live and move and have our being in death. Dealing out death is our ultimate recourse. The nuclear deterrent, the strategic-arms umbrella, the appeal to force: these things shroud our little lives as a race and as individuals. What is more, death comes nearer and nearer. The smell of terror moves slowly down our suburban streets. And what is new about that?

We have a vastly greater number of people today, of course, so we have the means to kill vastly more people. We have bright, shiny civilisation with brilliant technology to serve us, so we have bright, shiny weapons with brilliant technology to kill us.

But people are the same. The individual is no different. We all have our lives, our hearts, our loves and hates, our homes and our hopes. We have our causes, our clans, our classes and our creeds and they go deep, as do our prejudices, hates and fears. This was so at the time of Jesus, and Buddha, and Moses, and Mohammed.

Nearly three thousand years ago, King David felt as deeply on any issue or in any area of human life as any man alive today – and he put it in better language than most can today, if the *Book of Psalms* is any indication.

Terror and brutality were skies under which families lived at the time of Christ. The slaughter of infants whether in Vietnam or in Bethlehem; the massacre of a whole city, whether Jerusalem or Phnom Penh: the threat of death and destruction has not been newly invented in our day. This is the backdrop against which the whole drama of human life has been played out to this present time. The jungle is there still, in our veins, and it is a fallacy to think otherwise.

But there has been some progress. There have been times when hope has burned bright, when peace has come if only for a space, when fear has receded to the fringe of living, and beauty and love have been dominant.

What is more, we now have available to us an immense amount of experience and insight into the causes and conditions which have generated disaster. In a very real way the primary concern of mankind – until the last century or so carried us off on a treasure hunt of materialism, science and technology – has been to discern and clarify our goals, values and codes of practice with a view to securing a surer way, a deeper understanding and a better life for all. Until relatively recently there has been a widening consensus as to goals and values. Indeed, despite claims to the contrary, one wonders whether some of the modern materialist codes are not at least paying tribute to these same values and standards in the trouble they take to attack or avoid them! From the Code of Hammurabi and the Decalogue of Moses, down to the Atlantic Charter and the objectives of the United Nations, the attempts have been made to discern and strive for a better life for mankind, individually and collectively. Most particularly in the great religions of the world one sees both the hand of the master and the accretions of the camp-followers: things which are final and will stand for all time, and things which are transient, time-related, and doomed to pass.

A fascinating study for a modern psychologist of religion would be an examination of the expectation and anticipation of basic changes in people as the result of one regime or another, of this or that ideological initiative. Ché Guevara is reported as saying, 'If our revolution does not have the goal of changing men, it doesn't interest me.' Khruschev likewise has lamented the contradictions and frustrations in communist society, ascribing them to 'the inability to make a selfless man'.[1] The evils which have beset the world: exploitation, callousness, greed and class-repression, which have been and are fuel to the fires of the Marxists, are obviously held by them to be evil. If exploitation is wrong, then honesty and consideration must be desirable and right. If callousness and cruelty are bad, then caring and tender concern must be good. If greed is wrong, unselfishness is clearly desirable, as Khruschev admitted . . . and so the list could be extended. The more one studies the basic thinking of the Marxists the more one is forced to conclude that it was not with the standards and alleged goals and objectives of religion that the early communists had their basic quarrels, but with the hypocrisy and dishonesty of a system and its proponents who not only did not live what they preached, but who actually used religion to try to anaesthetise their victims.

The current revolt across the world against the standards and authorities of the previous generation stems from this same root.

The whites in South Africa are under attack for many reasons. Russia has her own strategic, economic and ideological reasons which dominate and determine strategy. In the non-communist West however there is a large proportion of transferred guilt, for there in that remote country is to be seen the final and logical outcome and result of the way we whites have lived. We can point the finger of scorn at people who claim deep religious faith but who exploit, ill-treat and humiliate their neighbours on the grounds of colour and race. There we see Bibles, gold and diamonds, technology and education, affluence and arrogance, all compounded into what is almost a caricature but more like a flashback from the way we have lived in the West for a century or more. They *are us*, in many ways.

We all know that that basis for society is doomed: that time is running out for racial overlordship, which is what we really knew all along in our hearts, but our hands and our gut-greed wanted more instant satisfaction. It was we who sent the flag, the gunboats and armies and police and then the traders to follow the missionaries. Not an integrated, ideologically deliberate scenario by any means, but a fair sample of the way we as nations have lived. We have so prostituted our priceless religious heritage that it has become an indecency in the eyes of some, an indifference in the view of many more, and a lingering, wistful longing in the hearts of those who still have hope.

But the synthetics haven't worked either.

'Workers of the world unite!' hardly describes the situation between Russia, Poland, Peking and Belgrade, or the comrades in Phnom Penh and Ho Chi Minh city. Solzhenitsyn was reared to all the privileges of and insights into the alternative way, and the whole world knows the result. It doesn't work.

Is there any way that will?

I have a friend in Australia who would be one of the least orthodox and least religious men I have ever met. He lives close to the soil, but he is a rustic philosopher. He has one saying which is full of wisdom, 'When everything else fails, read the instructions'. That strikes a chord in most people's minds. How often do we start out with a new gadget or a new product and only when it grinds to a halt or finishes in ruins do we ruefully go back to find out what the maker had set down as the rules for its use!

It is not my intention here to argue for the existence of a Maker, simply to set out some of the empirical results of some notable experiences and experiments I have encountered at first hand. However it seems to me that the Marxist who says 'in the beginning was matter and governing that matter was and is and ever will be a rhythm or law that will necessarily result in progress, and by means of the conflict of opposites lead to a new and higher synthesis', such a person seems to me to be pretty much a theist rather than an atheist.

The problems which beset the mind of modern man when confronted with the proposition that there may be a Creator with a plan, not just for the broad sweep of history, but for each individual life and for each detail of that life, are tremendous. First of all the sheer magnitude of the canvas is mind-boggling. We are talking not of Mao Tse-tung or his successors ruling the daily lives and thoughts of a mere one thousand million Chinese, but the God of all eternity dealing with all men who live. That is the point, of course; we are talking about an infinite and eternal being, so we must let that one pass.

There are other problems, to do with magnitude and numbers, and these we must come to grips with. What hope could there possibly be for the world if it depended on four thousand million people getting changed or converted from selfishness, greed, hatred, lust and the rest? It is a nice idea, but quite impracticable.

Yet is it?

In the first days of November 1977 very few people would have given any credence to the possibility that events could so shape that the vast majority of the Jewish and Egyptian people would be euphoric with joy at the prospect of peace; that Golda Meir would be glowing with goodwill as she pressed a birthday gift into the hands of the President of Egypt; that the Knesset would ring with the ancient words of Isaiah calling the nations to peace. But it happened, before Christmas. It did not take millions of lives to be deeply changed to a new concept of the will of God before those same lives opened, even if only for a time, to the sunshine of goodwill, peace and brotherhood.

What lay behind it?

It was no accident, to be sure. Behind the scenes were people with a commitment to peace which was 'just and lasting'. Anyone who listened to President Sadat addressing the Knesset must have felt Abraham Lincoln's presence breathing into that atmosphere from over the centuries, those immortal words of his inaugural speech '. . . with malice towards none, with charity for all, with firmness in the right as *God gives us to see the right*, let us strive on to finish the course we are in . . . to do all that may cherish *a just and lasting peace* between us and all men . . .'

So too were the cardinal values which should characterise peace as enumerated by Sadat: honesty, purity, love and peace. One saw here the peacemaker at work, and who can deny that to this action Jesus of Nazareth would have added his own benediction:

'Blessed are the peacemakers, for they shall be called the children of God.'

It may not be possible for the world to know the full story of the brief outbreak of peace in the Israeli–Egyptian field in late 1977, but there is one story which I have been able to examine in great depth. It relates to events still very much in the news in North East India.

CHAPTER 6

Neither the technological process that is forcing East and West together, nor the insurgence of the nationalist forces that is tearing them apart, can save the modern world from destruction. Salvation can only come through some power capable of creating a spiritual unity which will transcend and comprehend the material unity of the new world order.

Christopher Dawson, *The Revolt of Asia*

CHAPTER SIX

Peacemaking on the Borders of China

It would be difficult to imagine a more potential powder keg in international tensions than the North East frontier of India. When Mrs Gandhi was in power and Russia was a welcome guest and mentor, the Sino-Soviet confrontation formed the backdrop to its tribal and racial minority activities. I had heard stories of significant changes in attitudes and the consequent healing of tensions because of the decision by one of the minority leaders, Stanley Nichols Roy, to make the experiment of listening to the voice of God and obeying the imperatives which resulted.

Late in 1976 I was able to visit India and seek out a young man who was from a leading family among the Naga people, a hills tribe from the mountainous area surrounding the plains of Assam. His name was Niketu Iralu, and I came across him leading a conference between Indian Trade Union executives and their employers at the Moral Re-Armament Training Centre at Panchgani, some two hundred miles from Bombay.

I tape-recorded my interview with him, so this is the conversation just as it took place. I first asked Niketu to tell me something of himself and his people.

Niketu: I come from Nagaland, of the Naga tribe. My people live in the frontier between India and Burma. Some of my tribesmen actually live in Burma, while about half a million of us live on the Indian side and form the State of Nagaland, the smallest state of the Indian union. It is a very hilly region at the southern end of the eastern Himalayas. Most of the people live in villages, sometimes very big villages of one thousand houses or more, but we have no towns. Before the British came we were not part of India. We only became a part of India through the British in the third part of the nineteenth century. We are racially part of the Mongoloid race, and are called the Mongoloid fringe on the eastern frontier of India.

Nagaland itself was part of the old province of Assam, and after Indian independence Assam became a separate state. It was then that my people, as a tribal minority, started agitating for an independent republic. This resulted in insurgency wars that have continued up to this time, that is since 1947.

Active guerilla war started about 1955 and became very fierce about 1958 and 1959. It is gradually petering out but the hard-core of the resistance is still operating on the Burma border and based inside Burma.

Mackay: So the Nagas are very independent people at heart?

Niketu: They are expressing what they feel is an honest sentiment, that they are from a different racial background. This has resulted in the present political agitation. As far as they are concerned therefore they are not committing an act of treason, but from India's point of view it is treason, so India has sent in her army.

Mackay: I don't suppose your people, the Nagas, would be the only hill tribes in that area who felt the same way, for instance a new state Meghalaya has recently come into being. Could you tell us something about the Meghalaya people? Is their position parallel to your own?

Niketu: They are also a tribal people like the Nagas. Meghalaya today is a state made up of three distinct tribes, the Kashis, the Garos and the Jhantias, and they number about one million people. They live right on the Bangladesh border. They also began to fight for their own identity, and wanted to preserve their language, so they started agitating to have a state of their own. Then something very remarkable happened. Instead of the story ending in bloodshed and violence, as in the case of my people, Meghalaya was created because of the development of greater goodwill and understanding between the Assamese people (that is the majority people living in the valley, mostly Moslems and Hindus), and the tribal people living up in the hills.

Mackay: Had there been similarly tense and bad relationships earlier between the Assamese majority in the valley, that is in the fertile and perhaps one would say more developed part of the country, and the hill people?

Niketu: Oh, yes indeed! The agitation for the State of Meghalaya started in 1952 and gradually became a very dangerous movement, in the sense that it was about to become violent. By 1967 there was a real stalemate. Young people calling themselves 'freedom volunteers' started to send telegrams to the Prime Minister, Mrs Gandhi, in Delhi, stating that unless a Hill State was granted them they were going underground to 'follow the Nagapath' as they put it. Delhi was unable to give any decision because it was going to affect the Congress Party majority rule in the state of Assam, a state with about eight million people. The leaders of the hill people would go to Delhi, talk to the Government but would return frustrated because there was nothing conclusive, no decision made by the Government. It was at this time, towards the end of 1967, that the General Secretary of the Hills People's Party was a Mr Stanley Nichols Roy from the Kashi tribe.

Mackay: Now that sounds a very English type of name, Stanley Nichols Roy.

Niketu: Yes it is, because he, like many tribal people, is a Christian, so they had taken western names. Stanley Nichols Roy's father was a very prominent churchman and also a leader in the political field. In fact his father was the member of the Constitutional Assembly right up to Independence, representing the tribal people of India's North East. While in Delhi meeting Mrs Gandhi and the Home Minister, Mr Chavan, Nichols Roy met Rajmohan Gandhi, grandson of the Mahatma and some of his friends in Moral Re-Armament. He heard stories of healing that had come to situations in the world like the one between France and Germany after the war. How a French woman who had suffered greatly under the Nazis took it upon herself to bring healing to the wounds of war between the French and the Germans. That story in particular moved him very much and he said, 'If it is possible for a change taking place in the heart of a person to affect a larger political crisis, such as we have in the North East, then as the General Secretary of our Party, I must investigate.'

He expressed the desire to come to our Training Centre which had just been built in Western India, at Panchgani. A few weeks later Rajmohan Gandhi received a cable from him saying he was bringing thirty-three other tribal people with him, travelling from the eastern to the western end of India – about five days' journey on the Indian railways. This was a measure of his determination. He came, and stayed for five days. It was during that time that he made a very careful study of the people whose stories he had heard.

He was particularly interested in the practice of listening to the voice of God or 'the inner voice' as we say in India, and how by obeying that voice, change can come in human situations. On the fourth morning he got up very early in the morning and spent an hour making this experiment of really opening his life to God.

Mackay: How do you know that this took place?

Niketu: Well, as a man from the North East, I roomed with him in the new building, and I woke to find him sitting up at 4 am with a torch in his hand, and now and then jotting down things in his notebook. I was watching curiously because he sat like that, up in his bed, for over an hour. Later on in the first meeting that day he spoke, reading from his notebook, so I saw how it was being done.

Anyway, he said that morning that he had opened his life and heart to God and had told him that he would do whatever he asked him to do. He said he was desperate for a solution for his people's crisis. The first thought he got was to get completely honest with his wife about all the things that he had not told her including things that he had done in Calcutta and Delhi on his way to the political meetings in Delhi. The second thought he had was to apologise to two of his colleagues in his own party (nothing to do with the Assamese party). They were his political enemies and he felt he should apologise for his jealousy and rivalry towards these friends. He remarked that even as he planned to come to the conference with the thirty-three tribal people, he had made sure that neither of them came with him. He said that he always made sure that one of them in particular was not around to steal the limelight in any situation. So that was the second thought. The third thought was that, on his return, he should go and call on Mr B P Chaliha who had been the Chief Minister of Assam for over thirteen years, and a very highly respected man. Nonetheless he had been the chief opponent of the tribal people in the crisis in the North East.

Mackay: Therefore no longstanding friend of Nichols Roy!

Niketu: No, Nichols Roy was very hesitant to write this thought down because he felt it could be misconstrued by his followers as weakness.

But he had this very clear thought at that time in the morning, 'Go and see him, tell him what you have learned at Panchgani, and of your getting honest with your wife, and just get to know him on a human basis!'

So he had all these thoughts and he obeyed all of them, it must be said to his credit, on his return and immediately.

His wife said that the next morning when she went down town to buy things for the home she found herself waving to complete strangers on the street, she was so happy. The family was completely transformed. Soon after that I stayed in their home and I heard the other side of it all from his wife, and she told us all about it when she too came to Panchgani. As regards his apology to his two rivals he thought it was a risky thing to do, but it actually resulted in the party getting united. Later on, when they had to decide whether they were going to follow a violent method which could become a guerilla war or follow the peaceful Gandhian method, his two colleagues stood solidly with him, so the party adopted the non-violent method. He considered this a real intervention of God.

His meeting with Mr Chaliha also resulted in some most unexpected developments. He simply told him about his experiences and how he had started to change the management of his own life. Chaliha was fascinated, especially when he went on to say that he was sorry that as a leader of the tribal people he had not also thought in terms of what was right for the Assamese majority, that he had only thought in terms of what was right and good for his own people.

He said, 'From now on I would like my people and myself to start thinking of what we could do for you also and for the rest of India, and not always thinking of what we can get from Delhi as a tribal minority group.'

This pleased, intrigued and fascinated Mr Chaliha who had always thought of the tribal people as a minority group who always thought in terms of what they could get.

Then he suggested to Chaliha that they might jointly issue an invitation to all the members of the Assam State Legislative Assembly to see a film that he had seen in Delhi and that he had brought with him, the African film called *Freedom*. This is a film showing reconciliation and new hope for racial division in Africa.

He said to Chaliha, 'I feel this film has all the problems of our area in it and also the answers.'

Chaliha, to his credit, immediately responded, and the next day an invitation printed in their joint names went out. The press was, of course, immediately interested. Nichols Roy took that film and the projector to the State Assembly House and projected the film himself. Mr Chaliha brought his cabinet ministers and other members of the Assembly in and introduced the film. Although he had not seen the film himself he said, 'I'm proud to present my friend Mr Nichols Roy and also to introduce this film. I have not seen it nor do I know much about Moral Re-Armament, but my friend had wanted all of us to see it and from what I have seen so far in Nichols Roy's life, I want to support it.'

So the film was shown. That event brought about a change of atmosphere in the state capital.

Mackay: Could I ask a further question here, about the first thought he had concerning his wife? You say that his wife was overjoyed by his coming home and speaking to her as he did. But I imagine that the things he had to tell her were not exactly happy things, can you tell me a little bit more of what really happened?

Niketu: Yes, well, he has publicly stated what he said to her at our conference here so I'm not revealing a secret. He had to tell her things that he had kept hidden from her all the time about other women in his life.

Mackay: Was she surprised by all of this?

Niketu: She said that she had always suspected that he was doing something like this when he went away to Delhi, but he had never told her the truth so their family was full of tension. That's what she said, adding, 'With this new basis, from now on we can make a new start. If you had not told me this I had made up my mind that before long I was going to walk out, with the children.'

Mackay: That is a tremendous feature of this story, isn't it? – that there was a home that was potentially going to be broken and the children were already living in a divided home, which is one of the great problems of our age. That was the first thing that was put right. It started in the home.

Niketu: Yes. Soon after that the remarkable thing was that this home became a centre where people from various communities came almost every night, for example to see films that Nichols Roy had brought back from Panchgani, and to hear about what he had found in his life and in his family. From then on he started to bring the same experience to people after people: young people, people in administration, people in politics, people in business. He became possessed with a real passion for helping people.

Mackay: So his wife must have pitched in thoroughly on the whole programme?

Niketu: Yes, very thoroughly.

Mackay: A little earlier, Niketu, you said that there were various divisions among the tribal people themselves, and while there were those who were prepared to come to terms with the Assamese, others, the extremists and the guerilla fighters, weren't so easy to bring into this picture. How did Nichols Roy get on with the extremist leadership?

Niketu: One of the men who belonged to the extremist group was Huva Henyata, a great orator. He was a member of the Indian Parliament representing the tribal people of that region. In fact he was the man who first raised the cry for a Hill State in 1952. He had become very bitter towards Nichols Roy and others because of jealousy and because they were now running the Hills People's Party. In the elections he had lost his seat and so he became very bitter and very extremist. He took every opportunity to make it difficult for any approach to be made towards the Assamese people on the question of the Hill State. His speeches and his tactics always made it especially difficult for Nichols Roy and his colleagues to attempt any approach which could be interpreted as a compromise. So Huva was the one man that Nichols Roy wanted to win. He gave a lot of thought to this question.

One of the visitors who came to stay with Nichols Roy was a Welshman by the name of Sydney Cook. He had immediate rapport with many of the tribal people because they had become Christians because of Welsh Presbyterian missionaries.

Sydney Cook met Huva and after some time he had the very clear thought that Huva was meant to go to Panchgani and he said this to him.

Huva just laughed at it and said, 'That is utterly impossible. I'm physically unwell, I don't have enough money, and I really do not see how I can go.'

Sydney persisted, and really helped Huva over one obstacle after another.

The final hurdle that Huva put up was that he needed two truck loads of cow-dung in the dry winter months for his potato fields. He said to Sydney Cook, 'Get me two truck loads of cow-dung and I shall consider going to Panchgani, otherwise I'll have to spend the time finding them.'

Cook told him that God would provide those two truck loads.

He later discussed the matter with Nichols Roy and did nothing else about it except to pray.

Cook later met another friend, this time a doctor from the Assamese people who was also becoming interested in what had happened to Nichols Roy. Sydney Cook said to him, 'How do you find two truck loads of cow-dung at this time?' The doctor asked, 'Why do you need two truck loads of cow-dung?' He replied, 'My friend Huva says that he needs them otherwise he won't go to Panchgani.'

Now, unknown to Cook, the doctor was in charge of the TB chest hospital and therefore had to keep a lot of cows to get enough milk for the patients. He immediately said, 'No problem, tomorrow morning they will be delivered.' Sydney rang up Huva and said, 'Two truck loads of cow-dung arriving tomorrow morning.'

So the truck loads of manure were delivered and Huva finally said, 'You have won; what next?'

So they travelled together towards Panchgani.

On arrival at Bombay Airport Huva was very surprised to hear the name of Nichols Roy being called over the loudspeaker system in the passengers' lounge as they were getting ready to leave for the city. Now Huva had understood that Nichols Roy was in Delhi with other colleagues and that there would be no danger of his meeting his rival while in Panchgani. But Nichols Roy had come to Bombay because there had been a postponement of the meetings he was to have with the Prime Minister, so was planning to spend the intervening days in Panchgani. So Huva, to his great consternation, found himself travelling to Panchgani with Stanley. He decided to keep quiet about it but he was very angry.

On arrival in Panchgani Huva kept quiet and listened to everything, not saying much.

One day a young lady from Malaysia, a medical student studying at Calcutta University who had come to attend the conference, made a very brief speech. She said that she had great fear in making that speech but that God had made it clear to her that she was to put certain things right with her father and that she wanted to commit herself to do so.

The next day, when we were arranging a meeting, Huva said that he wanted to make a speech. We asked him, 'Would you like to take ten or fifteen minutes?'

He said, 'Unless you can give me one hour I don't speak.' So Huva spoke. He said, referring to the speech made by the young Malaysian, 'That little girl spoke and she has shamed me. Her story touched me, and I have said to myself, why be a slave to your own pride? If she can open up her life and speak like that, you can also, and you must do.'

He then spoke for one hour and it was a very, very moving speech. Quite a number of people had tears in their eyes. He talked about his life, how he had struggled as a youth leader, and how he went to Delhi as an MP. He even mentioned that the height of his achievement there was when he one day made a statement in the Parliament and got the Prime Minister, Mr Nehru so angry that Mr Nehru had to stand up and reply to him shouting. He said, 'After that, I felt happy.'

Anyway, Huva said to Nichols Roy sitting in the audience, 'I am sorry. All my life I have done my best to hurt you and your family. I enjoyed hurting your father who was such a great leader of our people, and I want to ask your forgiveness today. I want to throw all these things I have done behind my back, to leave them in the past.'

Nichols Roy came up, they shook hands in that meeting and a new relationship was established.

Huva left for home soon after that and he took with him the names of several people back at home whom he decided that he ought to see. He reached Gauhati Airport in Assam and from that airport one goes to Shillong, the Capital of Assam, by car or by bus. At the airport Huva found an Assamese who was known to him who said, 'I am going to Shillong (sixty-three miles up in the hills). May I give you a lift?' Huva said, 'Thank-you very much', and got into the car. They left the airport and entered the city of Gauhati and this Assamese gentleman said, 'Please give me a few minutes because I want to drive by my uncle's home in Gauhati city before we start climbing.'

Huva agreed. They drove into the home of the uncle of this gentleman and went inside. To his great dismay Huva found himself introduced to a man called Bishnuram Mehdi, one of the men Huva and all tribal leaders and tribal people always disliked intensely, because Mehdi was previously the Chief Minister of Assam and had always said the wrong things as far as the tribal hill people were concerned.

He felt that they were a nuisance, more or less, and created so many problems for his state that he tried to belittle them every time. And Huva found himself meeting this man whose name had come to him in Panchgani. His name was on that list. Huva said to himself, 'God, you have brought me to this place, this is the moment to act.'

So he said to him, 'Mehdi, I am meeting you today, but not according to my own plan.' Going on to explain the situation he said that he had just returned from Panchgani.

'When in Panchgani I thought of meeting you and of putting things right with you and the Assamese people. I'm sorry for having preached communal hatred against the Assamese people, agitating my people for my own political power and success. For this I need your forgiveness.'

Mehdi was very moved by the tribal leader speaking to him like this and gave him a very warm reception and hospitality in his home.

Huva returned to his home town Shillong, the capital, feeling that God had already used him.

Soon after his return to Shillong there was a reception, a meeting in the home of Mr B P Chaliha, Chief Minister of Assam at that time. About fifty people were in the official residence. Huva was one of those who spoke and he said to Mr Chaliha and the Assamese people present the same thing that he had said to Mehdi down in Gauhati.

This was a real surprise, because everybody in Shillong had known Huva to be a very extremist leader, always saying very hurting, bitter things against the other communities. Huva's change created a new spirit, a new atmosphere in the hill areas. This was an important element in the whole story of how the State of Meghalaya came into being without bloodshed and violence.

Because Huva began to co-operate in a very constructive way by giving positive leadership to the hill people at that very critical time, it helped talks which soon followed. Negotiations were soon conducted by the Government of India between the hill people and the plains people.

The major newspapers, unaware of all this, were already writing editorials and articles saying that only bloodshed was to be expected, and they did not see any hope of a settlement. In fact, the Chief Minister himself, quoted in a newspaper editorial, said that unless a settlement was found between the hill people and the plains people, Assam would become a second Vietnam. That was the middle of 1968.

At this time Nichols Roy and his colleagues had begun to make a fresh approach, and a very important meeting was held in Delhi. It was held in a hotel, and they kept the pressmen out. It was a meeting between the Assamese leaders led by Chaliha, and the hill leaders led by Nichols Roy and his friends. They spent the whole day just chatting and exploring the whole issue as between friends.

Soon after that, to the surprise of the whole country, what is now called 'The Meghalaya Proposal' was made by the Government of India and the leaders on both sides made public statements appealing to their people not to start agitations but to give the scheme a fair trial. It was given a fair trial and it worked. Eventually a full State for the Hill People was created.

The Governor of the North East Region, Mr B K Nehru (later India's High Commissioner in London) said, 'Seldom have such far-reaching constitutional changes been brought about with so much goodwill and understanding. I have seen the hate in the hearts of the hill people reduced before my eyes.'

He talked about several individuals.

Mr Chaliha, as the Chief Minister, said, 'This has transformed the climate of Assam. This is a fact, I speak as an administrator.'

That's how the State of Meghalaya was created without bloodshed and violence.

The real significance of this story is:

(a) Tens of millions of rupees of the Indian budget were saved because the struggle did not become violent. If the army had intervened and it had become a guerilla operation millions and millions of rupees every day would have been spent, to say nothing of the suffering.

(b) A tribal minority had demonstrated a new attitude toward racial problems. They found that they were a people who could give much to others rather than just receive, and they went about doing it, something which I think is of great relevance in the world today. Because so many minorities think in terms of what they are out to get this was a truly revolutionary development.

Mackay: Speaking as a former politician I can say that in the Cabinet Room one doesn't expect to see enormous changes take place without tremendous preparation and perhaps great political pressures brought to bear. You have told us a story here of very simple things. As simple as a girl being frank and honest about thoughts that came to her in a time of quiet, and her being courageous enough to tell a group of people about the relationship between herself and her own father, and how this actually led to the solution of a vital facet of an international situation, or inter-racial situation. The other thing that strikes me is the simplicity of what you saw at 4.30, was it, in the morning, of a man making the first experiment of his life of being absolutely definite about that voice inside himself that we all have, and how he was prepared to be as definite as black and white in a notebook and then to carry it out and how it transformed his home and his nation. I feel that we have underestimated the speed and the power and the effectiveness of this very simple thing.

Niketu: If I may add about Nichols Roy, he studied fruit technology in the University of California and he started the first fruit canning industry in North East India, so he was a very able businessman before he entered politics.

When he became the General Secretary of his party and negotiations were going on, the newspapers described him as 'A human steamroller'; so it was the case of a very able, dynamic man learning to listen to 'the inner voice'.

He was well equipped as a man and God used all that equipment.

CHAPTER 7

Our task is to utilise every manifestation of discontent, and to collect and utilise every grain of even rudimentary protest.

Is there a single class of the population in which no individuals, groups or circles are to be found who are discontented and therefore inaccessible to our propaganda?

Lenin

Selfishness is not by any means a monopoly of the rich. The same causes which lead the rich employer to lower wages or the rich landlord to raise rents operate quite as freely with working men when opportunity and self-interest dictate a like course . . .

[Class war] is a degradation of the Socialist Movement to drag it down to the mere level of a struggle for supremacy between two contending factions.

Keir Hardie

God is our guide. No swords we draw,
We kindle not war's battle fires.
By reason, union, justice, law,
We claim the birthright of our sires.

The Tolpuddle Martyrs

CHAPTER SEVEN

The Age of Ideology

In discussing the need for a new age built on values and incentives which will replace the competitive greed and selfishness which have brought both breakdown and revolution, the great question emerges as to whether it is possible to discern some of its hallmarks: specifically whether we see any more clearly the ways in which an answer could become more than an isolated set of incidents, a few gleams in a general darkness.

One of the things which Karl Marx and Jesus of Nazareth have in common is the fact that each held all he thought, taught and did in a global perspective. Whatever else one gathers about the qualifications Jesus demanded of those who enlisted as his disciples there can be no argument about the fact that he required their total commitment. It was a case of leaving all to follow him. This was literally true in the case of the Twelve. The rich young ruler might have been a disciple if he had been prepared to put discipleship before his wealth. For others in jobs and occupations it was a matter of the absolute primacy of the kingdom of God. Jesus taught:

'The kingdom of Heaven is like a collector of pearls, who sells his entire collection to buy one superb pearl – it is like a man who finds buried treasure and mortgages all he has to buy the field where it lies.'

'No man who puts his hand to the plough and looks back is fit for the kingdom of Heaven.'

Asked about the supreme rule of living Jesus said succinctly:

'You must be totally committed to God, to others and to yourself with every facet of your nature – intellectually, emotionally and in every activity.'

Such a quality of living has been all too rarely found among the generality of his followers.

God is given only a tiny fraction of the mind, heart, will or purse of most Christians today. Even then the 'God' part is often by proxy, a handout to some intermediary person, parson or cause.

Christianity is most frequently a bourgeois or middle class luxury, an optional extra attached to everyday life. It is certainly not life itself – all of it.

But there are others who are marching in their millions across the face of our modern world who *are* totally committed, in mind, heart, and will. They have discovered what it is to leave behind the old age of compromise, expediency, double-talk and lukewarm allegiances. They have a passion, a philosophy and a plan. They have an ideology.

Many of these people are young. Some of them are Christians; some are Buddhists or Moslems; many more are Marxists. Some go even beyond that to extremes which are utterly ruthless and fanatical. What happens when men and women who are ideologically committed to opposing camps come into contact? Who comes off best?

Here is a true story. The names and descriptions of people and places have been changed, but in its essentials it is precisely as it recently happened to young friends of mine. They were about to go on holiday and had visited a Chinese diplomat acquaintance in his home. As they were leaving the house the diplomat came out to the car to see them off.

'Drive carefully and look after yourselves', he warned with a smile. Was he a friend? they pondered, as they drove off. In a strange way they would have said yes, although he stood at opposite poles from them in terms of ideology. A cautious beginning to their relationship had warmed by mutual respect for the dedication of each to his cause and, with these differences openly accepted, it had been possible for simpler, more human and perhaps more fundamental factors to emerge.

They had first met when Ross deliberately sought out the Chinese officials at their Embassy who were in charge of the activities of students, ostensibly there to improve their English language, who were coming to the University in increasing numbers. Early in their relationship with this diplomat it had become apparent that each was deeply dedicated to a cause: one being a disciple of Mao, and the other a young scientist who, at Oxford University had made a thoroughgoing Christian commitment which had later led him to devote his whole life to taking that message to the world.

At first the diplomat had been bewildered as he recognised the clear, unmistakable dedication of the young Englishman to his mission, and the way he saw all issues as relevant to it.

'We Chinese know for whom we do things', was the way he put it. 'We find that most people in this country are doing things for themselves. But you, we cannot understand you, for whom are you doing all this?'

Ross replied in a way he knew would be understood:

'Where you are doing things for Chairman Mao', he said, 'my wife and I are doing them for God.'

The Chinese diplomat allowed this to pass without further comment; but as time passed it was obvious that something was building up deep inside him.

'Why don't you get a job and support your wife properly instead of living from hand to mouth in the way you are doing?' he finally burst out.

Ross smiled and asked, 'And where do you think your revolution would be today if Chou En-lai or Mao Tse-tung had adopted that philosophy?'

The diplomat got the point.

One evening as they sat around the fireside delving into each other's minds and ways, the Chinese diplomat seemed particularly interested to discover what it was that kept Ross and his wife on the rails, as it were. What was the source of their discipline? He questioned them courteously but firmly.

Ross replied in kind, 'What is it that makes your young men and women keep strictly to their training and mission, especially in the midst of the permissive student life in our universities?'

The diplomat replied at once, 'Every day each one of us must have a time of self-criticism when we read *The Thoughts of Chairman Mao*, and then review our lives.'

'But what if one of your workers fails to do this and starts to fall down on the job?' Ross queried.

'That would soon become obvious, because every week we have a period for group study and mutual criticism', was the reply.

Ross was still not satisfied. 'But what if someone appeared to be weakening in those sessions, what can you do about it?'

'We spend time going deeper into it and try to re-educate him', the diplomat explained, adding, 'and if that fails then he will be sent back to China for complete retraining.'

'Suppose that he had become convinced by other ideas and did not respond to that retraining?'

'Then we would kill him – something you have no courage to do', came the quick and almost angry reply.

Later that week there was an official garden party held by the Government, and Ross and his wife were included. They were making their way among the guests, renewing acquaintanceships and making new friends, when they saw their friend the Chinese diplomat obviously doing precisely the same thing. In a few moments they came face to face.

'What are you doing here?' was the Chinese greeting.

'What you are doing here', Ross replied with a grin.

Both understood the purposes of the other well enough now to enable the grin to be returned, and then they each turned away to continue a social activity which had behind it a serious place in the ideological battle in which he was engaged.

Looking around the well-dressed assemblage of that nation's leadership one might well wonder how many of them had the slightest inkling of the dominating purposes of these two men. The very word 'ideology' is elbowed out of the minds of most people in the still-free world as rather indecent, a word relating to the activities of lesser beings who are fanatics or cranks or somehow weaklings of one kind or another. Yet more and more of the nations of the earth, and already well over half of its population, are learning the hard way that this is an ideological age.

Sometimes a voice is heard which commands both respect and attention, at least for a moment. Such a voice is that of Alexander Solzhenitsyn. The monumental courage and intellectual stature of this man, the depth of his own experience and his passionate sincerity, cause most intelligent people to pause for thought when he says:

> All of us are standing on the brink of a great historical cataclysm, a flood that swallows up civilization and changes whole epochs. The present world situation is complicated still more by the fact that several hours have struck simultaneously on the clock of history. We have all got to face up to a crisis – not just a social crisis, not just a political crisis, not just a military crisis. And we must not only face up to this crisis but we must stand firm in this great upheaval – an upheaval similar to that which marked the transition from the Middle Ages to the Renaissance . . .[1]

Mao Tse-tung said that 'Marxist philosophy holds that the law of the unity of opposites is the fundamental law of the universe . . . between the opposites in a contradiction there is at once unity and struggle, and it is this which impels things to move and change.'[2]

Ross and his Chinese friend might well be seen as opposites in a contradiction where there is at once unity and struggle. The unity is important, perhaps as important as the differences in the diametrically opposed philosophies which separated them. Both were revolutionaries, and both were totally committed to vast changes in the world as we know it today, and both had confidence that they knew the secret of that change and the way to make it work. It was this unity in diversity which enabled them to develop a species of friendship, or at least a mutual respect, which was usually reserved for fellow-fighters in the ideological war.

Yet nothing of that altered the fact that they each knew in their hearts that they represented opposing sides in what would prove to be a total confrontation. The cataclysm of which Solzhenitsyn spoke lay immediately ahead, and such was the global significance of their work that each knew that only one faith or the other could survive.

It may not be precisely the form of communism which that Chinese diplomat espoused, nor yet again precisely the kind of religious activity that Ross embraced, but basically these two men represented ideological poles between which lies the tension within which all mortal men exist. The motive power behind unfolding human history is ultimately either the urge from below as man is essentially at one with the jungle and its laws of 'the sharpest tooth and claw' and 'the survival of the fittest', on the one hand, or on the other the urge from above as man reaches out for the consummation of his creation and sees himself as a child of God. Here by faith he cuts his ties with the jungle and reaches into the life of the spirit. The ideology of materialism versus the ideology of the kingdom of God, now, as always, is the true battle-line in all living.

At this point it might be as well for us to define our terms a little. What precisely is an 'ideology'? After all, isn't it just the set of ideas we live by? There are those who use the word in this way, of course, but on the other hand we in the twentieth century have been undergoing some rather salutary lessons in the nature of ideology.

Take the rise of Nazism for example. I well remember, soon after I was demobbed after the Second World War, meeting an older man who had been an officer in British Intelligence for many years. During the thirties he had actually been in Germany and had become a member of the Hitler Youth Jugendführer movement. He described the physical training, the hardening of body and brain to endure and to overcome great stresses and privation. The thing which fascinated me most however was his description of the assemblies which preceded the evening meal. He told how the trainees would file silently into a vast theatre-like hall to the sound of martial music or the strains of Wagner. Then, when all were in their places, an absolute silence reigned while they waited expectantly. Around the white wall were crimson Nazi banners with their white circle and within it the black swastika. Slowly the lights were dimmed until the only illumination came from a number of spot-lights which slowly traversed the room to come to rest on a marble bust of Hitler.

Then, with a sweep, the door would be flung open and the Commandant would be there, arm upraised in the Nazi salute. 'Heil Hitler!' The roar of response would surge from the eager mass of youth, and then, still standing, they would attend to the solemn reading from *Mein Kampf* or some other ideological text. Finally the whole scene would be played in reverse, as it were, and the company would file out silently to supper. The way my Major friend told the story gave me a thrill both of fear and admiration for the planning, the psychology and the depth of dedication involved. I had been given an inside glimpse into a militant ideology.

Yet Nazism was destroyed. How? There was a time when most of the tanks, planes, guns and armies were on their side, and Britain seemed to stand all alone. Arguments will always rage around the nature of the forces which finally stood together to defeat Hitler, but one thing is certain: the ideology of Nazism was not big enough to rule the world. It was a racist doctrine in essence, born of the desperation which attended the defeat of Imperial Germany in World War I and the terrible sufferings which followed it. If the basic conviction of the communists is that 'one class shall rule', then the philosophy of Nazism was that 'one race shall rule'.

There is much more to it than that, of course. The rise of Nazism as 'national socialism' was also a reaction, not just to defeat and despair and national chaos, but also to the rising tide of communism. Nationalist it most certainly was, but socialist? Hardly. The very term was born of a fear that the time of the ordinary man had come, that the masses were about to wrest final control from the traditional ruling classes. So several otherwise incongruous elements found common cause in a movement which, within Germany anyway, seemed to have enough of the ingredients of success to give it a future. Appealing to the fierce nationalism which was still smarting under defeat, rousing deep resentments and hatred against the Jews, and using all the techniques of demagoguery and mass psychology to bring passions to boiling point, the Nazis planned their bid for power.

It will be seen that there are three major elements in the structure of an ideology. In the rise of Nazism there was first of all the sowing of new ideas in the seedbed, the aching void of need, suffering and frustration which was post-war Germany. Hitler had codified these ideas in *Mein Kampf*, and had forged a force of committed people to carry them to the nation. Next came the deliberate kindling of the passions of the people, the enormous hysteria of the Nuremburg rallies and the exploitation of the fear, hunger, bitterness and longings in millions of hearts. Finally there came the massive structure of military and industrial planning which set the jackboots marching and the panzer divisions racing across Europe. Philosophy, passion and plan – three 'p's – and together these elements form the three sides of the one integrated triangle of ideology. Together, they relate to the millions as does the trilogy of mind, heart and will to the individual.

'Thou shalt love the Lord thy God with all thy heart, and all thy mind and all thy strength . . .' That is ideology!

So, ideologies are not new. Almost as far back as one might go into recorded history one sees movements structured in this way. The prophets of the Old Testament gave expression to ideas which, within the context of early Israel produced similar results. Moses came into the scene of misery, exploitation and hopelessness of the enslaved Jewish people sweating under Egyptian taskmasters and gave them a vision and a compelling hope. Their God had a practical and immediate plan by which they were to become a free and significant nation. After their escape across the Red Sea however, more than forty years were spent training and preparing them for national identity, and at the very core of that training was the Law, the system of ethical, religious and social ideas which was fundamental to their pilgrimage. When this ideological base was under attack, as it was continually, then Israel was weakened and in danger. When their zeal for their God and their national heritage waned, or when their resolve became weak, so too their very identity and integrity were in jeopardy.

It would not be too much to claim that the history of the human race can be written as the record of man's search for an adequate ideology. From the most primitive times to the present, one can trace his aspirations for growth – from family, to clan, to nation, to empire and finally to global alliances – all part of a pattern of man's outward urge, of his growing awareness of himself in relation to his environment. Through the ages, leader after leader has arisen presenting to each age new ideas, plans and challenges designed to rouse others to join in movements of change and growth. As communication, transportation and world relationships have shrunk the globe into one world, so there has emerged the corresponding need for leadership fired with ideas to match the challenges of this age. If ever mankind is going to live peaceably together as citizens of one world, then an inescapable requirement will be a global vision, a basic and relevant philosophy which is able to win the hearts, minds and wills of all men everywhere.

With this as background one could well ponder anew those prophetic words of Solzhenitsyn: 'All of us are standing on the brink of a great historical cataclysm, a flood that swallows up civilisation and changes whole epochs . . . similar to that which marked the transition from the Middle Ages to the Renaissance.'

To this one might add, almost as a corollary, that it was this Renaissance which helped in an essential way to give birth to the Reformation. The old ideas, philosophies and theologies which had been stagnant for centuries were no longer adequate for the expanding world being unveiled by the new knowledge. So today, as we are moving with increasing speed into vast social, economic, political and cultural changes on a global scale, it means that inevitably either a new great leap forward will take place in the world of ideas, in our philosophies and theologies, or the world will flounder in anarchy and nihilism. Nothing short of a globally relevant ideology will suffice for the fulfilment of the expanding hopes and needs of the hearts, minds and hands of men.

It is true that some of these philosophies and theologies have claimed world charters, but a glance at where they stand today indicates their failure. Not only have they come to present a divided and fragmented stance to the rest of the world because of inner divisions, but they have built up their own regional and sectional orthodoxies to the point that they are seen as exclusive and related to now decaying national, political and cultural systems. As the old ideologies, social and political philosophies as well as religions are weighed anew against the challenges of modern needs, the most searching question of all will be their relevance to man's, *every* man's, search for his common destiny.

It is this test which, to some degree at least, is already being applied in international courts like the United Nations. It is increasingly obvious, even to the casual observer, that we are already embroiled in the interplay of forces and influences which are global in their aspirations and which orchestrate many of the most important happenings of our time.

The tragic events in Northern Ireland and Rhodesia, for example, are fostered, fanned and inflamed by those from without who play for wider stakes. The blinding bitterness which has been spawned by past wrongs, by cruelty and exploitation in racial and sectarian dealings, is deliberately promoted so that those most involved rarely see clearly these international interests and objectives they are now promoting. And not only are the national interests of super powers involved, but other groupings of powers and interests emerge on the scene, all seeing their role within the horizons of their own ideologies.

It is little wonder then that the ordinary person today feels helpless in the face of this enormous complexity of forces which stand to play him like a puppet. He sees so many different kinds of force deployed in his own immediate situation. Overarching it all he is uncomfortably but rather resignedly aware of the spectre of nuclear war, and other forms of mass destruction equally horrible to contemplate. Even these dangers are continually being offset, or set over against a whole range of other naked abuses of power, from terrorism to trade. Some of the forces involved seem to cut right across all natural groupings, all national and racial boundaries and interests, yet in a tantalising way nationalism and racialism not only persist, but in some cases re-emerge to threaten the very future of professedly global ideologies and movements.

No area so amply illustrates the complexity and inter-involvement of this modern world ferment as does Africa. With the quickening of the struggles inside that continent one is aware of the great external forces acting upon it, many of them under the guise of internationalism or anti-racism or some kind of benevolence, but really with a view to their own primary interests. South Africa, for example, is bedevilled not only by the basic clash of races within the nation, with its tragic and explosive persistence with a tier system of races – first, second, third and fourth class – but both the past and the present in terms of super power strategy have a heavy hand on the possibilities of its solution.

There is no realistic view of the present which does not take into account the results of the Boer War. In those days, at the beginning of this century, the most powerful nation on earth sent hundreds of thousands of well-equipped troops to fight against tens of thousands of God-fearing Dutch farmers. They fought for their homes, while Britain, for all her professions of other causes, had a very keen eye to the strategic importance of the Cape of Good Hope and the wealth of gold and diamonds and other minerals which were being discovered. Is it any wonder that today the Boer prides himself on defying world opinion and regards himself through eyes glazed with isolation and resentment? Then too there is the enormous backdrop of the struggle between Russia and China and its possible growth into war. Russia looks increasingly to the strategic importance of the Indian Ocean in this regard, as well as the backing of the African nations, and so her pretext of anti-racialism sounds rather thin when she buys into Ethiopia or Angola.

The ordinary man has put all this together, more or less, so that he is not surprised by anything that happens any more, but he feels less and less able to come to grips with any of it. He is acutely aware of the fact that his own life and his own domestic situation are also under stresses because of new and unpredictable forces. He has become used to the interplay of more traditional interests, such as between labour and capital, between government and the unions, and these he expects and understands. Yet more and more his very right and ability to work and so his basic security are governed not only by these industrial factors but by a whole range of new political and quasi-political forces, promoting everything from environmental concern to women's lib. Political stoppages can now mean that he goes on or off work under orders with objectives which are more global than local, whether it be to protest against the persecution of another race somewhere or to promote a ban on mining uranium ore.

It is little wonder then that the average man feels like opting out; at best he is confused and finds his feeling of helplessness increasing. Where is all this leading? he asks himself. He sees his children growing up with an even more strident set of demands and imperatives dominating their lives, and often ones which lead to clashes with his own. Little wonder then that for many people the whole struggle is just put aside, and they settle for whatever the media prepare for them, and opt out of any thinking or significant actions of their own. They feel powerless to affect the events of the day.

At this stage it probably doesn't help in the least to inform such a man that the real reason for all this lies in the fact that he is living in an ideological age. That may only give him another convenient phrase like 'status quo' to describe the mess we are in. While the necessities of life are there and he does not feel too goaded by interferences in his life, he may remain purring away at his fireside for a long time to come. But come a tragedy, come a major deprivation or injustice and he will begin to stir. Despite all feelings of his own inconsequence, he will look around desperately for some way of action – and in that moment he is looking for an ideology.

That goes for man in the West anyway. It applies to a large percentage of that tiny minority of nations who still enjoy the bulk of the world's power, wealth and resources. Here there is every temptation to complacency and the pursuit of courses which will continue the status quo. In point of fact, however, the little group of the comfortably situated within the 'have' nations are living in a fool's paradise. 'Several hours have struck together on the clock of history', as Solzhenitsyn says. But the clock is an alarm clock, and it's time to get up!

CHAPTER 8

Once the lie has been dispersed, the nakedness of violence will be revealed in all its repulsiveness, and the violence, become decrepit, will come crashing down.

This is why I think, my friends, that we are capable of helping the world in its agonised testing hour. We must not seek excuses on the grounds that we lack weapons, we must not give ourselves over to a carefree life, we must go out into battle.

In Russian the most popular proverbs are about truth. They express the not inconsiderable and bitter experience of the people, sometimes with astonishing force. *One word of truth outweighs the whole world.* And on such a fantastic breach of the law of conservation of mass and energy are based my own activities and my appeal to the writers of the world.

Alexander Solzhenitsyn, *One Word of Truth*

CHAPTER EIGHT

Time for Change

Speaking of clocks and the time factor in history, the vital question arises, 'Is time on our side or not?' The answer can be given with absolute precision. Time is on the side of that ideology, that globally relevant life-style, which is able to satisfy most fully the needs and hopes of the whole man, not just some of the needs of most men. If there is in fact an inevitable and natural progression from the rule of the privileged few to the rule of the exploited majority, as Marx posits, if quantity is any criterion, then it follows that the ideology which most fully meets the needs of the greatest number of people will, in the end, prove victorious.

While confident of the inevitability of this process working out to establish the dictatorship of the proletariat, Marx believed that it was the task of communists to give a revolutionary push to history, to speed up the clock of change as it were. Behind the work of the Party in this regard, however, there was another consideration. Having decided what the needs, hopes and fears of the masses *ought* to be, Marx and his followers then set about exploiting and even creating conditions which would most quickly produce those very needs, fears, resentments and hopes among the masses, in millions of minds who had not as yet come to regard them as significant. Thus every conceivable area of discontent, every possible occasion of resentment or hatred, every disparity or injustice was seen not as something to be removed and solved but as a valuable asset to be nurtured and stirred into revolt – as the raw material for making a social and political explosive. Class war is made, inflamed and exaggerated by those whose whole *raison d'être* is claimed to be the bringing of an answer to it.

In the sphere of the trade unions many communists have made excellent officials, and have won better wages and conditions for their men. But the overarching motive has not been to oil the wheels of production and distribution of the world's goods and services, but to gain control and to lose no opportunity to promote the theme that the only real answer lies in total revolution and the destruction of the system.

But what of countries and situations where this revolution and change in the system have taken place, and not recently either? I will never forget hearing a veteran miner say bitterly in socialist Britain some years after the war, 'All my life I've fought for nationalisation, and now what do I find? We've still got the bloody bosses.'

In his book *Cancer Ward* Solzhenitsyn has his veteran communist, Shulubin, make the comment: 'We thought it was enough to change the mode of production and immediately people would change as well. But did they change? The hell they did. They didn't change a bit.'

Perhaps Khruschev was finally rejected by the Party in Moscow because he was too honest when he admitted those things, such as 'The contradictions in the communist society have their cause in the inability to make a selfless man.'

Indeed one might see what has so far been achieved by revolution and materialist effort to be the easier part. It is not hard to go to hungry, exploited, resentful people and stir up hatred, bitterness and revolt. The contradiction to which Khruschev alludes is very simple: when your revolution is over and you have wiped out all the enemy, how do you then go about converting the forces you have trained to hate, kill, divide, and destroy into peace-loving, co-operative, caring and creative citizens? A long time ago someone said, 'You can't get good fruit from bad trees . . . what a man sows he also reaps.' Perhaps the apparently enormous successes of such an ideology are unlikely to be stable, and contain within them the seeds of its own defeat!

Then again, the simple fact is that communism itself has relatively rapidly begun on a course of subdivision and fractionalisation into often bitterly opposed camps. This again illustrates an ideological weakness and inadequacy. Unless there is found some universal basis for unity and mutual progress then what seems so monolithic in terms of Marxist philosophy soon becomes frustrated in practice. The old, old history of man repeats itself – for without some better way he turns back to violence and reaches for the gun.

'Every Communist must grasp the truth: "Political power grows out of the barrel of a gun"[1] . . . "the seizure of power by armed force, the settlement of the issue by war, is the central task and the highest form of revolution."[2] This Marxist-Leninist principle of revolution holds good universally for China and for all other countries . . . The Army is the chief component of state power . . .'[3] These and other equally frank statements by Mao, and reproduced as essential doctrine by the Party till recent times, stand in strange contrast with his other assertions that ultimate power lies with the masses. 'The people, and the people alone, are the motive force in the making of world history',[4] he once declared. Can these two be reconciled? This is a question for a large number of the nations of the earth today, not just within the communist system. The place of force in a democracy is our problem today too.

In some of the western countries there is still an adherence in some degree to the basic myth of democracy – the concept that issues can finally be decided by a majority vote to which all will then adhere. One of the factors which varies widely in practice and is of great importance to the whole philosophy is in determining who has the franchise, which persons are able to exercise the vote at all. Then, even when this has been done, it is becoming more and more apparent every day that minorities are unlikely to accept the verdict. When defeated they increasingly look to whatever other ways they can devise to attain their ends, and in some cases blackmail, deprivation of services and violence are the weapons most ready to hand. Democracy today is in danger of becoming a far-off ideal unless there are elaborate structures and sanctions to back up a majority decision. In a body like the United Nations however there is little pretence of democracy. Majority votes there may be, but few feel bound by them, and behind all stands the veto, the symbol of naked strength by the biggest powers of all.

Yet what, after all, is the philosophical basis for the decisive power of a majority? It would be very appealing if one were to believe that it is born of a noble view of the value of the individual, of seeking the greatest good of the greatest number. In practice however it often seems to be little other than a relic of the time when it was simply a count of the number of available strong right arms.

The Communists try to bring the two concepts of power together by means of their own particular brand of semantics. One of the things which has always bewildered people in the non-communist world has been the speed with which the great, the orthodox and the powerful figures of today can become the despised, heretical and rejected figures of tomorrow. The fall of a Khruschev, a Lin Piao or a Chiang Ching illustrates the point precisely, but it is even more common in the humbler ranks of the Party. By definition the correct course is always that which serves the interests of the 'people'. The term 'people' however, much as in the days of ancient Israel, has a very special meaning. In Israel at least it meant all Jews, but in China it is by no means simply the sum of all Chinese. It is reserved absolutely for those who adhere to the currently accepted orthodoxy, those who fit the prescription of what a true member of the proletariat ought to be thinking, feeling and doing – in short, it means only the ideologically reliable. As the 'people' therefore simply reflect the decisions of the rulers they are in truth only a vast rubber stamp rather than an indigenous source of power and direction.

At first there would seem to have been a great, democratic spirit behind Mao's assertion that the people and the people alone are the true motive force in making world history. Indeed he goes further, 'We have always maintained that the revolution must rely on the masses of the people, on everybody's taking a hand, and have opposed relying merely on a few persons issuing orders.'[5] So far so good. But when one looks deeper one sees the prospect of the relatively few working upon and manipulating the masses rather like a small figure seated at the console of a great pipe-organ playing whatever tune he wills. This is made absolutely clear as Mao addresses himself to Party organisation:

> In the sphere of organisation, ensure democracy under central guidance. The leading bodies of the Party must give a correct line of guidance and find solutions, when problems arise, in order to establish themselves as centres of leadership. The higher bodies must be familiar with the situation in the lower bodies and with the life of the masses so as to have an objective basis for correct guidance . . .

Again he instructs:

> In all the practical work of our Party, all correct leadership is necessarily 'from the masses to the masses'. This means: take the ideas of the masses . . . and concentrate them . . . then go to the masses and propagate and explain these ideas until the masses embrace them as their own, hold fast to them and translate them into action.[6]

Speaking to the editorial staff of *Shansi-Suiyuan Daily* in 1948, Mao reminded them that as leaders they must be:

> good at translating the Party's policy into action by the masses, to be good at getting not only the leading cadres but also the broad masses to understand and master every movement and every struggle we launch – this is an art of Marxist-Leninist leadership.[7]

(The word 'we' would appear to be vital!)

Is this ultimate pragmatism, and some would say ultimate cynicism, regarding the power and voice of the masses the final word in political power? Is this crowded, impatient world now at the stage where it is necessary for some group of people with definite ideas about political and social philosophy and with the will and ruthlessness to enforce directives and arouse passions to take total control? Is such an ideological power-centre the leadership mankind awaits? Is this likely to be the final outcome of man's age-old pilgrimage in search of true freedom and social and political fulfilment? In a word, is dictatorship *to* the proletariat inevitable?

If ever that proposition has been put to the test it has been in China. Where events in Russia from 1917 onwards have frequently been decided on an ad hoc basis because a large section of the population, despite the purges and massive deportations and liquidations, is still imbued with ideals and values which are anathema to orthodox Marxists, in China this has been very different.

The Chinese had many years to study the Russian experiment and then to develop their own special brand of Marxist-Leninism. When the revolution finally succeeded they had large numbers of highly trained cadres ready to follow on the heels of the army and put a detailed plan into operation. The first task was to delineate, without regard to numbers or rank, all those elements among the people who could be expected to pose an ideological threat to the new regime. These included not only the old ruling classes and bourgeoisie, but all who had been educated to the values of the West, especially lawyers and other intellectuals of various disciplines. With precision and enormous patience and cunning the Communists set about detailing this evidence.

For the first few months after the shooting stopped and the last was seen of the Kuomintang armies, a comparative peace prevailed. It seemed for a time as though a new, happy and free society was being born. In the West many observers told the world that this new regime was no hard-line Marxist-Leninism, but rather it was merely a species of 'agrarian reform'. Everybody with ideas was encouraged to speak out. Children had more play periods at school and for the rest they spent much time writing stories and essays. In them they were asked to describe a day in their home, and especially the kind of conversations which took place around the family table. Churches were asked to continue their services, and even helped to get out to the people. Everybody heaved a sigh of relief. Peace had come at last. There came a great campaign to have every weapon destroyed in the name of peace, and they cheered to a man as lorries carried away the last hateful weapons of death which some of them had hoarded secretly for years.

Then the axe fell. A new group of hard-line cadres displaced the more popular figures in official positions, and mass arrests led to people's courts being set up in every district, town and village. Millions and millions, tens of millions were summarily tried and then publicly executed. Everyone, from the very young to the very old, was forced to participate in the trials and the slaughter. There could be no revolt, for there were no longer any weapons. The pattern of slaughter has been followed since in Indo-China, especially in North Vietnam after 1954, and more recently (indeed at this very moment in the south and in Cambodia), but for sheer size of the crime nothing on earth has ever resembled the butchery which occurred in China. The ground was utterly razed so that the philosophies of the new era could go without serious challenge. Propaganda abounded everywhere, and no voice could be heard other than the official one. With all the false doctrines of the capitalists eradicated, and with only orthodoxy in the truths of Marxist-Leninism remaining, surely within a couple of generations a new, free, happy, enviable society would be born!

But what has happened? Two generations later one of the exponents of this ideal ideology calmly admits that there are still people, and many of them young people, who want desperately to break free from the imprisonment of their minds and spirits and to think independently. Such is their conviction, and such the intellectual and evidential poverty of the system, that the Party cannot hope to persuade them, so they have to kill them. So one sees the spectacle of many thousands of young men and women who brave several miles of shark-infested seas to try to swim to freedom in Hong Kong. The racing tide as well as the sharks claim a high percentage of those who try, many of them unable to swim but buoyed up with plastic bags or even ping-pong balls. Today they find the free world's police there to hand them back for 'discipline' by the Chinese authorities because Hong Kong is over-crowded. There is no escape that way. The few who manage to escape across the Berlin wall, with its machineguns, snipers, Dobermans and boobytraps are at least assured of reception into a free society if they make their entry to the West. But even that is denied the freedom-swimmers now.

In other communist lands the persecution of Christians has recently taken a new and more ominous course. In Rumania as I write evangelical churchmen are harassed, and if they meet for prayer are often arrested on charges of vandalism or disturbing the peace. Church workers are sent to mental asylums for daring to meet with a handful of believers. What is it that the Communists fear so passionately from such people? There is only one answer: they fear their ideas. The Communists know that these people are more dangerous to the frightened men in the Kremlin than any material or military opposition.

Dr Ross Terrill, an Australian-born Sinologist of Harvard University has written an important book on modern China called *800 Millions – the Real China*. He was one of the principal figures behind the visit of Mr Whitlam, then the Australian Labour Leader, to China, and was himself politically aligned with the Labour Party. However he reveals in his book, which is a most sensitive appreciation of many things about China, that the thing which is guarded with the utmost diligence is the ideological base of the nation. He describes the less blatant propaganda efforts of today, and adds that nevertheless all information and all knowledge 'come down from the mountain top to the plateau'.[8]

He wryly comments that in Harvard they often feel that the only books the students really read are those written by members of the Harvard Faculty – but in China there is 'intellectual incest on a gargantuan scale'.[8]

Telling how they encountered military areas wherever they went, and remarking that today there are millions of militia who are allowed to have their own rifles, he adds: 'They can now trust them with rifles but they cannot trust them with their own minds.' His final summing-up is, 'I could not live that way.'

But why is it religion that is so feared? Why is it that people who give first place to a being whose existence the Communists deny are so important? The answer is quite simple, and one that anybody who has been tempted by power will recognise at once. The men in Peking or Moscow are beset by the same fears which threw Herod into a frenzy of rage and led to the slaughter of all the baby boys in Bethlehem; the same fears which were played on by the Jewish leaders to bring Pilate to concur in the murder of Jesus of Nazareth; the same fear which stalks an Idi Amin today. It is the challenge to final and absolute authority, that one day they will be held subject and accountable to a higher power. The paranoia of the dictator reaches a crescendo at such a prospect.

Mao once recalled for his followers an ancient Chinese fable called 'The Foolish Old Man who removed Mountains'. It tells of the plan of this old man to train successive generations of his children to dig away at two large mountains near his house. His arithmetic was sound. The mountains could not increase but must decrease with every basketful of soil removed. In time the mountains would be levelled. God, the story ran, was moved by this and sent down two angels who carried the mountains away on their backs. Mao concluded with the words: 'We must persevere and work unceasingly and we too will touch God's heart. Our God is none other than the masses of the Chinese people.'[9]

God, the masses – but a supreme authority? Only in a strange almost mystical way, for Mao saw the masses in need of being tutored, propagandised and constrained to the purposes decided by the Party for them. The 'divine' adjective is also most significant, for Mao never, in all his discussion of authority, deviated one iota from this same requirement: that the ultimate voice must be Chinese.

If we look for the source of the primary tensions within the communist movement as a whole, it is at this final focal point of authority that we discover the parting of the ways. The Chinese accuse the Russians of revisionism with regard to their philosophical foundations in Marxist-Leninism, but one feels that behind it all is this deeper question of final authority. Who is ultimately going to call the tune, who hold supreme power? The struggles which flared into the open after the death of Mao and led to the arrest of Madam Mao and her three comrades, is just one of a host of examples. It is the appetite for power which divides and destroys even in some of the finest of human institutions, and communism, being wholly based on materialistic values, is more prone to this corruption than most.

For the Chinese Communist it is unthinkable that the supreme head should be other than Chinese, and one suspects that the same holds true for the Russians, the Jugoslavs and so too for the Cubans, the Angolans and the Khmers.

If one of the major tests of an adequate ideology for the coming age is that it is able to overcome this divisive factor of the struggle for power between nationalities and personalities, then it may prove that Mao's instinct was quite accurate when he told the story of a God who would act to consummate the search of the people for the new age. But his definition was astray!

In the light of all that we have seen about the way the Party deals with the masses, whether through the observations of Marx, Mao or Terrill (and as the device of a majority vote clearly doesn't work unless there is the power to enforce it, the power of the gun), then there is very good reason to look more deeply at the reason why the Communists fear religious faith more than anything else. At least the consummation of man's search for an incorruptible and all-wise leadership, one with the power and the plan to offer bewildered mankind, if it be in a transcendent God, meets all the requirements of the ultimate in ideologies – provided such a God really exists.

Supposing there is a Creator behind this universe, a being who is intelligent, powerful, caring, and with a plan – then it may be that the ideology which alone will satisfy man both as an individual and collectively will be to find and serve that God for ever. At least this is what Jesus of Nazareth said when he gave his definition of the supreme task of man couched in the threefold structure which we have called an ideology: 'You must love the Lord your God with all your mind, and all your heart and all your strength, and your neighbour as yourself.' Could it be that all these other ideologies we have looked at are really corruptions of the one true and divinely appointed purpose for mankind? Can it be that the authority we are really seeking is not the dictatorship of race, not the dictatorship of the proletariat, but the dictatorship of the Holy Spirit?

There may be some who object to the use of the word 'dictatorship' in this connection, and that is understandable. On the other hand the point of using such an expression is to ensure that nobody imagines any longer that we can move into the future with thousands of millions of people all doing their own thing, all pleasing themselves and serving the ends of their instant pleasure. Let us make no mistake about it, the world today is the scene of a primal struggle between people with total commitments who put themselves fully in the hands of a leadership of one kind or another. These are the people who are deciding the course of events today in our churches and schools and every political party. Leadership rests with those with an ideological commitment.

An ideology is the enemy of the status quo. It is the motive-power of people who are on the march. It is born of a deep restlessness, a divine dissatisfaction, and it has its eyes on the horizon. Naturally it is feared and hated by those who want to rest in the status quo, just as much as by those of opposing philosophies. 'Don't think that I came to bring peace on the earth', Jesus warned his disciples, 'I came not to send peace but a sword . . . my followers may even find that their foes are within their own homes, members of their immediate families.' There speaks a revolutionary if ever there was one!

Mao Tse-tung told his followers: 'In any society in which classes exist class struggles will never end. In classless society the struggle between the new and the old and between truth and falsehood will never end . . . therefore man has constantly to sum up experiences and go on discovering, inventing, creating and advancing.'[10]

Describing the nature of the true Communist he said, 'A Communist should have largeness of mind and he should be staunch and active, looking upon the interests of the revolution as his very life and subordinating his personal interests to those of the revolution; always and everywhere he should adhere to principle and wage a tireless struggle against all incorrect ideas and actions . . . he should be more concerned about the Party and the masses than about any individual and more concerned about others than himself.'[11]

A true ideology is something which lays claim to the total devotion and commitment of its activists. It is in the heart of the policies and philosophy of his ideology that such a person tempers his moral standards and other values. Right and wrong are increasingly expressions for behaviour which either promotes or detracts from the purposes and interests of his ideology and its leadership. He accepts express instructions from a supreme authority and follows fundamental principles given to him. No matter what anyone else may think or do, no matter who or how many do otherwise, the person with an ideology finally accepts his right and wrong only in this way. All other standards and alternatives must be subjugated and hindrances to obedience rejected.

In the case of Marxist-Leninism it is held to be essential that any trace of bourgeois values and attitudes must be eradicated. Such serious 'errors' as to attach unique value to the individual; to think in terms of unchanging, absolute ethical values; or yield to idealism; these aberrations must be corrected or removed.

I have a young friend whose wife is the daughter of a Chinese medical doctor who lived in a large mainland city prior to the revolution. When the reign of terror began she was about nine years of age, and she tells how everyone in their village had to go each Saturday to the town square to witness the trial, torture and execution of others of the villagers. Coming from what was considered to be a bourgeois home, she and others of her young friends were forced to go each Sunday to a nearby burial ground and there to exhume decomposing bodies.

Her husband tells how, even after their marriage, she would wake up screaming after a nightmare, and eventually she told him of an incident when having uncovered a corpse she saw the skull start to move. She fainted but later discovered that this was due to a small lizard which had entered the skull.

It is important to reflect on the mentality of those authorities who could direct a child to this ordeal and to ask their reason. There is only one explanation, for sheer vindictiveness is not enough: they sought to destroy every vestige of bourgeois values and standards in her life. What was morally right or wrong for them did not exist, only the interest of the revolution. Human feelings to do with people and their value were dangerous errors.

The point of all this is not to bring a spotlight of criticism on a single nation. Indeed Nazi Germany, Chile, Russia and its satellites, to say nothing of Cambodia, North Vietnam and Uganda – and our own nation all too often – all countries have a history of horrors that disgust decent people. But until we in the West understand that virtually every sphere of life today has been penetrated by people who are being trained to regard such things as necessary to the revolution, unless we see the ideological reason why, in Northern Ireland in the recent past, men have had their throats cut, not with a razor but with serrated cheese knives, then we are living in cloud-cuckoo land.

People committed to an ideology have no time off duty. They use every resource they can command to achieve their objectives. They look on everyone they meet, everything they own, every relationship they form and every desire that rises in their hearts through eyes focused on their grand design. They covet everything that is, not for themselves but for their cause. Like it or not, this is a fact which will decide much of our lives in the days ahead. What is more, all too many of our own leaders, men and women with outstanding ability and qualities which would have been more than adequate for success in days gone by, are ill-equipped and poorly trained for this ideological age. They fail to see ideological strategy and purpose and go off on side tracks with great enthusiasm when encouraged to do so by those who are so trained and who seek to use them.

At Yalta we saw how a man with an ideology was able to mislead and make cynical use of some of the world's greatest leaders simply because for him the true war had hardly even begun, whereas they were at the head of war-weary nations anxious to get back to 'normal' after the defeat of Nazi Germany.

Even if Churchill did see dangers looming ahead he knew that he could not call on his nation to stand to arms in the way Stalin could order.

History is virtually repeating itself today. The great word, getting a little shabby by now but still there, is 'détente'. When he presented his détente policy to the American nation, Dr Kissinger told Congress that the only alternative to it was a nuclear war. Like so many words used in communication with the Communists however the word 'detente' has been found to mean different things for different people. Mr Brezhnev used no ambiguity when he described the Russian position in a report to the Central Committee of the Party after meeting with President Nixon at the very start of détente:

> In striving for . . . the relaxation of tension we realise that success in this important area in no way signifies the possibility of relaxing the ideological struggle. On the contrary, we must be prepared for the struggle to be intensified . . . to become an increasingly crucial form of confrontation between the two social systems.[12]

Four years later came Angola, and as they watched the burgeoning Soviet might reaching out to extend lines of support to the invading Cubans, the American and other western leaders fell back on empty words of protest, complaining that Russia was not observing the spirit of détente.

Mr Brezhnev again did not mince words. He spelt out the ideological position with great clarity:

> Some bourgeois leaders express surprise and raise a howl over the solidarity of the Soviet communists, of the Soviet people with the struggle of other peoples for freedom and progress. It is either naivety or more probably deliberate distortion of our policies. The relaxation of tensions does not in the slightest abolish or alter the laws of the class-struggle. No-one can expect that in the conditions of relaxation of tensions the Communists will reconciliate [sic] themselves with capitalist exploitation, or the monopolists will become revolutionaries . . . we are not hiding the fact that we see in the relaxation of tensions the way to create more favourable conditions for the peaceful construction of socialism and communism.[13]

This all means that, for the Russians, détente is reserved to the avoidance of armed clash at the international level, but that it has nothing at all to do with the ideological struggle at the political and party level. Having a little more time for their ideological offensives, and using their resources to breed and develop insurrections in country after country, the Russians see themselves as two-way winners. If ever it does come to a full-scale war then they will have created allies and established bases in many more areas by that time, for example around the littoral of the Indian Ocean. On the other hand, if their other local offensives combined with ideological struggle prove sufficient, they may yet take over without endangering their people in major, certainly nuclear, war.

Their acceptance of the concept of détente therefore is the measure of their confidence in their military growth and in the supremacy of their ideology.

There are two or three other factors, however, which the Russians must surely see as areas of doubt. The first is the growth of China, with its implacable, highly nationalist development of its own brand of communism. In dealing with a nation of one thousand millions one is dealing with imponderables in terms of warfare. Several years ago Lin Piao, then Chinese Defence Minister, published an important strategic and ideological appraisal in which he clearly outlined China's intentions of global conquest. In point of fact he merely amplified Mao's own philosophy that the revolutionary methods by which the Party had conquered China itself would later prove relevant to the conquest of other nations. The blood-chilling part of his speech was his indication that, when the time came to fight, the immense numbers of Chinese would inevitably spell victory. He spoke of being ready to see one hundred and sixty millions die in nuclear war to fertilise the ground of the new age for China. Lin is no more, but one wonders whether his philosophy is as dead as some would like it to be.

Another factor lies in the failure of communism with men like Solzhenitsyn and the Soviet dissident movement. Here are men who have been born and brought up in the heart of the Communist State, yet who testify to unbreakable, inalienable qualities of the human spirit which cannot be conquered by imprisonment, torture and death. They speak of a superior ideology to communism using the breathing space of détente to win the day.

Both Khruschev and Mao agree in this that all the changes which have been made to the system have not been successful in producing the new unselfish type of man. Indeed democracy will only work if the individuals who go to make it up are prepared to discipline themselves. Unless people in any group are prepared to abide by the inner sanctions of self-discipline then either that society decays or force must be used to compel obedience.

The search for freedom consists to a large degree in finding the secret whereby men and women everywhere freely accept certain values, standards and disciplines, voluntarily and willingly, and having accepted them live and die by them. Mao and others have come very near to the language of religion in describing the degree of commitment and devotion to the cause of the ideal Party member. Here and there one comes across selflessness and idealism in Communists which put to shame the commitment of many who claim to be religious. Yet the stark fact remains that the system in Russia, China and elsewhere has to be held in line with guns, dogs, mines, prison and death. At the top of the ladder Lin Piao meets with a convenient accident and disappears from the scene, Khruschev is humiliated and Madam Chiang Ching is arrested for treason.

There must be a better way.

CHAPTER 9

Soviet Marxism has never succeeded in reconciling the contradictions between its own nationalism and Marxian internationalism – either in its strategy or in its ideology . . .

Herbert Marcuse, *Soviet Marxism* (1958)

The Party considers the creation of the new man as the most difficult part of the Communist transformation of society. Unless we can root out bourgeois morality and educate people in Communist morality, renewing them morally and spiritually, it is not possible to build a Communist Society.

A resolution of the 22nd Congress (1961) *of the Soviet Communist Party*

The materialistic doctrine that man is a product of circumstances and upbringing and that changed men will be the product of different circumstances and changed upbringing, forgets the fact that it is men that change circumstances and that the educator himself needs to be educated.

Karl Marx, *On Feuerbach*, 'Man and Structures'

Marx and I are ourselves partly responsible that the young people sometimes put too much emphasis on the economic factor. Towards our opponents we had to stress the main principle which they deny, and there was not always time and opportunity to do justice to the interaction of different relevant factors.

F Engels, *Marxismusstudien*, Vol 2

We too belong to the devils – we too. Radical evil is asserting its mastery over all creatures all over the world. Whatever comes, we cannot complain. We sit peacefully and comfortably in our armchairs, we dine and we discuss, although we know that all hell is let loose.

Max Horkheimer, *Notizen* 1950–69 *und Dämmerung*
(Leading figure in the Frankfurt Marxist School of Philosophers)

You liberate man from the illusion of power and possession if you affirm the paradox of God's presence . . . He is the power to transform the world.

Roger Gratry: *The Alternative Future*
(Until 1970 the leading ideologist of the French Communist Party)

CHAPTER NINE

The Chips are Down

'Several hours have struck together on the clock of history', says Solzhenitsyn. What are they?

First the world has come together with astonishing rapidity, so great have been the effects of modern transportation, satellite communications and increasing economic and political interdependence. The four corners of the earth have shrunk to encompass an area within the reach of most men's minds. As a result the basic lifestyles, values and objectives of each part of the human race are seen as relevant and increasingly important to all. Penetrating all human society are the ideologies, the aggressive, persuasive or predatory philosophies which have as their prime objective the bringing together of all mankind under their various banners.

One race shall rule, said Nazism.

One class shall rule, said Marx.

All men are one, says Christianity.

And so on, but always with a world view. This process of global ideological enlistment or domination has raced towards its climax in the twentieth century.

Next, the end of the line for the appeal to war and violence is in sight in our age. 'They that take the sword will perish by the sword' has been qualified through the centuries into rationalisation of just and unjust wars, even holy wars; but the hour has struck when the entire process of violence and destruction stands to overwhelm mankind. Stage by stage the final sanction of war has been employed by those who have generally espoused values and philosophies of love and peace and forgiveness. Generations have lived with the conviction that, having tried the way of peaceful persuasion and failed, they could always fall back on violence in defence, or offence, with the claim that might would sustain the right. All that has changed.

In the century which lies behind us we have seen the escalation of war through its various stages until the consequences are so terrible that paradoxically the moral issue now emerges as the final arbiter of defeat or victory. No longer is it a question merely of righteous anger giving power to strong right arms, but of which side finally has least scruples about employing weapons of such horror that to survive might be less desirable than to succumb. The 'deterrent' strategies of the nations are like a giant poker game where calculations are made as to the costs of using force in aggression or even defence, compared with the gains. If one side is inhibited by the terribleness of the moral consequences of using such weapons as the diffusion bomb or chemical warfare and the other not, then the time approaches where might is no longer with the highest morality but the opposite.

This hour approaches in our lifetime.

Again the end of the road is at hand for economic and trade patterns and processes based on growth for some at the expense of others. Resources are no longer spoils for the exploiter, but this whole concept is increasingly challenged as they are seen as the birthright of the entire human race. 1973 heard a clock strike in terms of world economy which marks the beginning of a new age when the underdeveloped but oil-rich nations suddenly faced the industrialised world with their fourfold price increase and indeed the whole process of confrontation began a new era. Here was a species of trade-unionism on a global scale. Where Marx had seen the working class as having only their labour with which to bargain, now the poorer countries who had essential resources or power, liquid labour indeed, had united to demand and get at once an unprecedented rise for their product.

At first the majority of western nations could not believe that this was more than a passing phase and when the British Minister to the United Nations at that time wrote to his Foreign Office of his conviction that a new chapter was about to be written in economic and diplomatic history he was told by a Whitehall dignitary that he had been having nightmares. 'In eighteen months everything will be back to normal', he said.

But it is not.

In Berlin, Chancellor Schmidt was much more far-sighted when, in his 1977 New Year message he said, 'We have all believed that one day after the world economic recession has been overcome, things would go on as before. But only in the last few months it has become clear to us that nothing will ever be the same as before 1974. Germany has to be open to new ideas.'

There is, however, an even more important hour which has struck in our day, which includes many of these other factors but goes deeper still. There is today a crisis which I have described earlier as the choice between a reversion to the jungle and an uncompromising acceptance of a higher set of values and their requirements in terms of behaviour. In one sense it is a crisis of freedom. Freedom is the most dangerous concept to enter the mind of man, because it opens doors which lead to the lowest as well as the highest ways of life. It is the divine gift of freedom which can enable a man to become a saint or a fiend. In terms of social and collective behaviour it is this same demand for freedom which threatens every attempt to establish lasting conventions or patterns of behaviour which enshrine what the majority decide to be desirable and 'good'.

The twentieth century has seen global revolts not only against ethical structures which have been built up over thousands of years but against hitherto unchallenged concepts of right and wrong, good and bad, and even the existence of standards at all. Whatever the differences between the various developing religions and moral philosophies of previous ages, they have had discernible and basic presuppositions and values generally held in common. From the earliest known codes such as those of Hammurabi, Moses and Confucius, and in the heart of the great religions, there has been explicitly or implicitly a consensus as to such matters as the importance of the individual; the necessity for respect for life, property and authority, parental and civil; the fact of marriage; and deepest of all the necessity for individual integrity in some form or other. The most rapidly developing peoples have been those amongst whom broadly similar views and values of morality and social ethics have obtained. Natural Law was a concept with real meaning in the civilised world. There was no serious challenge to many of these concepts until the last hundred or so years. The Communist Manifesto of 1847 was far from being merely a document to do with political and economic matters, it crystallised the philosophy of revolt in the name of freedom in ways which struck directly at the heart of this civilisation, at mankind's fundamental values.

The basic unit of existence was changed from the individual to the group – the class or the Party. All rules to do with property ownership, with authority and consequently with law and order were to be regarded as expendable. Basic concepts such as of the desirability of peace, love, harmony, mutual co-operation and goodwill were not just ignored but reversed. When the new doctrine was too much for the masses to swallow a line of double-talk was developed whereby the old acceptable words, such as democracy, peace, freedom, became imbued with new and contradictory content.

The revolution in the name of freedom, begun by Marx, cannibalised by Hitler and advanced now by some of its progeny (who are consequently more representative of cybernetics than humanity in what we have held to be a reversion to the jungle), is bringing civilisation to increasing chaos. Nowhere is there the prospect of a great unifying force, such as was inherent in such slogans as 'workers of the world unite!' Rather there is the picture of so-called Marxists holding the rest of mankind to ransom for sordidly sectional and peripheral objectives. There are mindless killers at work who enjoy killing and gloat over the agonies of children and innocent people. More people have been butchered in the name of this freedom than died in all the wars of the twentieth century, and that in the brief period since the end of the last world war. The great crowds who demonstrated violently for peace and freedom for Vietnam and the journals who took their part in the anti-war movement, are running no campaigns now as the slaughter goes on.

This is the reality of the world in which we try to live normal lives and where our children have to try to find their way into the future. In many places even that possibility is denied millions of people. In China today Christian parents dare not try to teach their children even the basic truths of their faith until they are old enough to understand the mortal dangers of failing to keep their belief secret from their schoolmates and teachers. In Cambodia anyone who held Christian or Buddhist beliefs is probably dead, but if not, certainly existing under appalling conditions of 're-education'. In the affluent West millions of kids grow up as moral and spiritual morons in a decadent society which increasingly reflects the success of those whose purpose is the destruction or prostitution of the old values and the exploitation of the worst and lowest appetites of mankind.

The role of the Marxists in all this is basic. On the one hand it would be ridiculous to see reds under every bed so that all phenomena of decay or destruction of the status quo is ascribed to their activity. On the other hand it must be admitted that they are proving increasingly capable in selecting strategies for bringing the West to its knees. It is really a vindication of the negative and only consistent part of Marxist idealism – that it is possible to give a revolutionary push to destructive processes inherent in bourgeois society which will inevitably bring about its downfall. Those processes are already there, as nobody has ever denied, and the communist today has only to bring his trained insight to bear on the log-jams or set other seductive processes in motion and the natural course of events does the rest. It is not hard to hand the weapons for suicide to a man or a society already fascinated with the death-wish. 'When the time comes to hang the capitalists', Lenin is reported as saying, 'they will be found competing with each other for the contract for the rope.'

Living in Britain or Australia today one feels increasingly like a spectator at a series of rehearsals of parts of a play, a tragedy which has yet to have even the first dress rehearsal of its dénouement. Overarching the whole economic and industrial scene, for example, there is an aura of wishful thinking. There have been bad and hard times before, the argument runs, and one only has to wait for the pendulum to swing back and we will once more have booming economies and burgeoning productivity. There is little recognition of the ideological factor behind most of today's major strikes and stoppages, wage demands and other quasi-industrial issues.

A sixty-page manual for revolutionaries entitled *How to Win This Strike* has recently been distributed in communist circles in Australia.[1] It is not intended for wide circulation but is a detailed and directional set of guidelines on how the extreme left can use industrial upheavals for their own ideological purposes.

The ideal strike programme, it says, begins with the formation of a small 'central strike committee' from the ranks of the most militant shop stewards, 'likened to the Commander-in-Chief with his small group of advisory officers'. The first task is to form a reasonably accurate and highly secret estimation of 'the expected duration of the strike'. The attitude of the authors to rank-and-file workers is one of cynical manipulation. 'A balance must be maintained between inflicting the maximum damage on the boss as against straining the wage-earner to breaking point', it instructs. As for companies, the maximum hurt is to be inflicted on them. 'The company has fixed costs', the booklet states, 'The loss of sales could mean the difference between an overall profit or loss. Valuable customers can be lost to competitors'. Such results are seen as prime objectives for the strike-makers.

The manual goes on to describe how all strikes should be escalated and the workers kept militant by denying them the opportunity to take interim employment. Publicity for strike aims is vital and official trade union facilities should be used or, 'It could be better, especially in the case of a large strike, to simply commandeer Union office space, duplicators, typewriters and paper for the duration.'

Each day of the strike is planned. The first day 'is spent preparing and recruiting workers for battle', by placing pickets and making appeals to any not yet supporting the strike. The second day is used to form strong-arm squads of five members, ostensibly for the protection of strike leaders, but really to move in to expand any opportunity for violence. On the third day a march and occupation of the company's offices could be opportune, they say. Any signs of a stalemate developing should be tackled at once. 'A stalemate can be broken only by the strike being escalated.'

Short of major strikes the use of 'guerilla tactics' is advocated. 'The aim is to cause a climate of disorder and uncertainty by a planned campaign of sudden disruptions. These can range from lightning strikes in key areas, through the manufacture of faulty articles, to selective small-scale sabotage of equipment or finished products. In the building industry a walk-out during a concrete 'pour' is a good example . . . a small co-ordinated body is required, backed by the enthusiastic participation of the workers.'

The booklet says that it gives a 'framework which can be used in all industrial disputes irrespective of the initial militancy of the workers.'

What worker in Britain today, seeing the purposeful pattern of strikes in key industries, can have any doubt that the outcome will be and is intended to be huge losses in production, and thus a smaller income for the nation and for himself, plus lost commercial opportunities which eventually mean lost industries and lost jobs. The strike weapon, once the means of wresting a just wage and fair conditions from greedy ownership and indifferent management, is today increasingly in the hands of those who want not wage justice, but to destroy both the companies and the country.

The bedevilling fact is, of course, that in almost every instance there can be found cases of injustice or indifference which can be used by agitators to raise the workers' anger and so give apparent justification to the escalation of the strike.

While some sections of management and ownership have often gone a long way towards the changes that are needed to give just rewards and responsible participation in the developments of industry, huge areas of aggravation and inequity still remain. Each side is afraid to be seen to change or conciliate in case it be taken for weakness. Until there is a breakthrough in the sphere of human relationships, a change of climate wherein each comes to trust the other, backed by evidence of genuine consideration for each other, then 'counter-solutionary' forces who want conflict and not peace in industry will have an easy row to hoe.

Nevertheless it would be wrong to suppose that the Marxists are having it all their own way any more than the capitalists are. It is fascinating to hear some of the leading exponents of Marxian theory today forced to admit the inbuilt tensions and conflicts within its framework. In a world which has rejected religion, for reasons good or bad, reasonable or purely irresponsible, the basic void has been filled by a faith in scientific determinism. The other characteristic of man, the other face of his 'religious' nature which looks out from its secure base, be it in God or science, is his forward-looking expectation of a new age. The characteristics of this age are many and varied but always there is the basic yearning for an enhanced freedom, peace, harmony, and all the other resultants of discovering a surer way, a superior wisdom and a better life.

Marx clung to the thesis that capitalism was inevitably doomed to decay and to yield place to communism, and the true ideological leadership in this process would always emerge from the proletariat: the depersonalised and alienated working class who had 'nothing to lose but their chains'.

These two major components of Marxism, the existence of an impregnable, scientifically secure starting point providing a set of essential guidelines, together with the messianic expectations and strategic planning of a consequent new age, have replaced the fundamentals of orthodox religion in millions of lives. As we have seen, religion too has its impregnable and unchanging foundations in the laws and will of 'God' and it too looks out with expectation and missionary zeal to some form of new age – a 'kingdom of God' in the future. It too sees freedom as an essential characteristic of this goal, but freedom in the sense that each person has already chosen the values and objectives of living so that the freedom he seeks is that which enables him to move ever forward towards these goals. 'In his service is perfect freedom', the Christian apostle declares.

It is this sense of basic certainty together with a hope of the new age which carries the man of Marx or the man of religion through present perplexities. It sustains the more sensitive and intelligent Marxists through terror and totalitarianism of their own creation with the promise of freedom, peace and plenty in the end, the belief that this present farce shall surely end – at least for one class.

But it is a long time since Marx slogged out his theories in the British Museum. Time was his court of appeal as to the truth or otherwise of his tenets, and time has proved him wrong on many major counts. The scientifically impregnable and inevitably victorious issue of the decay of capitalism, especially in its most advanced forms, has not happened, as the most 'capitalistic' powers of his day, Britain and Germany, have not disintegrated into communism, despite all the pushing and stimulating of that process by the Communists. On the contrary, capital and labour have both changed so greatly that many Marxists have been forced to revise and restate their beliefs so that their Marxism is barely recognisable.

The Frankfurt school of revisionists, with Marcuse as its prophet *par exellence*, has tried to argue that Marx was an interpreter of the ongoing continuum of history, and thus continuing revision and restatement of his basic tenets are only right and proper. But this belies the fundamental scientific and absolutist basis of Marxism. It was precisely the capitalism of his own day which Marx avowed would decay into communism, and he was wrong. He spoke of the inevitable consequences of what he saw then and there, and claimed to proclaim the truth about future developments. It has been precisely because he has been proved so very wrong that innumerable schools of revision, reinterpretation and adaption have arisen. The pathetic thing about so much of it is that, even now, in the face of such vast challenges to the old simple 'one, two' of their philosophy, these people still revert back to the mumbo jumbo of their creed when cornered in argument.

Marcuse, when charged on the BBC recently with élitism, felt obliged to trot out an orthodox declaration of his faith in the belief that all advances and true growth would emerge from the working class, totally ignoring the fact that he had said half an hour previously that he doubted whether such a class any longer existed in the sense used by Marx. 'They now have a lot more to lose than their chains', he had said earlier.

Even more pathetic was to hear the way he referred to 'women's lib' as one of the most important and promising developments of the present day. Why? Because it stands for a basic change from the aggression, hardness and possessiveness of the patriarchial system, on which so much of our civilisation has been built, to the tenderness, compassion and peace-loving characteristics of motherhood. This, said Marcuse, could herald the fundamental change of values required for a new age.

But we can all judge for ourselves how real that is!

In my experience in political and ecclesiastical circles as well as in ordinary social activity one sees the New Left, the disciples of Marcuse and his Marx, using the term 'women's lib' to seek to destroy those values in woman as belonging to decadent femininity and they strive to make her also to be aggressive, hard and possessive.

Who is fooling whom?

Looking at the benign and ageing Marcuse I longed for him to be able to say, 'I've been wrong. I've been looking in the wrong direction. Tenderness, compassion and the love of peace are not to be found in the direction taken by Marx. As I have said, these values are essential to the new age for mankind. It is time for us to look elsewhere.'

Perhaps Marcuse, like many other persons who have hearts and souls as well as brilliant minds, will eventually come to that point.

Meanwhile the hosts of 'young intellectuals' (who seem to be the hope of the side far more than the proletariat), who espouse Marxism and venerate Marcuse, are like sheep without a shepherd. So many of them are really young persons who have lost their way and are trying rather desperately to find a path through the jungle of today. They are insecure and so are intensely conventional and wear the uniform of their peer group and chant its catch-cries. They respond easily to the most vociferous, most convenient or seductive lifestyles presented to them. More and more they have been conditioned at school for the coming of puberty when they naturally leave the security of their past environment for a world of their own.

In their history classes they may have had a Marxist oriented teacher and so have learned to despise personal leadership and reject the 'great man' concept of development. Yet somehow this does not apply to the figures of the left like Marx, Engels, Lenin or Mao – but only to those like Lincoln, Wilberforce, Shaftesbury, Wesley or Churchill! These men were only the by-products of history, youth are being taught in their millions, not the courageous initiators and prime-movers of change. The unspoken assertion behind all this is that it is to the masses, to the proletariat, that one must look for true leadership.

In the media they see the capitalists also bidding up and up the price for the 'rope'. It is doubtful if any leader at all can now emerge who cannot be set up as an object of a cruel and critical press campaign which lacks important factors of balance. The plain fact is that we are all mortal, all human, all sinners. There is no man alive who, if selected events and deeds of his life were to be exposed and distorted as to contemporary context and scale in the way only television can achieve, could not be shamed and possibly driven from public life. The media's essential right to probe has sunk to the right to intrude, to tear down privacy and disregard confidence. Such journalism is now growing to be a major cancer of our age, and it is big money. The capitalists buy it every time. The communication and entertainment professions thrive on it. The Marxists, who may have hardly had to give it more than a selective initial push, sit back and see the leadership potential of the 'other side' destroyed. That is all the communists in the media have to do, because the public want the product as much as the producers want the profit.

People are hungry to drag down anyone who challenges their own standards, their own lethargy, their own self-esteem. At the same time they dare to make to their leaders demands for a perfection which they would never dream of applying to themselves. They will even see traps and baits laid for the man up top, and never protest it. It possibly derives from an inverted hunger for God: people feel righteous and vindicated as their leaders topple, as the great men are seen minus their boots, with feet of clay. They have thrown down another idol! Little do they see the fallacies and the distortions, the propensity for falsification of fact inherent in judgement by the masses and the media which can eventually lead to the cry of 'crucify him' when a totally blameless person comes under attack.

Everywhere today there is the sour smell of blame. Professional blame-layers are at work in our schools and universities, in our media and arts, in our churches and parliaments. By professional I mean people who have been thoroughly trained in discerning and enlarging and fomenting causes of resentment and hatred, often in the name of truth and righteousness. Although the conditions have changed dramatically today in Scotland, which once produced the Highland Clearances, or the scandal of slavery in the mines right up to the beginning of the last century, or the old battles against the English, there are those today who are engaged as a major life work in stimulating those old hurts and horrors so that they live again in the hearts and minds of the many. The object is sheer cynical exploitation – to 'exploit every grievance' as *The Communist Manifesto* puts it. The drive for votes, strikes, divisions of society, the advancing of this or that personal or party advantage, is behind every instance of it. Yet so often it is fed out as of genuine academic, cultural or even Christian concern.

This is the kind of environment in which the young are educated today. The accent is on the curse not the cure. Like the media, only the negative is news. By the time they leave school young people are increasingly ready and conditioned for involvement in one or more of the fringe activities which will prove attractive to them in almost any sphere they desire or where they feel their deepest concern. Whether it be in sexual liberation, in concern for such matters as the environment, racial arrogance, peace, the plight of the underprivileged, the victims of exploitation: everywhere they look with the idealism and impatience of youth they find a Marxist front to ply them with facile answers. As they move into this orbit they can make rapid progress because it is easier to blame than to take responsibility oneself. It is easier to hate than to love or forgive someone who has hurt you, easier to lower standards than to build them up, easier to force change on others than to live to win them to see and accept change for themselves. Millions fall for this line of propaganda believing at first that they are on the road to a new age, only to be confronted sooner or later by the spectacle of the iron curtains, the massacres and the relentless tyrannies of every state which has finally fallen prey to this creed.

As the end of the twentieth century approaches it becomes apparent that a global contest will continue far into the future between those who, for as long as man is man, choose to see things through eyes focused by Marx and his successors and those who choose the road of religious faith. Marxism as it is emerging is more than a philosophy or ideology in the sense that fascism and Nazism were, it is an intellectual and quasi-religious framework for a materialist view of man. It seeks to give respectability to, and allay the consciences of, those who take up the easy weapons of the jungle, weapons well tried through history by all materialists. It claims a foundation in fact and an end to justify its means. On the other hand 'religion' is the name one gives to an equally wide framework based on a view of a man as a son of God, whose morally conditioned spiritual existence is his supreme destiny.

We have looked into a lot of corners of today's world in the attempt to get an adequate setting for the main thrust of our current search. It is time to face squarely some fundamental queries about this religious nature and destiny of man:

> What are the impregnable foundations for the religious life which are the counterpart of the Marxist insistence on scientific inevitability?

> What is the strategy which can fulfil the Marxist as well as the non-Marxist hope for a future wherein are found freedom, peace, harmony and compassion?
>
> What is the answer to the dilemma of the use of force in the cause of peace?
>
> What kind of leadership is able to avoid tyranny and yet provide an adequate global unity of values and purpose?
>
> These and a host of other questions are now before us.

The first and possibly the most important dilemma is with regard to religion itself. By the very results so far achieved it is evident that the existing great religions of the world such as Christianity, Buddhism, Islam, Hinduism and their various offshoots and expressions have nowhere proved to be universally acceptable. Two ways of approach are possible at this point. The one which has often been tried, and which has only resulted in yet more religions or sects, is syncretism – that is the amalgamation of the 'best' aspects of each, in the judgement of some new messianic figure. This savours very much of a patchwork mentality which has no greater hope to offer than those already demonstrated.

There is another and much more exciting possibility. What if all modern religions are, in fact, only the largely humanly-developed constructions and establishments of valid spiritual experience of the one and only God? What if the answer lies not without or beyond what is already available to mankind in terms of God's self-revelation, but in the coming together of all religious people with truly humble and selfless mutual concern and with such a confession as:

> We have been offered the Truth, but we have allowed our own sins, our own human greed, blame, envy and arrogance to distort and obscure the way.
>
> We have made our own fixed establishments, dogmas and codes out of the precious words given us by the prophets to point the way ahead.
>
> We have taken as our own what is truly the property of all as children of God.
>
> We have followed too much the devices and desires of our own unregenerate human hearts and have not been obedient to the voice of the Living God. The time has come for us all to unpitch our tents and move.
>
> So, let us bring the best we can to each other. Let us seek the mind and will of God together.
>
> Let us not close our minds and hearts to the deepest moral and spiritual truths regardless of which of us may be the vehicles of fresh insights and correction.
>
> Let us be fellow pilgrims bringing our varying gifts as together we seek the surest Way, the ultimate Truth and eternal Life.

Can it happen?

If it can, and I believe it can, then we are on the brink of one of the greatest breakthroughs in all religious history. We may see a fire lighted which will race across the globe and especially to the empty-souled hungry areas where materialism has choked spiritual freedom for generations.

CHAPTER 10

'I AM THE WAY, THE TRUTH AND THE LIFE: NO MAN COMETH UNTO THE FATHER BUT BY ME.'

John 14: 6

These last words of Jesus which at first sight seem to narrow the magnificent prospect on which we are allowed to look, do in fact only define it. They do not set limits for the access to the Father, but give us a wider view of the action of Christ.

They carry light into the dark ages and dark places of earth. They tell us that wherever there is heroic self-surrender, wherever there is devoted study of the ways and works even of the unknown God, wherever there is a heart yearning towards the undiscovered glories of a spiritual world, there is Christ: there is Christ, though we see Him not, and His name is not named, and where Christ is, there is the approach to a loving Father.

Brooke Foss Westcott, Bishop of Durham

All that is noble in the non-Christian systems of thought, conduct or worship is the work of Christ upon them and within them. By the word of God – that is to say by Jesus Christ – Isaiah and Plato, and Zoroaster and Buddha, and Confucius conceived and uttered such truths as they declared. There is only one divine light: and every man in his measure is enlightened by it.

Archbishop William Temple

I believe that the time has come when, if men are ever to achieve a common understanding, they must do so at a point which will only be reached by breaking, reversing or reframing a mass of conventions and prejudices that enclose us in a dead outer shell. We all now need something quite different. There is nothing Anti-Christian – far from it – in the direction my thoughts are taking; I see it simply as a call for the appearance of an even Greater Christ, and for that there can be no substitute.

Teilhard de Chardin, *Letters from a Traveller*

CHAPTER TEN

Jesus and the Non-Christian

At the outset of our enquiry we saw that there were certain preconditions of any adequate answer to mankind's present problems: it must be universally valid, everywhere available even to the simplest people on earth, and possessed of deep and compelling appeal – able to fire the hearts and minds of countless people and move them to act in response. Then, too, it must offer power to achieve its objectives and have accurate and adequate direction. Finally it must move towards increasing freedom, not the opposite.*

The proposal of these pages is that it is only in the sphere of religion that these and many other essential conditions can be met. Immediately however comes the rejoinder that it has been religion which is the great dividing force in many nations and situations. Countries like Ulster and India are surely a proof of this!

One of the questions asked of Roger Hicks at La Trobe University was on this very point. He had just stated that many Indians feel that corruption is one of their major problems as a nation. An interjector called out, 'What about religion? Doesn't that cause division and strife?' Hicks paused for a moment and then gave a reply which obviously came out of long experience and deep conviction:

'I have never known religion to be the cause of division', he said. 'It is always a matter of whether the individual is being faithful to his religion or not, whether he is obedient to the deepest voice within him or disobedient – and that applies whether he is a Christian, Muslim or Hindu.'

At the time I felt this was a rather adroit answer, but in the years which followed I have had many experiences which have borne this out. Let me just describe a few of them.

I was staying at a lovely old home in Chester in 1976 when an Indian couple arrived. The lady wore a sari and the man was immaculate in western clothes. After a day or two, as we had begun to know each other a little better, the gentleman proposed a walk before dinner and so we set off. The conversation moved from current affairs and the then precarious state of freedom in his country to the role of the individual in taking responsibility for national and international change. We agreed that there were far too many critics and advisers in the world who evidenced many of the causes of the malaise in their

* See pp 15-16

own behaviour, and that the only place where one could begin to rebuild with any justification was with oneself.

I was curious about his more personal and religious beliefs and assumed that he was a Hindu. I was somewhat taken aback when, after a longer silence than usual, he said very quietly,

'Would you like me to tell you why I believe in Jesus?'

Naturally I pressed him to continue.

'My wife and I are Parsees', he said. 'I grew up as a young man with a deep hatred in my life. You see my family had been very badly hurt by a certain man and I really longed to see him hurt in return. As I grew older I realised that this hatred was wrong, that it was doing me harm and that I ought to get rid of it. I tried everything I knew without success. It stayed on, hard and intransigent.

'Then some years later I went to see the first 70 mm wide-angle film – it was called *The Robe* – and showed much of the life of Jesus. As he was arrested and then whipped by the soldiers I found this same hardness and bitterness rising in my heart. I hope he never gets around to saying "Father forgive them", I found myself wishing.

'However as the film went on and Jesus was dying on the cross and when it came to the moment when he actually prayed that prayer, I found tears rolling down my cheeks.

'Nothing more happened at that time, but some weeks later I was in a meeting with some Christians and one of them was talking about resentments and hatred, when he said a very strange thing. He told of a deep hatred which used to dominate his life, and how, on reflection, he now realised that to nurse such feelings was tantamount to crucifying Jesus afresh.

'I thought he was talking nonsense; but later I pondered his remark and began to see how it was indeed human hatred which had brought Jesus to his death.

'We Parsees wear a white under-garment', he went on, 'and at that moment I felt as though I took this off and wrapped all my hatred in it, and then I took it all to the foot of the cross and prayed to God to forgive me for hating this man and to take it away.

'God did that', he concluded, 'and it has never come back. This is why I believe in Jesus.'

Some months later I was talking to a Roman Catholic Archbishop who is a good friend and I told him this story.

'Was that man a Christian or not?' I queried.

He replied, 'I would like to think that half the people who come to mass in my cathedral have as deep an experience of Jesus as that!'

This doesn't really answer the question, but it makes a very important point, especially in the light of a later remark of my Parsee friend when he said how much it had meant to him when it first dawned on him that when Jesus died on the cross there was not a single Christian in the world.

'He died for all men', was his conclusion.

Last year I was invited to the home of a very brilliant young doctor while travelling in India. He was a Brahmin and a devout Hindu. His wife was a Christian. As we talked about his work he told me how much faith in God meant to him. One of the hospitals he attended regularly was run by a Roman Catholic order. He had asked for a small room where he could snatch a brief time to be quiet and meditate during a busy day. 'I love it in that room – it is right beside their chapel', he explained, 'and I can really feel the presence of Jesus Christ there.'

When I was leaving he gave me a beautifully illustrated copy of the Hindu Gita.

Few people have not heard of the faith and courage of that modern apostle of love, Mother Teresa of Calcutta. It is told how Mother Teresa was called urgently to the hovel where a woman with several small children was starving to death. She took a small bag of rice and with one of her assistants hurried to the home. While she was attending to the pitifully emaciated children she placed the rice on the floor. When she looked up a little later she noticed the rice and the mother had disappeared. A little later the woman was back, but the quantity of rice had shrunk to half its former size. When she asked the woman where it had gone, the woman looked at her quietly and said, 'They are hungry too.'

They were a Muslim family living next door – also perilously close to death. The woman was Hindu.

I believe Jesus Christ went into that home with Mother Teresa. I am equally certain that he went into the Muslim home with the Hindu lady.

My wife and I were at a conference in Switzerland when a group of university students from a Middle East country arrived. Chosen by their education authorities, they were mainly Moslems. At first they were inclined to be aggressively strident about their own faith whenever the question of God and his will arose. When nobody argued or took up any points this subsided and soon they were all part of the group which included people from many faiths, and some with none.

A little later they moved to Scotland and stayed in the homes of members of an Edinburgh congregation of the Church of Scotland. There was one outstanding young lady, striking in her beauty and with a mind to match.

She was most articulate and a born leader. The men in her group tended to resent the fact that she was so often the natural spokeswoman for them.

One night, while she was sharing a bedroom with an Australian lass whom I know quite well, she sat on the side of her bed with a face like thunder, making no attempt to get ready for bed. My friend asked what was troubling her. There was a long silence. Then she burst out, 'How do I love my enemies?'

The Australian girl thought for a moment. It was obvious who the 'enemies' were. Then she replied, 'When I feel all uptight like that I often find it helps to read part of the New Testament.'

The other girl looked at her hard for a moment. Then she went to her case and took out a Bible given her some weeks before which she carried together with the Koran. As so often happens at such times (and by 'co-incidence'?), she opened the book at the place where Jesus was speaking about forgiving one's brother an indefinite number of times.

Another girl in the group became convinced that the Deputy Minister for Education, who had been responsible for getting them the trip overseas, should see for himself something of the spirit of the conference in Switzerland. She flew back to her country and found the Minister was about to leave for a UNESCO consultation in Geneva. She arrived on his doorstep at midnight and stayed until she had convinced him, his wife and two grown-up children that they should amend their schedule to get to the conference. By then it was 4 am!

My wife and I met them on their arrival twenty four hours later, and talked with them over a late breakfast. They were still a little stunned by the speed of the change in their plans. However, things were at a fascinating stage in the conference, and soon they were not only taking in all that was being said, but actively participating in the many tasks of running the conference shared by all the guests.

A week later they stood together as a family to make their farewells. The boy and girl, in their early twenties, spoke first. They told of a new and closer relationship they had found together and with their parents during the past week. Mother followed them to confirm and expand this theme, and all looked happy and relaxed. Then father spoke: a fine, handsome, big man in his early fifties.

'All my life, as a devout Muslim', he began, 'I have faithfully kept my times of prayer day by day. Since we had a family I have never failed to include prayers that one day we would be a united family in the way we have begun to find here in this place.'

There was a long silence. Then he went on to thank people for what he said was all the love and caring they had experienced there.

Another even longer silence.

Then, in a very quiet voice, he added, 'Above all I am grateful to God for coming into the world in Jesus.'

There was a long silence.

I felt a great lump in my throat and my eyes filled with tears.

Nobody had tried, at any time, to press a Christian viewpoint upon him. Somehow it was bigger than that. He had unerringly sensed the source and motivation of much that had transpired, of course. But the thing which moved me deeply was the vision in that moment of Jesus with his arms outstretched to all the world, not confined to the role of head of just one of the world's many religions, but as the light that lightens every man who comes into the world.

As my Parsee friend had said with deep emotion, when Jesus was crucified there was not a single Christian in the world – he died for all mankind. When he said it, he was clearly saying, 'He died for me too.'

I recently received a letter from a medical doctor friend of mine from India. He is serving as a Christian missionary, but is living in close community with people of widely differing cultural and religious as well as national backgrounds. When he heard I was engaged in writing this book he wrote:

'I hope you will have something to say about the relation of Christianity to other religions. I haven't the slightest doubt that among the "other sheep which are not of this fold" there will be many Hindus. I am sure many of our people worship Christ just as much as, or more than I do, though they may know Him by another name as orthodox Hindus. Now that I have got to know so many of them well, usually Brahmins, I realise that Hinduism is far more a cultural and legal system than a religion. As Nehru said, "It is possible to be an atheist and a Hindu!" He was himself, until near the end of his life. So that means it is possible to worship and follow Jesus Christ with a full heart and yet remain a Hindu.

'Christianity is, in the minds of so many, also a legal and cultural system – an extension of Western Life in general and the British Raj in particular. I think they have ample cause to think this way, starting with the forced conversions of the Goanese (first by the Church) during the Portuguese occupation and later by commercial pressure to adopt Christianity during British times. They haven't forgotten these things and many Christian missions since that time, by their patronising attitudes, have only served to confirm their ideas.

'On the other hand so many of the committed Hindus go to the New Testament for their spiritual food that it is almost, if not quite, universal.

We don't have to "sell" the New Testament, it speaks for itself, and they know it. I never realised before what an incomparable treasure we have in the Bible.

'Here is a passage from the *Rig Veda* (11.28, 1–9):

We praise Thee with our thoughts, O God.
We praise Thee even as the sun praises Thee in the morning.
May we find Joy in being Thy servants.

Keep us under Thy protection.
Forgive our sins and give us Thy love.

God made the rivers to flow.
They feel no weariness; they cease not from flowing.
They fly swiftly like birds in the air.

May the stream of my life flow into the river of righteousness.
Loose the bonds of sin that bind me;
Let not the thread of my song be cut while I sing;
and let not my work end before its fulfilment.

Remove all fear from me, O Lord,
Receive me graciously unto Thee, O King.
Cut off the bonds of afflictions that bind me;
I cannot even open my eyes without Thy help.

Let the dread weapons that wound the sinner hurt us not.
Let us not go from light into darkness.
Thy laws are immutable O God; they are firm like the mountains.

Forgive the trespasses that I may have committed;
Many mornings remain to dawn upon us:
Lead us through them all, O God.

'There is great inspiration in hymns like this that lift up the soul to God but for solid spiritual food the Bible is incomparable.'

The thing which first struck me about this lovely hymn of praise and prayer for help, was the highly developed concept of God. He is a God whom it is a joy to serve, a God who forgives sin and gives love to his servants. He is Creator, all powerful, and able to remove fear and temptation. His laws are absolute and immutable.

Wherein then can the Christian add more or bring additional strength to a Hindu with faith in such a God? As I pondered this question I found myself saying, nothing more can be added, other than this: we Christians can say to our Hindu brothers, 'All this is true, it is no longer a matter of hope and faith. We know.' In 5 BC a baby was born in Bethlehem of Judea who grew into manhood and as those around him came to know him they came more and more to the astonishing belief that he was not an ordinary man, though in one way he was every bit as human as they were. He spoke with an authority which no man can assume or pretend. His friendship unravelled for them the confused layers of their own hearts and souls until they looked on what cannot be seen and heard tones beyond human hearing. They knew that in him the Eternal God had fulfilled his ancient promises and come among men.

When he was finally betrayed and crucified, their first reaction was immense. The very base of their lives had been destroyed. If *this* man could be killed there was no longer any hope for any man alive. But a few days later their lives began to tremble in resonance to a wholly new and even more incredible experience, or series of experiences. Again and again, when their need was great but when they least expected any response, they met him – alive! Christ was risen! He had conquered the utmost that anyone or anything could or can ever hurl against the love and goodness and gentleness of God. It was no longer a matter of mere faith that God is love, that he is all-powerful over sin and evil and death, that he cares and forgives and recreates. Now it is utterly unquestionable fact. They knew because it had happened to them, there and then, in their own lives and in the evidence of their own senses.

So the Christian too is sent into history not to destroy the highest insights and aspirations of the men of faith, whatever their road from wherever on the circumference of human experience, not to destroy but to fulfil.

I was once invited by a Jewish Rabbi to take part with him in a 'dialogue sermon' in his synagogue. We were good friends and he was particularly keen for me to discuss the Christian attitude to the Old Testament, as we call it.

For more than half an hour we traversed a host of technical and theological questions regarding authorship, interpretation and relevance of the prophets, the writings and the law. We got on famously. Then, when it was obvious we should draw it all to a close, my friend suddenly hurled at me a question which was not only intended to throw me from any comfortable perch I had reached, but which also seemed to come from his own heart and out of a deep sense of hurt.

He said, 'Dr Mackay, in the light of the large amount of agreement we have demonstrated here today, don't you think it is an impertinence for there to be a Christian Mission to the Jews?'

Silence.

All the black capped heads were raised and hundreds of pairs of eyes looked directly at me. I felt the urgency and the sense of pain in so much history behind this question.

Then God spoke to me and through me. It was truly like that. I had no such answer ready, and it has always amazed me since, the truth of the answer which flashed into my mind.

'Rabbi', I replied, 'if you and I were scientists engaged in the search for a cure for cancer, and if one day we found the answer, the very first persons we would want to tell about it would be our fellow research workers.'

There was another silence, but this time the atmosphere had relaxed. A murmur spread across the congregation, and the Rabbi had a broad smile as he graciously closed the proceedings by saying, 'Well, I guess that had better be the last word.'

On 25th August, 1975, a significant broadcast was made by German South West Radio when Professor Hans Küng, a leading Catholic theologian from the University of Tübingen, had a similar discussion with Professor Pinchas Lapide of the Bar Ilan University and at the American College in Jerusalem. Christian and Jew came very close in mind and often in spirit as they traversed traditional differences. This is how that dialogue concluded:

Pinchas Lapide: Professor Küng, what unites us is everything that can be known and investigated with the tools of scholarship about this Jesus. What divides us are the things that divide not only Jews from Christians, but also knowledge from faith. One thing I know for certain: that faith in this Christ has given millions of Christians a better life and an easier death, and I would be the last to disturb their faith even if I could. Anyway I can't. What I can and will say is this: you are waiting for the *Parousia;* with you too the fullness of redemption is still in the future; I await its coming, but the second coming is also a coming. If the Messiah comes and then turns out to be Jesus of Nazareth, I would say that I do not know of any Jew in this world who would have anything against it.

Thus a legitimate awaiting of his advent or second coming – and the distinction here is really secondary – would not only be our common expectation of salvation, but in the meantime would enable both of us to concentrate on what can be known. And here the thirty-three earthly years of Jesus are a legitimate field of research for both of us. We should leave our faith to God, since neither of us can talk the other into it. We are living, thank God, in a religious pluralism. God alone knows, of all the ways which lead to him, which is the shortest and best. I have no desire to assume papal authority to decide which of us believes better, more prudently or more wisely.

Hans Küng: You have touched on a very fundamental point and theoretically there is little more to be said on the subject. You said that faith in Jesus Christ had enabled countless Christians to lead a better life. This I think, has all too often been forgotten in Christendom: that with Jesus it is not simply a question of a Christology, a doctrine, a Logos of Christ, but a question of following Christ. The whole history of relations between Christians and Jews would have taken a different course if Christians as practical disciples of Christ had made a better attempt to follow him instead of merely disputing theoretically with Jews how Christ is to be understood and how God is to be understood.

The decisive thing, however, is to attempt to live this message, which carries with it so many Jewish elements, which perhaps finds its most profound expression in the summing up of the law as it appears already in the Book of Exodus: to love God with all our heart and our neighbour as ourselves. I think, if we Christians had been more concerned with practice, we would have got further in the dialogue. Then the situation in regard to those lofty teachings would be fundamentally different from what it is now, after always speaking mainly about lofty teachings and largely neglecting practical discipleship. What is credible is only *being* a Christian and not simply any kind of doctrine held by Christians.

Pinchas Lapide: In a word, after living and praying *against one another* for nearly two thousand years, let us two study *with one another* and discover the earthly Jesus from below – as you say – and let us then see where God will further guide us both.[1]

In all of these encounters there has been a common factor, in that the Christian or group of Christians have been intimately involved. Yet is it not true to the express command and spirit of Jesus that the real way the world will be united in its greatest aims and motivations will be through the flowering and maturing of many, many faiths: and, with those in whom Christ is alive and regnant, humbly and sincerely serving, caring, loving, giving to our fellow seekers-after-God until we are united in our common pilgrimage, finding the way, the truth and the life together?

If so the 'religious' and historical anachronisms in which we have sought to confine Jesus will be shattered, for he will again be Good News for all men – news of liberation, cleansing, fulfilment. His disciples will be seen no longer as rivals or even enemies but as welcome colleagues bearing gifts of which they are not proprietors but are themselves fellow recipients.

Indeed it goes further than that. The sorely needed reformation of modern Christendom may well come out of the other faiths which are not hampered by copious rationalisations and other devices for avoiding the incisive ethics of Jesus, developments to which some of the best theological brains have increasingly been devoted.

I am sure many Christians shared with me a sense of deep shame at what a Buddhist from Sri Lanka had to say on the meaning he saw in Easter 1978 in a national broadcast in New Zealand. Vijitha Yapa began by asking:

> 'DOES EASTER MEAN ANYTHING to a Buddhist?' This was the question that went through my mind during a brief visit to New Zealand. I was invited to a Bible study group. It was the first I had ever attended. Instead of making the Bible relevant to the age we live in, many of those present were talking about the beauty of God's creation and the power of Christ nearly two thousand years ago.
>
> One lady spoke of how God put the right words into Christ's mouth when someone asked him, 'Should we pay taxes?' Christ asked for a coin, showed Caesar's head on it and said, 'Return to Caesar what is his.' I interrupted the discussion at this stage and said, 'Let's relate it to modern times. How many of you do not pay your taxes absolutely honestly?' There was a shocked silence. One bald-headed businessman, his face and head resembling the rising sun (when viewed from a Sri Lanka beach) as it changed colour, said, 'Well, we give it to the churches. They make better use of it than the Government.' I asked, 'Why didn't Christ say, "Give it to me, or to my colleagues?" Why did He say, "Give it to Caesar"?' The subject was quickly changed.
>
> When they discovered I was a Buddhist, they told me in no uncertain terms that I would not be saved if I did not accept Christ as my Saviour. This was when I began to ask myself, what does Easter mean to a Buddhist?
>
> To me, Jesus Christ did not come to earth to start Christianity. He came for all men everywhere. In Jesus' lifetime, the name Christians had not been invented. He showed all a road along which they could travel, an experiment if one likes to call it that.
>
> Jesus Christ came at a time when the Roman Empire was the mightiest nation in the world. It could be equivalent to America or Russia of today. Yet, Christ did not organise a revolt, though he was a rebel against the status quo. His revolution was through a change in people – and what happened to the Roman Empire as people lived Christ's standards is now history.
>
> Christ spoke to thousands but it was twelve men he chose to carry on His work. He spent a lifetime training these people. They saw lepers being healed,

they saw blind men see – they saw so many things we read about in the Bible. Yet, when it came to taking a stand, the apostles scattered in all directions. Peter the Rock denied him, thrice. In the long run, these apostles spoke fearlessly and spread Christ's word through becoming living examples.

To me, one of the most challenging parts of the Bible is when Christ prayed in that garden: 'Not my will, but thy will' – in other words, 'I do not want to die, but I know it is the divine will, so help me to obey.' He was human, just like us. It is so similar to the Buddha's life. The Buddha's father tried to prevent the divine will by keeping him locked up in a palace, but human engineering cannot prevent what is to be. The Buddha ventured out into the world outside. He was the reality of life and found the way to conquer desire.

When Christ says, 'I am the way', to me it means, 'I have experienced fear too. I know taking a stand will incur the wrath of people. My best friends may abandon me. Public opinion is fickle. But I am going to stand firm. The cross means the big I, what I want for my life, crossed out by the divine will.'

Many think of Judas as a crook. He was chosen as an apostle, not to betray Christ. He chose to mouth the right phrases, made the right noises in public and at prayer, but there was no moral decision to change. He may be the man sitting next to us at church or temple. He finally betrayed Christ but took his own life.

I am a journalist by training. If I had been at Mount Calvary and seen Christ crucified, I would have probably said to myself, Jesus was offered a chance to be king of the world. He refused. Now he lies helpless. Could he not have done more for his people if he had become king?

He was offered all the wealth. He refused. Could he not have done more for the poor people if he had used that wealth?

Just before he gained enlightenment, the devil (Mara) offered the Buddha virtually the same things, but the Buddha refused. In both the Buddha and Christ, they were deliberate choices. Both showed that it is not material things that count, but obeying the divine will.

To some who watched, the crucifixion was the end. Then came the resurrection. Christ's crucifixion is actually a paradox. It is in dying that one is reborn. To me the message of Easter is just that.

As the Buddha stressed, death to self gives birth to a new man. It is for each one to decide whether we, too, want to have that experience or not.

I have heard a Parsee pray and conclude his prayer with the words '. . . in the Name of Our Lord and Saviour Jesus Christ'. Yet he would politely refuse the title of Christian. Why? Certainly not because of Jesus or any lack of faith in him. Most probably it is because of what we Christians have done with the word, the content our lives and behaviour have put into it.

Mother Teresa recently discussed changing events in India with a friend of mine. In her long years in India this devoted nun has found the living God, whom we Christians know in Christ, regnant in the lives of many people other than those who claim the title of Christian. Talking of Morarji Desai she said quietly, 'I know him. He believes in God. It's good he's the one at the head of the Government.'

I recently heard a very senior minister say of Islam, 'It may be the Muslims who prove to be the real champions of Christian morality!' In the light of some of the developments in so-called Christian circles today, where perverted and decadent morality is seen as avant-garde, he may well be right. Actually, of course, it is the sensational and exceptional which always gets the headlines. It is one thing for a parson or a small committee of a church or council of churches to make some outlandish statement or a small group of people to start an heretical sect, but it is another thing to say that it is typical of the vast body of Christians.

That a global renaissance and rediscovery is needed in the sphere of religion, there can be little doubt. If Christians are right in believing that it is in the coming of Jesus Christ into men's lives that the fulness of God is to be found, then the time has come for them to ask themselves some honest and fundamental questions. The first ought to be, 'What was the nature of the preparation of Israel for the coming of Jesus?' Israel was the chosen seedbed for God's greatest revelation to mankind because of two essential factors: first their veneration and determination on the primacy of the Torah, the moral law, as given to Moses on Mount Sinai, and secondly their acceptance of the fact of the living voice of God speaking through the prophets.

May it not be that the fundamental prerequisite for the new great advance of religion across the world is for us, with all men and women of God everywhere, to agree that it is in taking absolute moral standards (such as honesty, purity, unselfishness, love and humility and dedication to peace-making) seriously? It is here that a beginning must be made and, at the same time, a turning to the one God who is our maker and Lord, to obey his voice.

To such as take this road, which can be denominated how you will, to those who seek the truth and commit themselves to live by it, God himself will come as the Way, the Truth and the Life – a living person. He has done so in Jesus of Nazareth.

CHAPTER 11

I had motives for not wanting the world to have a meaning, consequently assumed that it had none and was able without any difficulty to find satisfying reasons for this assumption . . . The Philosopher who finds no meaning in the world is not concerned exclusively with a problem in pure metaphysics; he is also concerned to prove there is no valid reason why he personally should not do as he wants, or why his friends should not seize political power and govern in the way they find most advantageous to themselves . . . For myself, as no doubt, for most of my contemporaries, the philosophy of meaninglessness was essentially an instrument of liberation. The liberation we desired was simultaneously liberation from a certain political and economic system and liberation from a certain system of morality.

Aldous Huxley, *Ends and Means*

In the first place, Christian faith turns on the reality of God's existence, His being there. Then it also turns on an acceptance of the fact that man's dilemma is moral and not metaphysical. Each person must face these two things on his own level as a matter of truth.

Francis Schaeffer, *The God Who Is There*

CHAPTER ELEVEN

New Forces Emerge

The exciting proposition now emerges that behind all these stories of the 'inner voice' in the lives of men and women and behind the actions or words of those Christians who were part of the 'environment' of their discovery, there was another Word speaking, another Person present. It would seem that in each instance a number of factors were focused at the right time to produce these important new spiritual discoveries. In the highlands of Papua New Guinea and in Bulgaria there was no apparent attempt to impose concepts of right or wrong or to propose rules or conventions. Nevertheless people moved rapidly and apparently independently towards ethical standards and values which are characteristic of developed religious experience.

This confronts us with the question as to whether moral standards and values are not, in fact, universal – part of the basic nature of man as man. Herbert Marcuse writes, 'In going through the enumerations of the highest moral values in Soviet ethical philosophy it is difficult to find a single moral idea or syndrome of moral ideas that is not common to Western ethics.'[1] It would be fascinating to know more of what lay behind the resolution of the 22nd Congress of the Soviet Communist Party when, in 1961, they asserted: 'Unless we can root out bourgeois morality and educate people in Communist morality, renewing them morally and spiritually, it is not possible to build a Communist society.'

The story thus far, however, has not yet taken into account another and one of the most powerful factors at work in each situation. Thus far each story has been told largely from the point of view of an external and uninvolved observer. Behind the facade of events as seen by such a person, or even by those who were themselves discovering the voice of God, there is another structure, involving other lives. For instance there was nothing coincidental or haphazard about the 'selection' of the people who became involved. It had been the clear direction of the Spirit that took the Abels to Kwato and later on each stage of their journey into the Owen Stanley ranges of Papua New Guinea.[2] It was this same voice which took Roger Hicks to Bulgaria and led him in the strategy he adopted there. This much we have seen, the voice or Spirit of God guiding and directing the way for those prepared to receive directions and obey. This was only the tip of the iceberg however, for permeating and undergirding it all there was intense spiritual activity on the part of many people who directly and indirectly beamed into each situation by means of prayer.

The mention of prayer brings a new dimension into all we have been discussing so far. What prayer is, its power and its vital role in our spiritual lives, and its relevance to the future development of human society is a matter we must soon discuss in depth, but meanwhile let us proceed with the story from the viewpoint of the discoverer.

As a Christian I would be more than happy to accept as a starting point President Sadat's crystallisation of the moral basis for peace, not only between Muslims, Jews and Christians in the Middle East, but for all mankind: love, honesty, purity and peace. These four words chosen by this Muslim leader to undergird his 'divine mission' broadly express the moral teaching of New Testament as well as that of the Jewish and Muslim scriptures. They are universal standards, and as God is absolute so they too are absolute – always unattainable but, like the Pole Star, they help to direct our course as we journey towards them. Because they are absolute they are continually breaking down the confines of the rules and regulations within which we try to make our religious ideals attainable. One day, as Jesus said, absolute love will encompass all the other requirements, laws, and standards, but that will only be when we have so grown in moral and spiritual maturity that the meaning and content of the word 'love' far exceeds our present understanding of it.

For the religious man then, for the seeker after the life of the spirit, the impregnable foundations for his faith are to be found first in these moral imperatives. One of the great scholars of Old Testament language and thought, the late Professor A B Davidson, wrote:

> The original relationship of man to God, being a relation of love, is ethical . . . man is a moral and independent being. The relation in which he first stood to God was a moral relation; the relation in which he is to stand anew is a moral relation; the means, therefore, used to bring him into this new relation must be moral means. Thus grace, or the scheme of salvation, is the great moral agency employed by God for bringing again His moral creature, man, into the perfect moral relation of the soul with Himself.[3]

Jesus said, 'Not everyone who calls *me* "Lord, lord" will enter the kingdom of God, but he who does the will of my Father.'

Schumacher, author of *Small is Beautiful*, comes to the same conclusion when he argues that 'Wisdom can be read about in numerous publications but it can be found only inside oneself. To be able to find it, one has first to liberate oneself from such masters as greed and envy. The stillness that follows liberation – even if only momentarily – produces the insights of wisdom that are obtained in no other way.'[4]

The very first Christian creed was simply 'Jesus is Lord'. This was the affirmation first required of those who wished to be baptised into the new way. Since then theologians and councils have expanded it into magnificent theses about God, Jesus and the Holy Spirit, the Church and much more besides. The grave danger is that much of so-called Christian evangelism ignores the method and teaching of Jesus and hurls such a set of doctrines and dogma at seekers-after-God with rigid insistence. Jesus knew no such way. Indeed the disciples were taught the 'Lord's Prayer' before they had experienced most of the events which are held to be so essential for a person to be converted today; most of the things which are so important in the great creeds had not yet happened! They certainly were not 'Christians', for the word had not yet been coined.

Jesus never demanded, as a beginning, belief in theological statements but a quality of life, of obedience, of preparedness to adventure in faith. He took men where they then were, and some of them were living lives which by any moral standards needed a great deal of reshaping, but the important thing was their readiness to hear his challenge to them and obey its implications. Christianity was a way of life (indeed, The Way, according to *Acts* 9:2) before it became a creed.

To me there is a tragic inversion in the methods of those well-meaning crusaders who go about the 'conversion' of others by putting to them a series of requirements of belief about the nature and person of Jesus, the events of the cross and the inspiration of the Bible. It is often as silly as setting a final degree examination paper to a kindergarten child. They may eventually get earnest and well-meaning repetitions and affirmations in return, and those with sincere intentions will unquestionably be blessed by God, not because of the correctness of their answers however but because of their need and sincerity. The danger is that such a confession has no roots, no foundations; and because of this it all too often becomes a hard, dogmatic orthodoxy which is defended with pharisaic intolerance because of its very insecurity. The doctrine, which is ultimately so vital, is not really their own but a second-hand orthodoxy.

Jesus said that it would be the Holy Spirit who would lead people to the truth, and teach them about himself. By whatever route people embark on the road of the Spirit they will, if faithful, be led to greater and greater insights. Nevertheless it is most important to consider again the methods of Jesus when it comes to leading men to God.

How is it that any person can ever come to the conclusions whereby he is able to make the assertion that Peter made to Jesus on behalf of the disciples at Caesarea Philippi, 'You are the Messiah – the Son of the Living God!'

How did Peter know or even dare to conceive such a thought? After all he was a Jew, schooled and reared in the uncompromising assertion of Israel that God is *one*. Everything in his training would have resisted the idea that this Master of theirs, no matter how beloved, was in any way to be called divine.

It certainly would not be because of the miracles. In those days, before scientific medicine and psychology brought explanations, diagnoses and cures, there must have been innumerable cases of afflictions which seemed to be due to demonic possession or intractable illness but which responded quickly to the ministrations of healers. After all, the many prophets of Israel were credited with mighty miracles without any suggestion that they were divine.

There is one overarching explanation of the disciples' conviction about Jesus which begins at the moral level. It was as these men set out to live with Jesus, to hear his teaching, to face the implications of his friendship, and as they heard his insistence on taking moral perfection as their rule, that they began to develop a new dimension of need and humility and so too new organs of moral and spiritual perception. It was one thing to keep the commandments of Moses as to such things as adultery or theft or covetousness (which could be managed), but when Jesus demanded such absolute purity that to entertain lustful thoughts was to sin, then their sense of moral need grew deeper and stronger. They could never meet his challenge on their own.

But all the time Jesus *was* there, right in the centre of their lives – and somehow he *knew* all about it. He saw, before they did themselves, the plain truth about their natures, their thoughts and deeds. He felt their hopes and their despair. He came into their defeats as well as their victories, not as a fellow sinner but in a unique way. When he came he healed them, cleansed them, re-fired their resolve and brought them back to a wholeness of spirit in a way in which only God can act. He was always there, going on ahead, patiently building them up and pointing the way for each one. He fulfilled the deepest and most intimate function of God in their lives. 'Their hearts burned within them' in his fellowship. In their moral poverty they found the divine abundance; in their dry and arid lives they found living water, in him.

When Peter confessed this faith and asserted his conviction that he was uniquely divine, Jesus rejoiced greatly. 'Blessed are you, Simon,' he said. 'Flesh and blood have not revealed this to you, but my Father in heaven.' At that moment the centre-point of all history had been reached. God had broken through absolutely. For the first time human lips gave expression to a conviction which declared that the end of the long, long road of mankind's moral and spiritual pilgrimage was within sight.

And where did this central drama begin?

It was with Abraham and Moses and Isaiah and John the Baptist: these and other faithful prophets and men of God had helped to shape the moral and spiritual environment. It was their obedience to the divine will which prepared Israel for the coming of the supreme revelation of God. The road to Caesarea Philippi led past Mount Sinai. The Sermon on the Mount stood firm on the Ten Commandments, which Jesus averred he had come not to destroy but to fulfil.

So in our own search. If any man is to know God he must begin in the same way, by his readiness to bring his life under the cleansing scrutiny of the highest moral code he knows. His insight into the moral requirements of Almighty God for his own life will expand and grow every day as he hears and obeys God's voice, as he reads and watches and shares his new life with new friends. Each new moral conviction will bring Jesus closer to us, more real, more divine.

The New Testament too is a book which grows for us as we grow. It is new after every new spiritual experience; its familiar words hold new depths and meaning for us every step of the way. There will come the day when we will form convictions about that too, but not at first. The words *about* God gradually come to be heard as the words *of* God and the experience progressively deepens until we hear this book speak the very Word of God: the Word which became flesh and lived among men.

But the starting point for the seeker after the spirit is the moral law, just as the starting point for the Marxist is what he believes to be a scientific, socio-economic law. But the Marxist also has his messianic hope, his belief in a brave new world which will emerge out of obedience to the Party, and he also believes that in some almost mystical way the Party will always express the infallible word of the proletariat, the will of the masses. So too the religious person cannot stay long merely on the level of the moral law, for this too is set in the context of belief in a brave new world which will emerge out of obedience to the Spirit, to the voice of Almighty God.

I once conducted a service in a small church in the countryside of New South Wales and spoke of the experience of receiving direction from God and the effect it had had in many situations. After the service a woman in her early forties came up to me with a child of about ten years of age at her side. She seemed most anxious to have a personal chat so we waited until others had gone. Then she said, with almost breathless anxiety, 'Do you really think God would tell me what to do?' She paused, then seemed to retreat from saying any more.

I felt strongly that I should not probe but simply tell her what I had found. I replied, 'If you are prepared to pray to God for help and then sit down quietly to allow him to speak to your mind, with willingness to obey any thought which comes, provided it does not transgress the standards of Jesus, I am absolutely certain that God will make clear to you the very next step you must take.' Then, out of the blue, this additional thought came pounding into my mind so that I blurted it out, 'Almost certainly it will have to do with your relationships with another person.'

She looked a little startled but said no more than 'Thank you', and left. Two days later my telephone rang and she was on the other end. 'I want to tell you', she said, 'When I went into that church on Sunday night I was absolutely desperate. I had left my husband and my home that day, determined never to return. I had taken my youngest child with me. Then you told me about God being ready to talk to me. He did. He showed me where I had been wrong in several places, and that I must go home and put things right with my husband. I did, and it has been a wonderful two days since.'

'That is not all', she continued. 'Next morning I woke early and felt I wanted to ask God for the next steps. Again he spoke very clearly. He told me to go to our next-door neighbours and apologise for something where I now see I was largely to blame for a difference which meant that our two families had not spoken for more than two years. That was very hard to do, because the man of the house was liable to have a bad temper. I left it until I was going out, but I couldn't pass their house without obeying God's instruction. I sat another twenty minutes in the car trying to get courage, but in the end I went to their door and knocked. To my dismay it was the man who answered the door. However I told him I was sorry for the things which had happened and wanted to put them right. He invited me in and he and his wife were particularly nice to me and our two families are now friends again.'

In two days, obedience to God's voice had mended a broken marriage and united two families with eight or nine people involved and faith was alive in a new situation! Looking back on the incident, that compelling thought I added about relationships with another person was not so surprising because it was virtually axiomatic. It may not be the first thought which comes to the listening mind, but very early in the new life of the spirit there emerges an astonishing chain reaction between people so that new relationships, new friendships, indeed more than that, a new 'fellowship' emerges.

The word 'fellowship' is a wonderful old Anglo-Saxon one which is used to describe the intimate, blood-bought, love-impregnated relationship which characterised the disciples of Jesus and which the Greek New Testament calls *koinonia*.

It is one of the most amazing and generally uncontrived phenomena among the hallmarks of the developing spiritual life. We products of the affluent West who have seen neighbourliness and friendship decrease and even degenerate to the level of mutually protective class groupings, mutually exploitive business groupings, or highly transitory groupings of convenience for some cause or another, are very often starved of true friendships, let alone this heart-filling commitment to each other which unites people who have the greatest of all objectives in common.

It would be a mistake however to suggest that there is primarily a realisation of a shared objective and then the consequent decision to develop such a relationship. I can only describe the experience of *koinonia* as a gift of God. It brings together the most astonishing variety of people. It transcends every human barrier of which one can think: colour, class, creed, race or even the iron walls of inherited hatreds. Long before any rational or reasoned basis for mutual involvement is developed people can become so deeply interwoven in their spiritual lives that their unity becomes among the most significant of human relationships. Indeed, unless a person has experienced *koinonia* he is at a loss to understand some of the most important phenomena of the spiritual life or the true nature of the Christian Church.

On one occasion Jesus and his friends were making a long journey back to Galilee from Judea by the most direct route despite the fact that it passed through the hostile area of Samaria. 'The Jews have no dealings with the Samaritans', as the New Testament succinctly puts it. About noon they were skirting a Samaritan town and rested in the shade beside the village well. The disciples went into the town to buy some food while Jesus rested. As he sat there in the dappled shade he noticed a woman coming alone to draw water. This was unusual, for the cool of morning or evening was the normal time for this chore and at such times the well would be thronged with gossiping neighbours. Clearly this woman wanted to avoid company.

Jesus drew her into conversation and soon saw all the symptoms of her problem. She was little more than the village prostitute. Step by step he brought her to the point that there was an adequate and abundant answer to her needs. Before long he was pouring out to her some of the greatest riches of his spiritual teaching. The woman was profoundly moved and leapt into a wholly new life. She raced off back to call the villagers, no doubt lethargic in their early afternoon siesta, saying, 'Come and meet a man who knows all about me (knows the worst about me indeed). Can he be the Messiah?'

Her reticence was gone, she was a new woman. Her experience began a whole chain of events which later meant a strong centre for Jesus' work in that part of the country. Meanwhile the disciples had returned with lunch. They found Jesus alone. When he was offered food he seemed to have lost both his weariness and his hunger. 'I have had food to eat you don't yet know about', he told them.

Such is the absorbing joy and fulfilment of true spiritual sharing of lives, of true *koinonia*, that it transcends all lesser merely human desires.

On another occasion Jesus was deeply absorbed in a life-changing, faith-giving encounter with a whole group of people when someone tried to call him away with the message that his mother and brothers had arrived and wished to speak with him. Jesus said that must wait, so important was the task he had in hand, adding: 'Anyway, who are my mother and my brothers? These here. Whoever is truly doing the will of God is to me mother or sister or brother.' Not for one moment were his family ties and filial affection less than those of other men, indeed all we know is to the contrary, for no son could have loved his mother more or been worshipped more by a younger brother, but rather he was here using the very depth of this love for his own flesh and blood to describe the tremendous love and caring he had for those who were willing to hear and obey the voice of God.

'No-one who is truly guided by God ever works alone', is indeed a wise and experienced testimony. Even in solitary confinement, or as a lone disciple amidst a crowd of unbelievers, one is never alone. Like yeast, wherever a man of the spirit goes, his faith begins to germinate and so a new *koinonia* emerges.

If the moral law is the starting point for a journey into the life of the spirit, as the consensus of experience indicates, then the development of *koinonia* follows hard on its heels.

Across the world today there seems to be a reaction to the growing centralism and unification of the human race. New and strident forms of nationalism or tribalism are emerging which tend to draw man back to his roots, to bring him once more within the perimeter of a social unit small enough to give him a sense of belonging, of personal significance and identity. It is this phenomenon which works for the breaking down of the massive ideological movements as it has in the great religious ones. It is one of our very important considerations when looking ahead towards any potentially global movement or evangelical or ideological framework for the future of our increasingly crowded planet. No matter how universal is the appeal or application of a set of ideas, a philosophy or a strategy, unless men and women can feel a fundamental sense of belonging and of personal significance it will always be fraught with the danger of disintegration from within.

When communism was in its early stages the sense of comradeship and unity between groups of committed men and women ran very high indeed. In contrast to the vague and superficial relationships, the mere nodding acquaintanceships of most members of the Christian churches, the communist cells presented a picture of something much more akin to the fellowship and zest of the early Christian community. When to this was added the demands for the depth of commitment and self-sacrifice which characterised the early communist movement, just as in the days of the *Acts of the Apostles*, the parallel between the two forces in their days of greatest enthusiasm became even more significant. No wonder many Christians were attracted, especially by the carefully prepared fringe or front activities which espoused desirable causes and ends.

One of the very important problems which emerges as one considers any movement of great or global proportions is that of leadership and cohesion. It is one thing to have masses of people sharing the same philosophy, practising similar ethics and seeking to know and obey the voice of God in their hearts; but how does it all become directional, purposeful and relevant to specific planetary problems and challenges? Especially, how can it work in a religious context?

Ideally, of course, it might be argued that if God is one, and if this almighty, all-prevailing and all-knowing source is available to each individual, then this is all that is needed. Each person would then be directed to his or her place in a vast mosaic of activity as it were, and no other directing organisation would be required. It is an interesting point of view. Indeed, more than that, it is at least partly true. The great obstacle, however, is the fact that mankind is made up of people at all stages of spiritual development or counter-development. It is true that the potential is there for total individual freedom and initiative when each one is both totally receptive and totally obedient. Yet even within the activities of a highly dedicated group of a mere two or three hundred people all seeking God's way for their daily and detailed activities there soon emerges the need for organisation and experienced leadership. Not that there aren't sufficient instances of remarkable 'coincidences' to convince the most sceptical of observers that there is a great deal more to it than an imposed plan or a shared goal or logic, or even a chance pattern of activity proving effective – but at its best it remains an ideal. The practical solution is to find that kind of leadership, that kind of organisational framework and that way of informing and enthusing the whole group which still caters for individual initiative and conviction.

This is even more imperative on a bigger scale. The larger the numbers involved the more needful is both a degree of devolution of authority and control over details and minor issues and at the same time the need for a common discipline and basic obedience. The parallels are many. When there are very few vehicles using a road system, such as in small country towns, the rules of the road can often be ignored without much danger of an accident. Come peak period however, or a sudden increase of traffic for whatever reason, the more imperative is adherence to the rules. On a high-speed road system in a great city at peak usage there is virtually no place for individualism or any deviation from the rules of the road at all.

So too in a ship at sea. In a trampship there is a high degree of individual freedom for each crew member within the simple framework of his watch-keeping routine. He can generally wander about the ship, do his laundry when he wishes, take a bath or go to have a talk with a shipmate or even wander off to see the captain, as needs be. In a highly crowded warship such as an aircraft carrier however, where a thousand or more men have to live their daily lives, an enormous increase in organisation and rules for behaviour are essential if each person is to have some time in which to take a stroll in fresh air, do his laundry, have a bath, or have a chance to bring a matter to the attention of senior officers. The freedom factor for the ship's company depends on all obeying the rules.

As spaceship earth sees her crew multiplying in numbers so that scores of millions are added to her complement each year, it is obvious that only chaos and disaster (to say nothing of unequal opportunity) will result from each person demanding the right to 'do his own thing'.

While working my way through university, in days before government grants and bursaries were available, I took a vacation job in a city store in Adelaide. It is an interesting experience to stay in one spot in the city for seven or eight hours a day watching the passing parade of human beings all intent on their Christmas shopping! One woman I recall was dragging a howling boy of about five or six years of age with one hand a push chair full of baby and parcels with the other. Opposite the counter where I was selling men's wear she stopped and gave the crying boy a great smack on the ear, which raised an even louder howl. 'I brought you here to enjoy yourself', she hissed at him indignantly, 'and you are bally well going to enjoy yourself!' With a savage drag at his reluctant hand the little family moved on through the shop as the loudspeakers sang 'God Rest You Merry Gentlemen.'

In some vast and overcrowded countries there are millions of adults as well as children who will 'bally well' enjoy themselves when they are told, fight when they are told, work, eat, marry and even think when they are told and produce the results they are told to; or else. At a certain level of totalitarian control they are like the crowded warship: at least everyone generally gets enough food to exist, enough to wear, a job to work at and a roof over his or her head, as long as they obey. That stands in contrast to other overcrowded countries where there is much less control, but much more chaos and much more danger of starvation and homelessness, at least from time to time.

Yet if man cannot live by bread alone, if he longs for personal identity and significance, for personal relationships in terms of heart-to-heart friendships and even fellowship as a basic need of human existence, if he must have a group small enough with which to identify, what does the future hold for our crowded earth?

Thus far we have come to some important aspects of the answer and it might help to recapitulate them once more:

1. The 'Maker's Instructions', the guidelines or fixed principles of human behaviour, are found in the moral law, and particularly in such cardinal standards as love, honesty, purity, and peace: the ethical crystallisation of the Law of Moses, the Sermon on the Mount, and the great majority of religious and ethical teachings. At first the precise meaning and content of these concepts may differ, of course, and this is a problem to be faced before we proceed much further.
2. There is an 'inner voice' available to the simplest or most sophisticated man on earth, to guide and direct him in pursuit of these moral goals as first steps toward a new spiritual life and the recreation of human society.

   This voice does not depend on race, class, colour or creed and is the birthright of all mankind.
3. As each individual follows this way he will come to see more deeply into his own religious heritage, his own people and the part he and they can play in the universal search of man for God, and in building a better future for mankind.

   We are all engaged on a journey from the wide circumference of humanity to the centre, which is God. We begin where we are, but as we journey we not only draw nearer to God, but to each other.
4. The life of obedience to the Spirit brings us not only to fundamental changes in our own personal lives and values but also to revolutionary changes in our relationships with others, even those with whom we may differ most or with whom there have once been barriers of hatred and mistrust. These changes can be the raw material of radical changes to the existing system of society, the basis of a more thorough revolution than foreseen by communism.

Inherent in this last discovery is the most powerful and revolutionary ingredient of them all, something which stands in absolute confrontation and contrast to the methods of the Marxists. All too often in recent years we have seen people of religion confused and misled because they have failed to see the importance of this factor. Many widespread Christian activists, for example, have seen evils and injustices in our present world which have moved them to compassion and righteous indignation. They have seen racism or exploitation or other undesirable forces at work and have felt compelled, as Christians, to tackle and confront them. So far so good.

At this point however they have often turned to methods which as members of a materialistic, power-bedevilled, affluent society they find most apparent and easy of adoption. They have turned to the weapons and methods of the militant materialists and especially of the Marxists. They no longer see the way of the cross as the supreme power. They have little or no faith in a force able to change men's and women's hearts from materialism to higher values. They have apparently had little experience of discerning and discovering the 'coincidences' which obedience to the voice of God brings into strategic living, and so they hold a meeting, or a world assembly. Then they turn to money, to numbers, to protest, to blame and even hate, saying that force and violence may be necessary to achieve 'Christian' ends. In short, the end now justifies the means, a direct contradiction of the moral teaching of Jesus.

The BBC recently quoted a black Christian minister commenting on race antagonisms in Britain as saying that answers were too slow in coming. 'Before they have learned to love we may have learned to hate', he said. Frustration, failure and finally infidelity were stripping him of his faith and his divine commission.

Is there any hope of a really effective alternative to hate? What does a Christian do even if he could 'sheet home' blame beyond question? What is his remedy? Can he really still call himself a Christian if his answer is the same as the Chinese diplomat – 'We kill them'? Or if he merely subsidises those who kill? or gives them his backing as a churchman? The vitally important factor which undergirds true Christian strategy, which characterises the heart of God's approach to this sinful world, and which is essential for the moral and spiritual life of his children is 'forgiveness'. To me anyway, and I find to most people, this is one of the most difficult things to practise in everyday life because blame with me is an automatic and immediate reaction to any mishap. Why? Well, there is a fear, going back into my childhood of *my* being blamed. No doubt my own children inherit the same problem! Then there is pride. My attitude to others so often is one of demand, whenever they affect *my* convenience, *my* well-being, *my* possessions, *my* concept of right behaviour.

Blame can even be almost wholly justifiable and still be wrong. Why? Because it is one of the most important ingredients of a hopelessly impractical philosophy of life. It is quite unrealistic because it creates increasingly insoluble positions when it is taken up in homes, industry, politics or international society. The problem is that it is so very natural, so apparently logical and so readily justifiable. It is nevertheless part of the buildup of a stockpile of fissionable materials which today stand to destroy mankind.

If you want to discover something of this, just raise some controversial or contentious topics in any group of people and watch the temperature rise. For example: China and the Opium Wars; the Boer War and the Afrikaner today; colonialism; the rights of women; the previous generation; trade and the developing nations; the environment; racism; class war. We all know that these and a thousand other issues can make ordinary decent men and women burn with indignation, with anger and even with hatred and blood lust. That is why approaching such matters from the viewpoint of blame can be like taking a tinderbox to our already inflammable world. What is more, we are living in an age when highly trained incendiaries are at work trying to produce exactly that kind of holocaust, and in an increasing number of areas.

If we want to be reasonable however, even if we *are* embarking on the road of blame, we must surely hesitate when the question is raised of where blame really begins. After all, in each of the above list of areas of resentment there were other and underlying or causal factors which, in all honesty, must be taken into account. If we are honest we will come to admit that perhaps one of the wisest judgements in such a situation is 'let him who is without sin cast the first stone'. Each of us has been blameworthy at some point or another, in so many things. The chain of blame goes back to the beginning of time.

It is important that we do not get lost in a semantic jungle at this point, that we are quite clear as to the intended meaning of the word 'blame'. I use the word to indicate something very different from the recognition of responsibility or even the condemnation of guilt. Let me try to explain.

Blame begins in the instinctive flash of the mind when one's own self feels endangered and reacts to deflect or redirect the threat. It has within it first and fundamentally this fear of personal involvement or responsibility for something which has gone wrong or which is unpleasant or reprehensible. This aspect of personal involvement may not even be entirely conscious. It can be born of attitudes and opinions built up over many years within families, clans, classes and nations. In every case however it will be found, on close and honest analysis, that there is this defensive mechanism at work. The urge is there to protect the self or group in terms of pride, reputation, hide or possessions.

Blame rarely waits to discover whether the attendant condemnation or retribution are truly just. It is the result, not the cause of an action or situation which matters to it. Judgement is biased from the start, for the individual or party making it is not disinterested.

The injunction by Jesus, 'judge not', is of particular interest here, for one implication of it is that he is insisting that only God can know and assess all the causal factors involved. Try as we may to discover the tangled strands of our motivation we can rarely fully understand even our own actions at times! How much less then can we be sure that we judge others aright?

Blame is a wholly undesirable and counter-productive element in any attempt to seek and sift the facts in order to solve problems and cure hurts. When the parties bent on blame are removed from the bar the true task of justice begins, beginning with looking for the facts, the unbiased evidence. Only when the full dimension of the action and its results have been revealed is it possible to turn confidently to discuss the question of cause. Behind the persons involved there reach long lines of influence due to heredity and environment, the impact of many other factors as well as those of deliberate and responsible choice.

Having derived such a picture it is possible to point to causes, to denounce utterly actions, attitudes and concepts in such a way that the person involved is not utterly rejected. Indeed, ideally the person may be won to complete concurrence in the assessment made. It is certainly possible to hate the sin, to do all in one's power to eradicate it and the conditions which make it possible, and at the same time to love the sinner.

It is the rejection of the adjudged defaulter which is such a terrible part of the process of blame. Closing one's mind and heart to another person is forbidden by Christ – yet it is so easy to do, even in the best of circles. The deeper the true relationship between persons the more destructive can be the refusal of fellowship, the rejection of association. Its results can be demonic. It not only frequently jams shut the door to true repentance and so to redemption, but it wounds the blamer with the ugliness of self-righteousness and self-justification. Blame for the Christian is OUT.

But this in no way means a passive, supine acceptance of evil and the status quo. Precisely the opposite. What we are discussing here are the preconditions for the only truly effective way of approach to diagnosis and cure of these ills of mankind. It is only when we have deliberately refused the self-protection of blame, and have let down the drawbridge of our citadel of self-preservation to become personally involved in therapeutic action, that victory can even be contemplated.

When we are completely honest, and especially when we are prepared to seek the mind of God upon us and the circumstances in which we are now involved, we begin to see things in ourselves and others which are necessary areas of change if there is to be true healing. Courage and commitment are certainly required to reject blame and to accept God's gift of love and insight into the lives of others, no matter how much they are involved in the wrongs and errors of the case. This courage and this love and insight are themselves gifts of God. They do not come naturally, but as we begin to see ourselves as fellow-sinners, as individuals equally needing the forgiveness and love of God, then we can begin to forge relationships which will reverse the grim march of blame, terror, violence and human degradation which bedevils our lives in this age.

Perhaps nowhere in all life is there a more definite and stark challenge and reversal of the laws of the jungle, the instinctive reactions of the natural man. This is high folly to those who have never known its power. It is here that the 'weakness of God is stronger than men'.

When we turn to the Bible we find that Jesus insisted on this revolutionary approach to the question of blame. He taught his disciples to pray: 'Forgive us our trespasses as we forgive those who trespass against us'. He warned directly: 'Judge not, that you may not be judged'. In short he taught that it was an absolute duty for his followers to practice forgiveness, not once or twice but infinitely, and not to indulge in blame. He himself did not blame others, even on the cross, although, unlike us, he was totally without blame or any kind of causal guilt himself.

If we are going to join in his great and revolutionary way of reconstructing men and human society, therefore, one of the areas where we are called upon to be most revolutionary is in this area of blame. What then is the new and practical approach to past wrongs and injustices? What do we *do* about present wrongs and wrongdoers?

The first thing a surgeon must do before he starts an operation is to make sure that his own hands are thoroughly clean. Hypocrisy at the point of dealing with the problems of others was castigated by Jesus. 'First be sure you have the beam out of your own eye before you try to remove the speck from your brother's eye', he warned.

But when I start to try to put my own part right I soon find that, while there are some things which I can and must do, there are other things which it is quite impossible for me to mend. Clearly I have to ask for and rely on the forgiveness of both other people and of God himself. It is God's limitless readiness to forgive us when we are really sorry and want to begin again which is at the heart of the great good news Jesus brought.

Having honestly made the first step oneself, it is only at this point that one can properly turn to others. Now what about them? What about some of the most obviously evil or unjust persons we know? What is the new and revolutionary way of dealing with them?

The thing which we have found is that blame must not be the motive or source of action here. This does not, of course, prevent our taking any action at all, even to total opposition and confrontation. Jesus was unflinching and implacable when it came to opposing the heartlessness of the Pharisees, even though it sealed his own doom. Jesus was free from blame or the attitude of blame himself, so he was able to stand absolutely firm on those issues where God told him a stand must be made. This was a vital, even *the* vital ingredient of his whole strategy. It was never a case of 'the end justifying the means'. Indeed the more tense and urgent the crisis the more time he spent alone with God, seeking his mind and direction. In the final hours of his life he did bloody battle with fear and desire for his own safety, but he went to the cross certain of the rightness of his course. When self and blame are crossed out, then God's inspired plan of action can be discerned, and this spells the difference between defeat and victory, even though it led to the cross. Mahatma Gandhi knew the secret of this course of inspired action, for example, when he rejected violence and waited for the inner word which finally led him out on the Salt Marches.

Again, there is the need never to lose sight of our greatest objective. This is not in achieving retaliation or vindictive punishment, but in bringing about renewal, a transformation of men and circumstances based on repentance and forgiveness. The very worst man or woman on earth can change, can repent and be forgiven and received into God's family as a beloved brother. This is true. It is of the essence of the Christian gospel.

The supreme source of power in this revolutionary way of living is found in the cross of Christ. It is here that final victory is already made sure, and where we find our strength to take the way of the cross ourselves. (See p 236, below.) This is the secret of continuing and permanent revolution.

CHAPTER 12

If he is free from lust and hatred
A man can walk safely
Among the things of lust and hatred.

The Bhagavad – Gita

Hatred ceases not by hatred at any time.
Hatred ceases by love.

Gautama (the Buddha)

No man shall drag me down so low as to make me hate him.

Booker T Washington (1856–1915)

Hate is the weapon of reaction.

Dr Paul Campbell

Love seeketh not itself to please
Nor for itself hath any care;
But for another gives its ease,
And builds a heaven in hell's despair.

William Blake (1757–1827)

Through violence you may murder the hater, but you do not murder hate. In fact violence merely increases hate. So it goes. Returning violence for violence multiplies violence, adding deeper darkness to a night already devoid of stars. Darkness cannot drive out darkness: only light can do that. Hate cannot drive out hate: only love can do that.

Martin Luther King

CHAPTER TWELVE

The Cancer of Hate

If love merely consists in 'turning the other cheek' at any time by anybody under any circumstance, then in my view it is more of a recipe for a sucker than a saint, for a coward rather than for a Christian. In the Sermon on the Mount Jesus was speaking to his disciples, to men and women who had chosen to go his way.

Those who try to make out that St Luke was a leftist radical because he recorded Jesus as saying 'blessed are the poor', whereas St Matthew had it 'blessed are the poor in spirit', simply fail to see these words in context. Jesus is not discussing what later came to be known as the working class, but people who had the basic characteristic of 'dependence' for the supply of their needs rather than any form of self-reliance. 'Poor' is not a pretty word when used in an economic or sociological context, but in the realm of the spirit it says exactly what St Matthew wrote: the people who had come aside with Jesus, the people who were his disciples and who knew their need of help spiritually, were blessed indeed.

So too for Jesus' saying about turning the other cheek. He was not giving a general instruction for human behaviour in any environment or setting, but was speaking to men and women who had decided to become his disciples, those who had 'put on the whole armour of God', those who were possessed of new powers and weapons which would ultimately prove victorious over the worst that evil could do.

There will be many churchmen and those of other religions who will want to argue that all this is otherworldly, impractical, and deserving of the gibe about 'pie-in-the-sky'. But perhaps it is not so lacking in guts and gumption as may appear at first sight. Love may truly be the only force that can finally resist and reverse the cancerous growth of hatred in our modern world, the hatred which is the deliberate product of the Marxists and which is so cynically exploited by materialists of the Right as well as of the Left.

When those two courageous women, Betty Williams and Mairead Corrigan of Belfast, were given the Nobel Prize for Peace in 1977 they bore in their hearts a full measure of understanding of the demonic and deadly power of hate.

Early in the development of the Peace Movement, they had had encounters with hate-filled men and women that threatened to scar their very souls.

Under the headline 'Hate Hurts' a Belfast newspaper described the results of their attempt to tell a women's protest meeting that they stood for an end to violence. This is how the newspaper described what happened to Mrs Williams:

> She started towards the platform. And then the first woman stepped into the aisle, kicking her and hitting her sharply above the ankle – she registered surprise before pain.
>
> The hall was full of shouting and faces coming in close to her to scream invective and hate.
>
> And for the first time she really felt that cold edge of fear telling her that maybe they weren't going to listen to her, all these women, that maybe Betty Williams who could get her message across to foreign journalists and international TV stations, who could be flown to America to say what needed to be said, was not – going – to – ever – make – it – to – the – platform.
>
> 'Whore, whore, w-h-o-r-e!' shrieked a woman, her voice rising an octave in her frenzy.
>
> 'Whore! whore!' the shout echoes around the hall, bouncing down on Betty Williams and her husband as the audience, surging with menace, push around them.
>
> It was the faces, the faces with their contortions of hate and eyes filled with loathing and anger. They headed back to their car. The spotless Cortina they had owned for less than a week, a car with only 9,000 miles on the clock.
>
> But they were never going to make it. Both Ralph and Betty knew that if they ever got inside that car they would never get out alive.
>
> Through the mob she became aware of another movement. A group of men, armed with heavy sticks, were pushing and smashing their way towards them.
>
> Then suddenly, the men were around them and she realised that they were friends, not enemies, and the little group began surging over to the church. The blows were still coming.
>
> The church door was near when Betty began to go down. Someone had got in a savage blow to her stomach and she was doubled up, being half dragged into the portal of the church. Then came a rabbit punch on the back of her bent-over neck.
>
> She felt the bile coming up into her throat and her mouth and then the flashing lights exploded briefly in her eyes and almost instantly the noise and the pain stopped as the comfortable blackness of unconsciousness engulfed her.
>
> She was out for ten minutes. When she came round she was on the floor of the vestry. Mairead, and Ciaran McKeown (another peace organiser) were with them.
>
> Two men came into the church. They said the cars were wrecked, that it was very dangerous.

> The men explained. They would tear a gap in the church railing near a door and back a taxi right up to it. Then the peace organisers would have to get into that taxi which would move away very fast. Were they game?
>
> They were game. They moved and as they did, they prayed, they got into the taxi and its engine was racing and Betty Williams was chanting the Lord's Prayer as it roared away.
>
> The car took them to the Williams home, a nice comfortable semi on a new housing estate which used to seem a million miles away from the violence and the death of Ulster.
>
> Ralph, who is on leave, tried to snatch some sleep. He is a Protestant, Betty a Catholic.
>
> He remembered the days when Betty spent all her time cooking for him and the two children. He remembered how different she looked before all this started.
>
> Now the strain was showing on her face, and grey hairs were appearing. Even though she is only 32.
>
> And he told himself sternly, that all this was necessary if their children were to have a future.

That was a long time ago. The Peace Movement has been world news since then, and the Nobel Prize a fitting symbol of its recognition, but the killing still goes on. It continues, not because of the sectarian or even the political hatreds of the past, but because dedicated and highly trained soulless killers are at work who see this as just one more place where hatred can be promoted to tear down the present civilisation. It has even been claimed that the men who do the killing sometimes cannot speak a word of English – or Irish – and that they are international operatives trained in East Germany, the Middle East or North Korea.

Whatever nationality, they are deliberately killing women and children now. Bestiality increases.

Where will it end?

Can love really exist, let alone succeed in changing the course of these rivers of hatred? Can it do more, and bring about changes to the evils of a system which has too often been based on greed, arrogance, envy and exploitation?

In London in 1977 I heard Saidie Patterson, a little stocky, grey-haired lady from Belfast, tell a story which at times moved her audience to tears, at other times to laughter, then again to horror and finally to faith. I was able to get a tape recording of her talk, and I will let her tell it in her own words. It is a document which forms part both of the social history of Britain at the beginning of the twentieth century and of the true power developing within the Christian community:

Well friends, I am glad to be here with you this afternoon to tell you something about Ireland because it is very much on the map at the moment. It is a very small but a very difficult country. I myself come from a past which denied the fulfilment of life to so many people. I come from a textile background. There are two things for which Northern Ireland especially is famous and that is shipbuilding and linen. The shipbuilding has mostly employed men folk and the textile industry mostly women. In my area we were doubly related because the shipbuilding men marry the textile women. We have been one of another. But it has been a struggle in our country. No country in Europe ever had the struggle that Ireland had for bread and for work.

I had a wonderful mother. Mother said to us each evening as we said the family prayers around her knee: 'Children, if you see something wrong in this world and you do nothing about it', pointing to each one of us, 'you are committing a crime against the whole of humanity'.

My parents were really before their time because today most of us know or should know that you can be quiet and still and that the 'still small voice' can speak to you. As a very small child I can always remember a jotter on our kitchen table and mother occasionally went and made a note on this jotter. My father was very good at making speeches, provided he had the material to make the speech. So mother provided the material and father delivered the speeches in the streets of the Shankhill Road. I used to be sent out as a child with a candle in a lamp, and father would be making these speeches and I would hold the lamp up for him to follow his notes.

Now what were those speeches about? About the right for a child to go to the university. The right for free school books. The right for free dinners, etc etc. Because they were so distressed about the background that we as children had to put up with. In my early days we were not allowed to sit in the school. We stood back to back and we just had a slate and a slate pencil. Now that is all altered today, thank God, and most of the school curriculum in the part of Ireland that I come from is today really based on things such as my parents talked about when I was a young child so many years ago.

When I was twelve my mother died. She died in childbirth and left a baby two hours old. The simple reason was that we could not afford adequate medical attention. But being a good woman my mother knew she was dying and told me – I was brought to her bedside before she passed on – and she said: 'I know that I'm going to meet the Saviour that I have taught you about for so many years. Take that baby and rear that baby for the Master.' I was twelve years of age and my schooling finished then, at twelve years of age! I was taken from school to look after the baby and to look after seven other brothers and sisters and father. When I became fourteen I went into a linen factory. And what did I find there? Poverty was the order of the day. We were just a pair of hands, or a number on a payroll. We didn't count. They built the mills and the factories wherever there was water, then they simply built the worker's houses around them. If you'd got a job in a mill or a factory and occupied a firm's house, you didn't speak out of your turn when injustices were done.

Today in my country it is the fear of the bomb, and the fear of the bullet, or that midnight knock at your door. But in my time it was that if you spoke out of your turn you were not only sacked, but you lost your home as well. Now it didn't matter whether we were Catholics or Protestant, we were all paid the same pittance. It was most difficult to organise women within the trade union movement because there was always the fear of losing your job and losing your home. Now history can only really be written after fifty years, and when the history of women in the trade union movement in the North of Ireland is written it will be seen that Ernest Bevin, one of the greatest men that England ever knew, played a very great part in it. Bevin came to my humble home to ask me if I would take on, with other people, the organising of the tax-paying workers. And we did.

Today in our country I could stand outside any mill or any factory and speak to the workers. But fifty years ago you did not do that. It would not be the first time that I have been beaten up by police and taken away in their van for standing outside mill factories and gates trying to organise the women. We eventually got the women very well organised but we had to have a very big strike. (I want to preface my remarks today by giving my conviction that sacking and striking are largely out of date. The great strikes of the past for the right for bread and the right for work were understandable. But not today because agreements are there where people can come around a table and discuss the problems on the basis of what is right, not who is right.) Over the years we were able to get ninety thousand women organised, and many of the wrongs have been put right. Incidentally it is one of the advantages of having more than a nodding acquaintance with over ninety thousand women that it has been a great help in our peace work at home.

Our present troubles started seven years ago. I want to make it perfectly clear that we in the North of Ireland asked the British Government to send the troops into my country. Our MP and our local priest came to my home because our country was on fire and we hadn't a large enough fire brigade, we hadn't enough police to cope with what was happening. So we asked the troops to be sent in. So if you hear this business about pulling the troops out it's certainly not coming from the Irish, not from ninety-five percent of them, anyhow.

Well, this trouble started, and it started quite near where I live. We have four beautiful schools there. My parents would have been very proud of those schools. But we have had the children fighting all the way to school. And this is where I want to say to mothers how important is the part that they have to play, because every mother sends – or should send – her child off to school in the morning. Yet when the children came on to the streets to go to school they were fighting and using language that is certainly not in the English dictionary. They had to put soldiers on to guide the children to school, to do what we call lollipop men's duties.

Then we had three young soldiers who were nineteen, twenty and twenty-one murdered by snipers. Quite a number of us were distressed about this. We thought that we should do something about this because the mothers brought the children to school and then the mothers fought. And believe me friends, you might see children fighting, but to see women fighting is dreadful. The women were worse than the children. So one or two of us got together and we felt we should try to mobilise the women. We put an advertisement in our morning and evening newspapers and called a meeting in one of our big halls in town asking all women who were interested to do something about bringing peace to our country to come along on a particular evening.

The meeting was called for eight o'clock. And at eight o'clock there were only six of us on the platform and we thought that the women were not going to come. But at half past eight the doors of the hall burst open and dozens and dozens of women came in.

Now, when trouble starts in Belfast, the teenagers often set fire to the buses. They seem to have any amount of tins of petrol and they throw them on the buses, set matches to them and the buses go up in flames. When that happens our City Corporation calls the rest of the buses off the road. And that was why the women were late – they had to walk to the meeting. That was a most moving evening because a few of us had said what we were there to discuss. Where do we go from here? What can we do to help?

One little Roman Catholic woman from the Falls Road (and to get the story clear I want to make this point, the Falls Road is entirely Roman Catholic. The Shankhill Road is entirely Protestant. The streets on the Falls Road and the Shankhill Road dovetail into each other. And it's the heart of the textile industry). Well, this little woman – a little Catholic from the Falls Road – got to her feet and said: 'Oh how I would like to shake hands again with a woman from the Shankhill Road, a Protestant.' Well, friends, you wanted to be in that hall just to see how that happened. People shook hands and people were crying. It was out of that beginning that our Women Together movement was born, and it is into its sixth year now. Wherever you lived, you started a group, and each group looked after the problems in that area. But, friends, it is not easy to look after problems in some of the ghettos. It is not easy because you can be watched and reported to the organisations. Especially when a mother has a home and a family she is afraid to stand up and speak out because her child could be intimidated going to school, or the husband could be kidnapped or murdered. That is literally true. But we kept on working and working.

Just before the Second World War, thousands and thousands of new houses had been built, with the result that we were integrating our Catholic and Protestant neighbours. Then when this trouble started intimidation began.

If it was mostly Protestants that lived in an area, the Catholics were intimidated and vice versa. Many and many a night I, as a Protestant, was in the Catholic areas with others and we sat and talked with the women. When people came to the homes to order folk out or to burn the houses we went out on the streets and sometimes took a floor brush and beat the youngsters – and they were youngsters, teenagers from other areas, not from the area we lived in.

That lasted for about two years, but then it became so bad that people had to get out. Protestants left, Catholics left, and unfortunately we were back to where we were many, many years ago. Catholics are all living together, or Protestants, which is not good. It is better to integrate the people. Much better. But our Women Together movement still kept going, visiting where we could and we visited every home where there had been a murder. Remember that in my country one in every thousand has been murdered, and one in every hundred maimed, and when I say maimed I mean such as losing limbs or eyes. Yet with it all there is no bitterness in those people. There is not one of those afflicted homes that we have not been in, and especially when a husband has been murdered, because the children have to be clothed and fed and the rent paid until the claims come through from the Government. Often it's a year or even longer before the claims come through. Many a time it even comes out of our slender purses and many of us are pensioners, but if you do this kind of thing the Lord always helps. Practical sympathy is a language that most people understand, and above all it's building bridges. I believe, and I've said it before and I'll say it again from any platform, the answer will come to our country, but it will not come in retaliation – it will be done person to person, and this is how we are working.

The recent Peace Movement with Betty and Mairead developed in an area where they both live. Three children were killed. This taxi was coming along and the army called on it to stop because it was wanted. Well the army called on the taxi to stop – three times – and it refused. On the fourth time the soldiers fired and the driver was wounded (he died afterwards) and the car swerved and went through some railings. Mrs McGuire was coming along with her children. Mrs McGuire is a sister of Mairead Corrigan whom you all know, and three of her children were killed. The fourth one was not, and she herself was badly injured. It is an awful thing to say, but it had to happen to really arouse women. Betty Williams came out with many other people and started to go around and knock on doors to ask for support and ask for signatures against all this violence. Then it just started to snowball, it went all through our country and beyond. In Belfast we've had some wonderful rallies for peace.

You might say 'What good do rallies do?' Well, many a time I'd start out walking under a Shankhill banner. (The banners were made with material out of Protestant homes and now I've hardly a sheet left at home.) The banners say nothing except the district where you come from. Our Catholic friends painted the banners so you see we had unity even in the banners, the

Protestants provided the material and the Catholics did the printing on the banners! As you go along people are talking as they are marching and it really does something for them because for the first time they know how thousands are thinking especially our women folk. Now, God love our men folk, we couldn't do without them and I'm speaking as an undiscovered treasure, but I am very glad to say that many, many of our men folk are now not only marching but doing baby-sitting and what-have-you in order to let the wives out, if their wives can't go out and leave a small family at home.

The paramilitary organisations – that is the extremists on both sides – are beginning to take notice. They are beginning to take notice because this is something new that has been begun and I believe, and I know in my country, women who normally were afraid to stand up are now standing up and being counted. It is amazing when you go to the meetings (I speak at many of our *Women Together* meetings) because if they're held in the Falls Road many of us from the Shankhill go, and if they're held in the Shankhill Road many of our friends come from the Falls Road.

We had one march that took place on the Shankhill Road about ten weeks ago, (and friends I have been standing at the barricades for over fifty years fighting for the right for bread, fighting for the right to work), but for this march to the Shankhill Protestant area Mairead and Betty asked me to take on the organising. Believe me we pulled out every stop on that Shankhill Road. It wasn't easy, it was a difficult job, and we took the hardliners first.

Now I don't know if you know what a 'hardliner' is. It is a person as narrow as their name indicates, it's either this for them or it's not, and it's most difficult to change their mind. Well, I called at the house of one hardliner whom I had had great trouble with in the trade union world. I went to her on this particular morning and the moment she opened the door she just stared at me and said: 'What the hell. What the hell's gates brought you here?' I said 'My feet.' So she looked at me and said, 'I hope you're not going to tell me that the Catholics are going to walk up the Shankhill Road.' I said, 'Oh yes. You know we are living in a democracy and anyone has a right to walk on the Queen's highway.' Now I think she thought I was insulting our Queen and it wasn't too pleasant what was said and then she just spat upon me. So I looked at the spot where she had spat upon me and I said to her, 'You know, that's just the spot where the Queen of England pinned a medal on me some years ago for the work that was done for women and children in our country.' And I said, 'What's more, the greatest peacemaker this world ever knew, and I refer to Jesus Christ, he was spat upon. And who am I? Good morning.' So I walked away. Not too happy, but you know the Devil gets busy on you sometimes and I felt like kicking all round. But as chairman of the Peace Group I know kicking is not the answer, although you feel like kicking. So I went to number two.

I was invited into number two's home. But when I told her what I had come about she said, 'Miss Patterson, I am not going to help get the Catholics to come up the Shankhill Road.' 'Well', I says, 'Now you're a great churchwoman. Let us get down and have a word of prayer about it.' So we got down to have a word of prayer, and believe me friends, I don't know whether the Lord smiles or not when he hears some of the prayers we utter but she was telling the Lord in no uncertain manner, 'O Lord don't ask me to help the Fenians to walk up the Shankhill Road. I'm not going to do it.' However, her own daughter saved the situation. She came into the living room with her two small children and we got up off our knees and I said to the daughter, 'What kind of a world do you want for these two children? This country of ours is dreadful – they're robbing banks, they're murdering people, there's drink, bingo and gambling all over this country. It's not the country that I want to build nor help to build.' So the daughter said, 'Well, I'll come with you, Miss Patterson.' So of course when the mother heard that she said, 'Oh, I'll come too.'

So coming onto the road, going home again, I met number one coming down the road. She saw me fine but she didn't want to see me. So as one who usually carries an umbrella with me – I'm not too steady at times on my feet, and an umbrella comes in useful in more ways than one – I touched her on the arm and I said, 'You will be glad to know that Tilly is coming to help me.' Well, she nearly collapsed. And it wasn't said in reverence, but she just said, 'Jesus Christ, if Tilly is coming to help you, I'm coming too.'

This was how we started. The next day we had the press and the television of the world at our park. And I brought those hardliners along. And Mairead and Betty were there and I said to them, 'Look, put your arms round these two lassies and give them a kiss, and it will maybe melt their hearts.' And the girls did. And the press of the world caught this. It was terrific.

Well the march came off. I said to Betty: 'I want you to do something and I want everybody in this audience to listen to this, because it is a very important thing. There's one little word in the English dictionary and it's a word that I don't find it always easy to say. But oh! when you say it it works wonders and miracles. I said to Betty and to Mairead: 'As well as having the place banners, could you get two children to carry a small banner with that magic little word on it?' And that magic little word was 'sorry'. I added, 'When you come to all those buildings on the Shankhill Road', and I had the numbers: seventeen murdered in this building, six in another, children murdered here when bombs blew the building up, 'when you come to these buildings will you dip the banner and bow your head.' And the girls did that. And friends, you wanted to be on that Shankhill Road just to see forty thousand people marching to that park, another thirty thousand lining the streets. The church choirs came out and they were singing, the church bells rang on every church – and we've no shortage of churches in the North of Ireland. It's not a question of too many Roman Catholics or too many Protestants, it's too few Christians. That's our problem. Too few Christians.

But on that road that day I never saw anything like it. Right at the park gates there's a big church and I went to the rector and asked him for the loan of his fine drawing rooms to throw the drawing rooms open and we would have a cup of tea for everybody who wanted it. And all the hardliners baked – you talk about feeding the five thousand, it wouldn't have been in it!

And something new was born that day. When I came back to my own home afterwards I got down and I thanked the good Lord for such a day. And I wouldn't have minded if I had been called home that night because what I saw on the Shankhill Road was the crowning experience of my life.

The seed has been sown and we're going to go from strength to strength. I won't say the trouble is over because peace has to be made every day. You don't make it today and it's there for ever after. It's got to be made every day. And the wounded have to be looked after, the widows have to be looked after. And we are opening homes. We have a house, 'the house on a hill', and every woman that has been left a widow now goes to this home. And it's wonderful to see there's no bitterness there. You may say, well, they've every right to be bitter. That's true. But bitterness doesn't bring the answer. Hate doesn't bring the answer. Because hate has a million children. What we are working for now at home is our children, because they were six or seven years of age when our troubles started and now they're teenagers. Don't forget they are tomorrow's Mums and Dads and it's these children that we are working for. We have so many of the leaders of the violence in jail that now the children are used. And God forgive any mother, or father either, that knows that their children are involved in this and do nothing about it. We have tramped the streets of our city for years. Luckily I have something that many people haven't because of organising them in the textile works.

Well it didn't matter who they were I could go into their homes. And if I didn't believe that there was hope for my country, at my age I would be sitting with my door closed catching up on my reading. But I always remember what mother told us, 'If you see something wrong in this world and you do nothing about it, you are committing a crime against the whole of humanity.'

Miss Patterson, who was the first woman to be elected Chairman of the Northern Ireland Labour Party, was awarded the 1977 World Methodist Peace Award – and a few hours later heard that her nephew's son had been murdered by the IRA.

The *Yorkshire Post* quotes her as saying:

I will continue to fight the good fight. It was a terrible blow to hear of a relative's death so soon after being told about winning a peace prize.

What keeps me going is the fact that more and more of our women, both Roman Catholic and Protestant, are telling the men that it is better to sit round a table and talk than stand around a graveyard and cry. Those tears are not coloured in orange and green. They are tears of sorrow.

I never believed in judging a man by the church he attends on Sunday or

> the colour of his skin, but by his character. Hope is the greatest word in the English language. I have that hope because many years ago Ireland gave Christianity to Europe and I believe in my heart we will come again to practise Christianity, not only as an example to Europe but to the rest of the world because, believe me, the world needs it.
>
> Basically, the Irish people are kindly people and I believe they will prove it again. It is not being a Roman Catholic or a Protestant which will create peace. It is being a Christian. Peace is not going to be achieved either by the politicians or the army. It is going to be done by personal contact. That is what I believe in.

The citation for her award says that she 'has sat with the men of violence and dissuaded them from bombing and shooting'.

The worrying factor which emerges when one ponders such a stand as this is the fury of retaliation which so often results. There are those whose anger is roused more by the hand of friendship than by the mailed fist. Soon after I spoke with Miss Patterson she was set upon by a group of children, many of them not yet in their teens, and was knocked to the ground and was being kicked and battered when a group of Catholic women came to her rescue. She believes the children were paid to act in this way.

The response to the Nobel Peace Prize has been the extension of slaughter to include women and even tiny children. It is terribly logical, because this is a total war being fought – a war of basic values and philosophies. The disciples of violence whose hate-blinded dupes are found among nominal Catholics and Protestants alike, know full well that the things which have to be ruthlessly expunged are all evidences of love, forgiveness, mercy and goodwill.

Mikhael Borodin, in conversation with Madam Chiang Kai Shek, once put it plainly:

> The real motive of our atheism resides on a loftier plane. It is because of a little word, forgiveness. The Christian doctrine of forgiveness, so little practised, yet so often preached and seemingly so innocuous, is the single greatest enemy to the dissemination of Communism. We too are capable of love for those who follow our tenets and discipline. But forgiveness is not love, it embraces love, hope, faith, charity, and all other human foibles of penitence; therefore with forgiveness forever troubling the being of a person it could not make a truly new and unblemished Communist man. Forgiveness throughout the ages has proven to be the ready-made excuse for sloth, sloppy wilfulness and compromise which incidentally also exist in the Confucian teachings of Chung-she. It counters and negates all that we wish to instill in the people. The debilitating germ must be quickly and terminally purged – decimated – so that the moulding of the paradigmatic man can go forward apace without let or hindrance.[1]

If this is the motivation of the destroyers – then what is the response of the man or woman of God? Facing this question for myself there are several things which emerge.

First there is the fact that hatred destroys the soul. Nothing must be given such stature in my life that it can make me hate. 'What does it profit a man if he gains the whole world but loses his own soul?'

Second, I believe utterly that God, who is almighty, who cares about his world, and who will be finally victorious, is a God of love and not of hate. He holds the ultimate power, and will never forsake me – 'even though it be a cross that raiseth me'.

Third, I know that, whether I win or lose by this world's judgements and standards, there is really only one way for me to live, one way which satisfies my heart, mind and spirit, and that is the way I see supremely set forth in the life of Jesus of Nazareth. Then too there are the 'coincidences', the amazing ways in which God comes to his own – in veritable hell if necessary.

Admiral Denton of the USN spent seven years in the hell of a communist prison in North Vietnam – much of the time being tortured and in solitary confinement. At the time he had the rank of commander.

In his tiny cell there was only one book, a book of communist propaganda. By code signals and tapping he could exchange a few words with fellow prisoners. A tiny window, high in the room, did not permit him to see out but it gave a little air and at times a dim light, and he could hear some of the prison activities through it. By these means he set about making entries in the middle of the book to keep a record of new arrivals in the prison. In the book too he kept a precious symbol of his faith: a cross, skilfully woven from bamboo broom strips, a gift made and smuggled to him at great risk by a fellow prisoner.

One day his record of the prisoners was discovered. There was fury as he was hauled from his cell and civilian workmen were brought to brick up almost the whole of his tiny window. He says that he didn't much mind the list being discovered for it would make the communists realise that there were those who knew the names and numbers of prisoners. He was utterly devastated however when the propaganda book was searched and his little cross was discovered. With fierce anger the North Vietnamese officer flung it on the ground and pounded it to nothing with his boot. Denton said that in that moment it seemed his last tangible link with hope and faith were gone, and he felt indescribably bereft. Then he was pushed back into the cell, and the propaganda book replaced.

A little later he thumbed through its pages and there, hidden in it, was another exquisitely woven little bamboo cross! To this day he has no idea how it came to be there, but he thinks it was placed there by one of the workmen with the courageous help of his mates. Whatever its human source, it was God reaching into his cell, and his strength was renewed like the eagles.[2]

As I write these words I feel thrilled with a telephone call from my daughter, who is studying in Edinburgh. She rang three nights ago with a story from Rhodesia. A mutual friend had received a letter from Salisbury from a white girl whose parents own a farm in a dangerous area of the country. The girl is a strong Christian, giving her whole life to bridging the barriers between black and white and bringing change on a moral and spiritual basis to her country. She had gone home for the weekend only to find that her parents had left to go to another area for the night. She felt a little afraid, but went about her chores until it got dark. Just as darkness fell she found to her horror that she had left the washing outside on the line. It was dangerous to leave it all night as it would let any wandering guerillas think the farm was deserted, but it was even more dangerous to go out into the darkness. What should she do? She prayed for help and direction and God gave her a very clear thought: 'Go out and get the washing in as quickly as possible and keep praying all the time.'

She did this and she got back inside without incident. The night passed peacefully, but next morning a security patrol arrived and anxiously asked if she was safe. Was she disturbed during the night? When she said she had not been they appeared amazed. 'Then who was with you last night?' they asked. She replied that she had been quite alone. The officer then told her that they had captured some guerillas who told him that they had been about to attack her home after dark the previous night and were watching from nearby bushland. Then they had seen her come out to take in the washing and with her was an armed man and the whole scene was brilliantly lit. She had been conversing with him all the while!

Not for a moment do I believe that God always works by intervening continually and miraculously like this in human affairs but there are so many instances of his refusal to let evil expunge goodness, so many 'co-incidences' that have to be explained, that for me anyway they are more than enough to give a valuable shot in the arm to my faith, to give me one of those glimpses of a lighthouse during foul weather at sea such as enable the sailor to feel secure in his course.

The vital issue for the man or woman seeking the larger life of the spirit is not whether pain and suffering are to be avoided but whether the whole is encompassed within the love and purpose of God. Obviously the gift of freedom of choice must mean freedom for evil to attack and inflict grievous pain on others. Any religion which offered immunity from such suffering as an incentive for the spiritual pilgrimage would be a contradiction in terms – it would be offering a material bait for an allegedly spiritual endeavour. The whole point of the Christian answer to the attacks of evil and violence, to pain and suffering is not that the individual is offered a way of escape by his faith, but two things:

First, as he faces these trials for the sake of his faith he will be given new strength and spiritual discernment, new experiences of the presence and love of God such as more than compensate for his suffering, indeed, which it may not be possible for him to discover in any other way.

Secondly, he will find he is not alone, that there is someone with him, someone who has been through it all, and who has proved beyond any doubt or query that when evil and pain have done their very utmost, even to death by torture, there too is the victory for the man or woman of faith who refuses to hate or blame. Love never dies.

This may well be seen as an argument for pacifism, the refusal ever to bear arms or to use force. Having been both a minister of religion and a Minister of State I have obviously had to give this much thought. I find pacifism being supported by stronger and stronger arguments as the years go by and we see war and the possession of weapons of terror developing into unthinkable threats. At times I wonder whether if a century or so ago the 'Christian' nations had renounced war as a way of meeting aggression, there might not have emerged a 'victory through defeat' which would have enabled those with a true faith and love of others to live and develop their faith inside a captive situation.

Today we see an Idi Amin or a Baader Meinhof gang actually enjoying the torture and killing of the defenceless and innocent. There is little ideology in their motivation, often it is psychopathic sadism. 'I enjoyed killing people. I liked it best when their hands were tied behind their backs. I liked to watch them twist and turn and roll about in agony. Men and babies were easy. Women I didn't like so much unless they were soldiers' women', gloated a twenty-one year old member of the Khmer Rouge then ruling Cambodia, in an interview with a leading Australian journalist in 1977.[3]

He knew nothing of Marx or Lenin but only that 'Angka was always right' – (Angka being the supreme organisation which ruled every facet of their lives). He may know nothing of ideology but he is the deliberate and perhaps inevitable product of an ideology which inverts moral values, destroys the concept of the value of the individual and denies any spiritual reality. That is the true source of the germs infecting mankind today and rightly or wrongly, we have arrived at this primal confrontation.

What should we do?

To me it is unthinkable that such bestiality, or the force which produces it, should go unchallenged. Jesus said, 'They who take the sword will perish by the sword.' It is an interesting statement. It has tremendous implications. What Jesus said was that it was a rule or law of human behaviour, a law which had the authority of Almighty God behind it, that those who turned to violence to achieve their purposes would be destroyed by violence. Pacifists read this as an injunction against taking up the sword and, if it is in the category of taking the sword to enforce or achieve one's own purposes, then it does clearly mean that such people will be destroyed. But the second half of Jesus' pronouncement states equally clearly that Almighty God has ordained it that another will, in the face of such a use of force, use the sword to destroy the aggressor. There could be no 'perishing by the sword' without someone else to wield the sword of punishment or justice. The wielding of the sword in such a case is clearly stated to be the intention and judgement of God. So there is a tension.

As a disciple of Christ, one who wants to do the will of God, I am taught personally to turn the other cheek, to forgive, to love my enemies. As a citizen of this world in which evil is being done, I also have a role to play. I cannot take myself off to the desert and seek a cave to escape from the fury of history. This is my Father's world. I am not permitted to hand it over to his enemies. Jesus drove out the defilers of the Temple and cleansed it of those who wanted to wrest it from its divine purpose.

Today we have a mortal confrontation with evil, and my own decision is quite clear. On the one hand I am a man, a white man, a Christian, British of Australian citizenship, and I am inescapably part of all that white British Australian 'Christians' have been and have done and are today. I cannot escape that fact, nor do I wish to do so. For better or worse I have my roots in this soil. Where my people have been wrong I share that guilt. Where we have done well I enjoy that knowledge. It is me and mine who have been entrusted with certain values, standards, concepts, facts and heritage of faith for which we are responsible. I believe I must do everything possible to safeguard that heritage and pass it on to my children; and that may even mean using force in its defence. But what is 'possible' has strict limitations.

There are, at the same time, values, standards, concepts and facts which supersede and have a prior claim to all others. Some of these I have already tried to elucidate. They are essential for the wellbeing of my eternal soul, and for the spiritual weal of all who, with me, have embarked on the supreme pilgrimage of man towards God. I cannot hate, for example. There may well come the time when my primary loyalties mean that I cannot proceed with some course of action which seems essential for victory in the material sense and if so, then the end will never justify the means. 'What will it profit a man if he gain the whole world and lose his own soul?'

I do not know the way ahead. More than human wisdom is needful in this battle. I can only say that the older I get the more certain I feel about the profound wisdom of St Paul as he faced these very issues and wrote to the Christians at Ephesus: 'We are not fighting against human beings, but against spiritual forces of evil in the highest places, against the rulers, authorities, and cosmic powers of this dark age. So take up God's armour now! Then when the evil day comes, you will be able to resist the enemy's attacks and after fighting to the end you will still hold your guard.' St Paul went on to outline God's weapons and armour as being primarily moral. Truth, righteousness – these qualities of life were primary and so too were faith, salvation and 'the word of God as the sword that the Spirit gives you.'

The grave danger confronting men of God from all faiths is that they use their very limited capacity to try to evaluate and assess the spiritual forces available to effect a change in the world of today and find them apparently overshadowed by materialist methods. Then, in desperation, they turn to expediency in achieving their ends or safeguarding what they hold to be essential, and all too often these adopted means threaten and even destroy their principal objectives.

There are two processes unfolding in today's world. The first we may think of in 'horizontal' terms. It is development of human history and thus of the individual's part within it. In this dimension a global struggle is taking place wherein forces of many kinds battle for supremacy. For example, tyranny, which seems so powerful and formidable at times, is always under attack from without and within as it has been all through history by those factors in human nature which resent injustice, deprivation of freedom, lies and propaganda and all its other dehumanising attributes. Exploitation and injustice face increasing challenge within the political, national and international processes of the day whether by race to race or class to class. These processes are the business of all mankind and they are shaped and fashioned by our natures and ideas, our beliefs and our values. It is on this horizontal level that the sword of retribution meets and destroys the sword of aggression and oppression, or at least it always has done in the long run and there is no reason to doubt that it will still do so.

On the other hand there is a supreme strategy which has its major axis vertically. It relates to the primary purpose and commitment of those who have accepted the proposition that this is God's world, that he is their Father, that he cares for all his children and has a plan and purpose for it and them. Such people are those who may be likened to germ carriers by a Borodin, for Jesus himself saw his disciples as being like yeast, which only needs a little to germinate and grow to proportions sufficient to leaven the whole mass. 'Yours is the task of being the salt of the earth, or the light that is set like a candle in a dark room', he told them.

Each individual has to face the fact of a potential tension within himself between these two forces, horizontal and vertical.

As a student in Edinburgh I used, on occasion, to visit the old manse at Inveresk. Around it ran a high stone wall. Above the small gateway at the rear a sandstone block bore the inscription (in Hebrew!) 'I am a stranger in the earth'. I wondered then at this rather strange choice for a greeting above a manse gate, and frankly tended to think it rather morbid. However, I now see more and more clearly that this material world is not man's true home, that his supreme purpose is not simply to make it a place where perfect political, economic, social and other regimes are built up. Earth is an arena within which human beings are enabled to grow in stature, morally and spiritually and in personal relationships with each other and with God as their Father. The material world is only the framework, the scenario for the greatest experiment of creation. People of God care deeply about war, tyranny, hunger, exploitation and the other social, economic, political and environmental evils not because they are the products of some defective system or because they are contrary to certain beliefs or ideologies, but because they afflict, dehumanise and debase the lives of people, stunting them physically, mentally and spiritually. No person who holds such values for mankind can feel 'at home' in the materialistic world of today. He knows he is basically a stranger in the earth: a foreigner in a land which he seeks to see conquered and ruled by the King in whose kingdom he is a citizen, where he is truly at home.

'What is *my* role in all this?' This is the question each one must ask in open honesty as he stands alone with God in moments of solitariness. Some may discover that he directs them to involvement in politics, in economics, in defence activities, in commerce and so forth. Others will find that they have been called, as were the disciples of Jesus, to a full-time and total devotion to wider moral and spiritual activities. But for everyone who accepts the call and commission of God, the same imperious objectives, the same hierarchy of standards and values applies. Wherever we are in this battle there are standards which can never be lowered, values which are always supreme. Above all there is a new society to which we now belong, the fighting fellowship of the Spirit of God, the *koinonia* of the committed.

There is yet another sense in which Jesus' saying about 'taking and perishing by the sword' must be seen. 'Whatsoever a man sows that shall he also reap', he said on another occasion. As one sees the way in which the moral and spiritual fibre of twentieth century society has been eroded, not only in Christian but in other lands as well, it seems that the old, old story of the rise and fall of civilisations continues apace. It would be totally unrealistic and indeed immoral to expect that Almighty God would intervene in the situation simply to save us from the just deserts of our behaviour. For example from beginning to end the story of ancient Israel tells of this process of nemesis at work. Judging by the evidence presented by the statistics and other ways by which we can attempt to assess modern behaviour, mankind faces the stark alternative of 'change or be damned'. Another dark age lies directly ahead, unless a great new cleansing force sweeps into the situation. Unless the power of God is released on a global scale.

While Jesus asserted that his kingdom was not *of* this world; nevertheless he prayed, and taught his followers to pray, 'Thy kingdom come on earth as it is in heaven'. He sent them out to make disciples of all races of mankind, proclaiming the good news that God was alive and active in his world, still all-powerful even if temporarily suffering. He asserted that it was not his will that a single human being should suffer hunger, want or destruction. He gave a global charter with a global responsibility. The object was not a system, a structure, a politico-economic establishment, not a 'kingdom' in the human sense but the reign of God. An age when God would have the supreme allegiance and become the directing force in any and every human situation. Jesus asserted that any structure built on the moral and spiritual truths which he came to reveal would be like a house with granite foundations, but the most ingenious of human structures built on rejection or disregard for those standards and values would be like a foundationless house built on sand, destined to destruction when stresses arose.

Jesus made no attempt to hide the fact that he was calling men and women to do battle. 'I came not to bring peace but a sword', he declared when he saw the claims of God making costly and difficult demands on his disciples. 'In the world you will have suffering', he promised, adding 'but don't ever lose heart for I have already conquered the world.'

CHAPTER 13

Notoriously the religious orders are nowadays short of vocations, nor has permitting lipstick and the wearing of mini-skirts served to reverse the trend. On the other hand, the Missionaries of Charity are multiplying at a fantastic rate: their Calcutta house is bursting at the seams and each year three or four new enterprises are started, in India and elsewhere. As the whole history of Christianity shows, when everything is asked for, everything – and more – is accorded: when little, then nothing. Curious when this is so obvious that today the contrary proposition should seem to be more acceptable.

Malcolm Muggeridge, *Catholic Herald*, 16th May, 1969

CHAPTER THIRTEEN

Finding a Person

It was the late Archbishop William Temple who said, 'When I pray coincidences happen – when I don't, they don't!'

Thus far we have used the term 'God' to designate the source of direction, of moral instruction, of the 'inner voice' to which any and every man can turn. This mortal life is primarily a time of opportunity for us to establish contact with the divine word which is always ready and eager to speak to each one of us, from the worst to the best man on earth.

I was staying for a few nights in a Benedictine Abbey at Clairvaux in mid-1977 and had risen with the early morning bell to have my own time of quiet devotion in the little room allotted to me. Idly, I opened the desk drawer at one point and found a number of pamphlets designed to help the occupant in his meditations. My French is minimal, but I could read enough of one leaflet to encourage me to study it further. This is what it said, in part:

> God is not silence . . . it is because he is Word that men keep silent. Absolute silence is only justified among men because God speaks. Because all words emerge out of silence they must have silence for their reception. The fuller and richer the words to be received the more profound must the silence be . . .
>
> We keep silence in order to listen to God. He seeks our total receptivity, our ears kept alert for his speech . . .

This monk described the way in which the 'desert' of St Benedict is available for all men everywhere – at every point of their need, even amidst the clamour of everyday life. It is God's eternal nature and purpose to be available wherever anyone is in need. To everyone in search of him comes his command: 'Be still and know that I am God!'

Our cry for help, for direction, for strength or for someone to care is an instinctive human cry when we feel lost, alone or unable to cope. When Britain stood alone against Nazi Germany after the fall of France in 1940 King George VI expressed this cry on behalf of his people when he broadcast to the nation quoting the poem by Louise Haskins:

> I said to the man who stood at the gate of the year
> 'Give me a light that I may tread safely into the unknown'
> And he replied 'Go out into the darkness and put your hand into the hand of God.
> That shall be to you better than light and safer than a known way.

But God as Word, inner voice, source of direction or power – none of these expressions can long prove sufficient to describe the experiences which follow obedience of the one we come to know as the source of the coincidences. The Buddhist monk said that, when he listened to his inner voice, 'There was some*one* there', not some*thing*. The Moslem politician discerned that it was God working in certain people's lives through Jesus of Nazareth which had made so much difference to him and his family.

St John, the disciple who was perhaps closest of all to Jesus, tried to sum it up when, as a very old man, he wrote of his own experience of life in the spirit. He described how the 'Word' of God – God as initiator, communicator and source of all that exists in the created world – became a human being and lived among other human beings so they could experience not only the truth, the moral instruction and the eternal source of direction, but a gracious and ever-deepening personal friendship.

Jesus formed a relationship with his followers which was deeper than anything yet known or experienced by them. When found and shared with other friends of Jesus in the new *koinonia* or family fellowship of believers. The word *agape* was raised to a new level to describe this divine quality of love.

The depth and power of this love relationship has bewildered and exasperated those outside the spiritual fellowship as they have tried to understand its source and nature. As the first inner circle of disciples were all males, some people have subjectively seen homosexual reasons as a source for Jesus' and his friends' fellowship. Others, like the pathetic 'Children of God' have, raised a furore by proclaiming 'sex for Jesus': encouraging recruitment by offering a sexual incentive when they know nothing of the source and conditions for the experience of the quality of such love as is called *agape*.

Jesus, nevertheless, recognised our difficulty in progressing beyond the early experience of God as a directing power. 'If you do not love your neighbour, whom you have seen, how can you love God, whom you have not seen', John later reasoned. When Roger Hicks said to me, his face alight, 'Jesus is my best friend', I know I envied him that relationship.

How do we find it?

The first step is surely to find, as did the Buddhist monk, that there is a person there. To do that we must first of all establish communication. One cannot form a personal relationship with a book of rules, a television set or a radio. It is only when there is a person-to-person response, when each person begins to share common experiences, reacting and responding to each other, that the possibilities for friendship emerge.

So it is with God.

My own reaction when I heard the news from my estate agent that he had sold my house for me at precisely the figure to cover my asking price plus the contribution I believed God had directed me to make to others' needs, was a delighted chuckle, not just in a remarkable response to prayer and obedience, but as I said at once, 'God has a sense of humour'. I meant it, he has. He began to come alive for me in a new dimension in that 'coincidence'. I felt a new confidence in establishing dialogue with him.

In her exciting account of the beginnings of the work in Switzerland where she and Dr Francis Schaeffer established a centre for study of the Bible where the students live together in a family atmosphere, Edith Shaeffer tells of their early struggles to get permission to remain and teach in Switzerland. They were at first actually ordered to leave the country because they were engaged in unorthodox religious activity. They finally found one of the cantons which would permit them to stay temporarily if they had a place of residence within its bounds. Final approval for permanent residence in Switzerland would be a difficult and complicated matter for the Federal Government and its many relevant committees.

The first hurdle confronting the Schaeffers was to find a house they could rent at a price they could afford. At the last moment an amazing set of coincidences brought to light a suitable chalet, but it was not for letting, it was only available for sale. Mrs Schaeffer continues the story:

> As I asked for God's guidance concerning the chalet which had seemed such an exciting answer to prayer that afternoon and now seemed so impossible, my own logical sequence of thought brought me to begin a sentence in which I expected to ask that the owner change his mind and let it. It was after a length of time during which I had been inwardly struggling for reality in my sincerity of wanting God's will, when I came to this specific request concerning the chalet. It was then that suddenly I became flooded with a surge of assurance that God can do anything, nothing is impossible to Him. My sentence changed in the middle, and I ended my prayer with a definite plea, which even startled me as I asked it, 'Oh, please show us Thy will about this house tomorrow, and if we are to *buy* it, send us a sign that will be clear enough to convince Fran as well as me, send us one thousand dollars before ten o'clock tomorrow morning.'
>
> The following morning as we went through new layers of fresh snow to the train, the postman – his packages and mail-bag on a sled – handed us three letters. We opened these on the train, as the morning sun suddenly slipped over the rim of the mountains and poured light and warmth over the light wooden seats. One was from Paris, the next from Belgium . . . and the third was from a man and his wife in the United States. Mr and Mrs Salisbury had been following our work with interest and prayer for quite some time, ever since they had been spiritually helped through Fran's messages in a conference

they had attended. However, they had never given financial help to our work in any way, nor were they wealthy. They knew that we had been told to leave Switzerland, and had been following the story up to that point. It was Mrs Salisbury who wrote the letter:

'I have a story to tell you that will interest you,' she began. 'Three months ago Art came home from work with an unexpected amount of money. The company had decided to pay the insurance premiums for all their employees, and this was made retroactive for those who had worked there a certain number of years. Art's amount was a great surprise to us. We decided at first to buy a new car, then came to the conclusion that we didn't need a new car. Our next thought was to invest in buying a little house, which we would rent. We went to look at houses, and as we looked over a very likely small house I suddenly saw signs of termites in the beams. "Look, Art," I said, "Doesn't that remind you of the verse in Matthew which says, Lay not up for yourselves treasures upon earth, where moth and rust doth corrupt, and where thieves break through and steal: but lay up for yourselves treasures in heaven, where neither moth nor rust doth corrupt, and where thieves do not break through nor steal." I then asked, "Art, would you be willing to take this money and invest it literally in heaven? . . . rather than investing it in another house on earth for added income? Would you be willing to give it to the Lord's work somewhere?" He replied, "Yes, Helen, I would."

'Well . . . that was three months ago, and all during these three months we have been asking God to show us what He would have us do with this money. Two or three times we almost gave it to some cause, and each time we felt stopped from doing it. Now tonight we have come to a definite decision, and both of us feel certain that we are meant to send you this money . . . to buy a house somewhere that will always be open to young people.'

The amount of money was exactly one thousand dollars!

You can imagine that my tongue was suddenly loosed, and I poured forth the story of both my prayers, and the fact that the house was for sale. As the train arrived at Ollon, and we stepped on to the yellow bus . . . both of us were convinced that God was leading us to buy Chalet les Mélèzes.

Later we discovered that Helen had been ready for bed when she finished writing that letter, and suggested to Art that he mail it on the way to work the next morning. However, he felt such a strong urge to mail it that night, that as she got up from her knees where she was praying by her bedside, Art said, 'We must mail it now,' and getting out the car, they drove through a blinding rain storm to the main post office to mail the letter right then. The perfection of the timing of its arrival, the *timing* of both my certainty at the moment I prayed, and his certainty of the need of mailing the letter were amazing. Then her statement that it was for buying a house, 'That would always be open to young people' was almost a prophecy of our future work. Neither she, nor we could have known at the time what an accurate prophecy it was.

Chance? Coincidence? Luck? To us it was a tremendous instance of answered prayer, a wonderful demonstration of the existence of a Personal God who deals with His children as individual, meaningful personalities, and in an individual way.[1]

Possession of a house, however, might only prove a further hurdle for them if permission to reside permanently was refused. Then began a series of events which defy any recourse to so easy an explanation as mere chance or coincidence:

That week a telephone call from Lausanne brought us the news that a *décision favourable* had been taken by the Committee on Religion and Education, so one more step had been given. Now the rest of the authorities would have to make their decision and then the whole dossier would go to Berne for the final word from the Federal Government. The news gave a temporary feeling of relief, but we knew there were many possibilities still of a negative conclusion. It was at least a mild case of living under a hanging axe.

We could not make any changes in the chalet, nor have a phone put in, until the permit were a more certain thing. The lack of a telephone meant that I had continually to be going next door with twenty or sixty centimes in my hand, to use the neighbours' phone. I discovered that these two maiden ladies had a little *pension*, and one of them also did embroidery which was photographed for a magazine. We exchanged a few sentences each time I went, and Debby frequently sought their help for difficulties she had in her school homework, (as Priscilla was not there, and she was our only 'authority' in French at that time).

One afternoon the two Mademoiselles asked me whether we would be staying long, and why we had come to Huémoz. I felt it was only fair to take the time to tell them the whole story.

As I was telling it they shook their heads, and looked at each other with shocked glances. 'Mais . . . Mais . . . we'll have to tell our brother about this.'

'Oui, oui . . . we certainly will, I'll telephone him tonight.' 'This surely can't be allowed, you shall surely *stay*.'

I thanked them warmly and went home a bit puzzled, and not too impressed, thinking, 'Dear ladies, wanting to do their best to help, and probably their brother is the one person who always "fixes" things in their lives.' It gave me a warm feeling that one gets when someone is being really thoughtful – but that was all.

When Alice the post-girl brought the mail the next morning, I asked her, 'By the way, who is the brother of these two ladies who live in Beau Site?'

'Why, don't you *know?*' she asked by way of response. 'He's Monsieur Chaudet, the head of our national defence. He is one of the Council of Seven!'

I was duly impressed and drew in my breath with an exclamation of surprise 'Really? Well then he *could* do something.'

'He certainly *could*, he is one of the alternating presidents of Switzerland.' . .

At that time Monsieur Chaudet was President! The sisters calmly told m that they would telephone the President to tell him what had taken place!

Switzerland has twenty-two *cantons*, so from only seven of them is there man on this Council of Seven. Each *canton* has many cities and villages. Th villages of Huémoz had at that time seventy houses. In all the land, what 'coincidence' that we should have landed in a house next door to the sister of one of the men on the Council of Seven!

Coincidence? Chance? Luck? It spoke to us of the One who could tur back the Red Sea, of the One who could shut lions' mouths.

A slightly bent little old man, with white hair and twinkly blue eyes, passe on the back road each day, as I was hanging up the wash. With a shovel an rake he went to his vegetable garden, a plot of land some distance from h chalet. We spoke to each other, and sometimes he stopped to talk a litt longer. One day I thought it would be only fair to go to his home to tell hi the story of what had brought us to that place, as Alice had told me he was retired pastor, and a respected man in the village. He had not only been pastor for many years, but this nature-loving, gentle man had also become fully accredited Swiss mountain guide, having passed the difficult tests his youth so as to be qualified to take young people on climbs without hirin an expensive guide.

It so happened that this pastor had trained a man from Champéry as h porter, and he had grown to love and trust this man. When we told our sto to him, his reaction was to call his old porter, now a leading guide himse and ask his opinion of the case. That Champéry guide turned out to be fine friend, Mr Avanthey, who gave a very favourable report concerning and said in no uncertain terms that we had many friends in Champéry w were quite upset about our being put out!

The pastor turned to us in his deliberate way, a slow smile coming fi to his lips and then his eyes, and said, 'I will write to my nephew about th I shall tell him the story, so that he may look into it.'

And who was his nephew? He was the Chief of the department of t *Bureau des Etrangers* in Berne. He was the one who would do the final signi of anything to be signed concerning our permit. We found out later, throu the pastor, that this man had been away when the edict against us had co through his office, and the assistant had signed it. This man had power sign papers when his superior was not there. But a thing of such importar and so contrary to normal procedure would not usually be signed with the Chief knowing about it.

This pastor was our neighbour . . . two doors away on the other side Les Mélèzes! Who could choose such a chalet, situated between relatives

> two such people? *Coincidence? Chance? Luck?* Again let me tell you we believed it to be a miracle of answered prayer, by a Personal God.[2]

The accent placed on the word *personal* is no accident.

As these miracles (for that is the word which more nearly meets my own need for a better and more rational word than 'coincidences') unfold, it is impossible to remain aloof from the proposition that, by communication with God, both by speaking to him and by listening to him, it is possible to establish an intensely personal relationship. His care for details, his refusal to lower standards, his power, his lavish provision, his concern for us as people gradually build up to an amalgam of trust, admiration, affection and expectation which are all absorbed into the rapidly expanding word 'love'.

CHAPTER 14

In Jesus, and in Jesus alone, there is perfectly revealed to men all that God always was and always will be, and all that God feels towards and desires for men.

William Barclay, *The Gospel of John*, vol 1

CHAPTER FOURTEEN

Jesus and God

Towards the end of 1976 when we as a family were about to move from Australia to Scotland, my wife had the conviction that she should visit her doctor for a checkup. To her dismay she heard his verdict that an operation was needed, a radical one to remove certain tumours, probably non-malignant. He would have preferred to perform a large operation, but as time was against this he arranged for and carried out a lesser procedure.

By the time we arrived in India, Ruth was having a considerable amount of pain once more and by great good fortune we were able to consult with a highly experienced Australian doctor, a longstanding friend who had senior qualifications in surgery. He made a most painstaking examination, then called me in to hear his verdict. He confirmed the earlier diagnosis and, taking a piece of paper, he drew a diagram to illustrate the position of the growths causing the pain. He advised that we arrange for a specialist surgeon to carry out an operation as soon as possible after our arrival in Britain. It was then mid-December.

We spent Christmas in Switzerland. I was alone one day pondering the future, especially the prospect of arriving in a new country, to an empty house, trying to establish a home – and over it all the spectre of Ruth's need for major surgery, possibly in a remote city. I was quite depressed. Then came a sudden and convincing thought. It wasn't an audible 'voice' but a deep conviction surfacing in my mind. It was, quite simply, 'Why should we have this dark cloud over our arrival on the next stage of a journey directed by God?' (for it was the definite and shared decision that it was God's will that our family move to Dumfriesshire). The thought came, 'This complication is not God's will. Ask him to heal Ruth now.' It was so imperative that I did just that. Then and there, on my knees, and I never told a soul. A weight seemed to lift from my mind and the gloom was gone.

Two weeks later we were in Cheshire and I found that one of Britain's leading specialists in Ruth's kind of problem was in practice in a large city not far away and that, *by a coincidence*!, he was the father of our host. Ruth and I decided to consult him as to the next steps and discuss surgery. We drove to his home and I talked with his wife for what seemed an interminable time as he examined Ruth in a nearby room. Then they both came in, Ruth smiling and the surgeon a little puzzled, and he said 'She's a perfectly healthy woman. I can find no sign of any abnormality or growth.' He strongly advised against any surgical measures. Ruth wondered at the way I didn't register any surprise, until I told them of my earlier experience and my prayer.

More than a year later I can report that there has been no sign of any recurrence of the trouble.

Coincidence? Miracle? Call it what you will, but there is no doubt in my mind that we have a Father who not only cares but who is in full command.

It would be very wrong however, to suggest that prayer is a means of avoiding or obviating the suffering and pain in life. I do not find it possible to explain why, for example, my wife was not intended to undergo that operation while thousands of other people suffer.

When you have watched someone you love very deeply suffer, perhaps die an agonising death; when you have seen a little family blighted with disaster; or have seen a brave and battling nation brought to its knees with ruthless power and bloodshed; you must have asked, as I have asked, WHY? In God's name, why?

Having brought the name of God into the matter, the next question then naturally follows. If there *is* a God, and if he is really all-powerful, and if he is all-loving, why on earth does he allow it all to happen? Why do good people, and especially innocent people, little children, suffer?

Only God can know the whole truth, but I have found many aspects of these questions which have helped me greatly in my own faith. I have watched both my parents die of cancer. I have seen the terror and misery of people facing hopeless prospects as a ruthless enemy draws the net around their nation. I have tried to share as a friend and pastor in the lives of many people who have faced death and suffering in their many forms.

The first thing which comes into my mind at such times is that it is essential that we do not lose sight of the nature and destiny of man. Christians believe that God has created man 'in his own image', and for a very special purpose. God is spirit, and the most important thing about human nature is that it is intended by its creator to be the forerunner of a being who is destined to share in the eternal spiritual existence of God. All that happens in man's physical and earthly life is part of the process of 'soul-making'.

Yet even as we say that, we must make haste to add another parallel fact. We are not saying that the only fruit of living according to the Maker's instruction in this life will be a reward in the hereafter. On the contrary, I make this assertion with every conviction of which I am capable: when a person lives according to the will and direction of God, when he makes that tremendous experiment of saying 'no' to himself, and 'yes' to God, then, and only then, does he begin to find out what real happiness, what true security, what love and the fullness of living are all about.

In Britain, in the seventeenth century, Christians compiled a catechism in which the very first question was, 'What is the chief end of man?' and the required response was, 'Man's chief end is to glorify God and to enjoy him for ever.' We must discuss the fact of human suffering in the light of the belief that everything which happens here and now must be evaluated in terms of its importance to man's supreme good, to his eternal destiny as a child of God.

The next thing I try to remind myself when I see undeserved suffering and innocent people hurt or killed, is that God could only create a world in which people could grow into individuals if he gave them freedom to obey or rebel as they wished. God has not made us mere puppets. Part of that divine spark, that nature of his own which is with us, has to do with a sovereignty of choice.

This, of course, means that if God's intended purpose for us is that we should find the love and joy and fulfilment of spiritual unity with him, then it must also be possible for us to experience the misery, the pain and the emptiness caused by disobedience and sin.

Once more, I must make haste to add a rider to that statement, for I am not saying that when a person suffers it is due necessarily to his own faults. Far from it. I have already used the word 'innocent' suffering. Jesus was questioned about this kind of thing on several occasions. Under Roman rule there were continual outbreaks of revolt and insurrection, and nothing provoked this more than when Rome interfered with Jewish religious affairs. On one occasion Pilate gave orders that a new water project should be built, and that 'Temple money' should be confiscated and made payable towards the cost. This immediately roused the Jews to arms, and none were more ready to take up the fight than the Galileans.

When the mobs gathered, Pilate instructed his soldiers to mingle with them, disguising their battle-dress under cloaks, and carrying clubs rather than weapons. At a given signal they were to fall on the mob and disperse them. But the result was a riot and much bloodshed, and a considerable number of people lost their lives.

What about those who died? Were they greater sinners than those who escaped? This was one of the very important questions put to Jesus relating to our theme. Jesus never hesitated in his reply. 'I tell you, no!', he said. But he went on at once to point out that the cause could be traced to the actions not of individuals so much as of nations. He could see the hatred and bitterness building up around him which were to lead to the revolts prior to AD 70 when the Roman armies would retaliate by wiping out Jerusalem in an enormous slaughter. Jesus asserted that, if the Jewish nation kept on seeking an earthly kingdom and rejecting the kingdom of God, they could only come to one end.

One of the most wonderful things about God's world is that he has not simply created it, enshrining certain laws of cause and effect, and leaving us to our fate so that our own disobedience is the cause of suffering and death. God has gone much, much further than that. He has given us a way of stopping and indeed reversing the process of cause and effect which is within the reach of us all.

During the past few years I have lived and talked with people who have first of all learned to take full responsibility for their own race and its part in the world's suffering, and then to move out to translate into healing and hope-giving activity the faith they have found. The results have been miracles of change. I have met Egyptian students who have found the change of heart which has enabled them to rise above their hatred for the Jews and to pray and work for friendship with them. I have lived with black and white South Africans who have done the same. I have found people whose nearest kin have been foully murdered, actually giving their lives to help the people responsible, to help them rise to the stature of sons of God.

To me it is an enormous mystery, but I know this for sure, that when God comes into a situation where there is suffering and pain, he is able to transform those involved so that they become bigger, deeper, more caring and more fruitful than would have been possible before.

There is little profit, in my opinion, trying to speculate and philosophise on the origin of evil. For me it is enough to know that darkness is a negative state, it is the absence of light; cold likewise is simply the absence of heat. Thus I find it enough to ascribe the existence of evil to the absence of the goodness and love of God.

God is primary. He is the Creator of all things, the powerful light which can shine in the deepest darkness and that darkness is at once beaten and its terrors dismissed. God is able to stand before the worst that sin and evil can do, and speak with utter and final authority as its conqueror. The cross, the grave and the empty tomb need only happen once in all history. There one who was utterly undeserving of suffering because of his own sinless life, nevertheless paid the utmost penalty of sin, taking on himself not just the sins of his own nation, but the sins of all humanity whose flesh he shared. He, the Christ of God, accepted full responsibility, without complaint, without blame, with only rich out-going, forgiving love, for the whole sorry story of our failure. He did it through suffering, suffering which was the will of God.

Many people ponder the power and effectiveness of prayer in the face of suffering, sickness and pain. Does it not say in the Epistle of James that the prayers of the believers will heal the sick? Did not Jesus commission his disciples to heal and cast out demons? Was not this healing ministry an integral part of the first century Church?

Yes, of course! The amazing results of faithful, believing prayer are so frequent and so well-attested that there can surely be no hesitation in our agreeing to this much. But it is important that we do not stop there. We must never forget that Jesus prayed, before his crucifixion, for God to save him, if it were possible, from that ordeal. God could not grant that prayer, but in that hour it was God who disclosed his agony to the world, the pain he bears continually seen for a moment in time.

As a young man I once worked aboard a tramp steamer which sailed past the island of Stromboli whilst it was erupting. It was night and all we could see was a vivid red scar of molten lava, like a gigantic neon sign, piercing the blackness. For a few minutes we were able to see revealed something of the searing heat buried for ever in the bowels of the earth. In the cross, mortal man sees momentarily in the life and death of the man Jesus of Nazareth the passion and pain of Almighty God as he experiences the waste, suffering and sin of human misery, which is the result of man's rejection of him.

Then again, when we are confronted with pain and death, we quickly fall back on our humanity, on our human and physical values. We tend to think of death as the great evil, and are seldom able to evaluate suffering over against other considerations. It may very well be that God has a far vaster, and much more important consideration for the person for whom we can only see freedom from pain or continuing human existence as of outstanding importance.

It must surely be agreed that Jesus came to prepare us for a life which would be far beyond this physical life, and even its great joys such as courtship and marriage would be surpassed. If that be so, then does it not stand to reason that there must be objectives for our lives which go far beyond freedom from sickness and suffering? Indeed, if the greatest life of all be any criterion, it is certainly true that it is *through* enduring, suffering and dying that some of the very greatest things can be achieved for God and his kingdom.

Prayer is not a magical ritual to placate or change the intentions of a remote and stubborn deity, it is a person-to-person relationship between God and his own family, about the family business. It is not a matter of reminding God of things needing to be done that he may otherwise forget, nor is it a matter of badgering an unwilling God into activity. Prayer is a powerful activity. It is here that, in the spirit, man completes a circuit with God, the source of all power, so that new forces can be released and directed in situations in which God has deliberately given responsibility into our hands.

Time and time again I see God as being unable, or at least unwilling to act in a given situation because he is bound by a higher consideration: namely, the free will and independence of his children. When we do come to him and begin to build the intimate response of prayer, bringing resonant life into new circuits, power surging into new situations, then God begins to work as he longs to do. But without us he chooses to wait, to wait for us to grow up into the stature of children becoming adult in the life of the spirit.

Prayer is a partnership. It is the definite and direct exercise of a God-given power. It is not just what our hands can do if directed by God, but what our spirits can do together with God, when we have come to him along the way he has shown us, seeing the truth as he reveals it to us and seeking to live the life he directs. It is this way, this truth and this life which lead us to a Person.

CHAPTER 15

Next to losing the sense of a personal Christ, the worst evil that can befall a Christian is to have no sense of anything else. To grow up in a complacent belief that God has no business in this great groaning world of human beings except to attend to a few saved souls is the negation of all religion. The first great epoch in a Christian's life, after the awe and wonder of its dawn, is when there breaks into his mind that Christ has a purpose for mankind, a purpose beyond him and his needs, beyond the churches and their creeds, beyond Heaven and its saints – a purpose which embraces every man and woman born, every kindred and nation formed, which regards not their spiritual good alone but their welfare in every part, their progress, their health, their work, their wages, their happiness in this present world.

Professor Henry Drummond, *The Programme of Christianity*

CHAPTER FIFTEEN

The Ultimate Battle

There are two completely different ideas of the end or goal of this material world. One view is optimistic: it looks for the coming of the millenium, a period when 'the lion will lie down with the lamb', when 'swords will be forged into pruning hooks', and the kingdom of God will 'come on earth as it is in heaven'. It is this view which refuses to despair and goes on patiently and determinedly lighting even a single candle when darkness threatens on all sides.

The other view is cataclysmic. It too derives its warrant from scripture. It holds that the last phase of the created world will be fraught with disaster, plagued by wars, insurrection, moral breakdown and the apparent triumph of evil. In the days of the great prophets men of God frequently warned against the optimistic view. 'Beware', they cried, 'the day of the Lord will be darkness, not light!'

When the forces of evil rise in great strength there is always the temptation for Christians to assume, quite contrary to the express instructions of Jesus, that the end of this world is at hand. It is sobering, at such times, to look back carefully into the past and see how many have been the occasions when similar darkness has threatened to engulf mankind, without the promised end. For those who lived in Jerusalem there could hardly have been a greater disaster, a more terrible happening than the sacking of that city by Rome in AD 70. The inhabitants were reduced to cannibalism as they starved to death. Finally merciless Roman swords decimated their numbers. One million, one hundred thousand died in that bloodbath, leaving less than a hundred thousand alive. But the expected end did not come. Instead this very event, this attempt to quench a fire, merely sent a thousand sparks flying to the four winds to kindle even greater flames. 'God works in a mysterious way his wonders to perform', says the hymn-writer. 'He makes even the wrath of men to praise him', says the man of God.

If God is a God of love, – absolute, unyielding love – then it is hard indeed to see him as the one who will cry 'halt', and thereby damn for ever the unrepentant and disobedient members of the human race. There is another possibility, and it is seen in perfection in the Easter story. Having given men freedom of choice, to choose evil rather than good, to opt for death rather than life, may it not be that God foresees the day when, despite all he and his forces can do, men will so pursue the ways of rebellious hate that they themselves will effect the final destruction? When all God's goodness, wooing and pleading are rejected, and hate, violence, lust and terror are the deliberate choice of men, might it not be that God (and now God's faithful friends and followers as well) will be brought with the whole of the created world to the consummation wherein the only comment remaining will be 'It is finished'?

There is another aspect which must never be forgotten, and that is the complete command which Jesus exercised over even the smallest detail of his passion and death; God is still in command even when men are doing their worst.

Jesus deliberately went to Jerusalem on that last journey when it was teeming with pilgrims for the Passover. He lingered in the countryside until the crowds, including many of his friends, were gathered. An earlier arrival could have seen him isolated and arrested without the furore which the authorities were anxious to avoid. There was only one time in such a crowded city when an arrest could be made clandestinely: that was at the moment when the law demanded that everyone must remain indoors, at least for the duration of the Pascal meal itself. Hence the crucial importance of the part played by Judas. If the authorities could only discover the house in which Jesus would celebrate Passover, then such an arrest could be made. So Jesus took elaborate precautions to prevent this knowledge getting to Judas.

One can imagine the frustration of Judas as he waits to learn of the venue only to hear Jesus call two others and send them to prepare the meal, making no mention of the address, but giving them a pre-arranged sign whereby they would recognise their host: he, a man, would be carrying a water-pot, not an impossible thing, but very rare in the East, where this was 'woman's work'. Judas has no alternative but to go along quietly with the rest. Not until they are actually entering the very house does he know its location.

Then Jesus keeps him sitting right beside him throughout the meal. Jesus has much to say, and does not intend to have this climactic night in human history disturbed by premature arrest. Only when he is ready does he turn to Judas and say, 'Go and do what you have decided to do.'

All the way, to the very cross itself, we see Jesus thus in command. He goes steadfastly ahead because it is God's will that he suffer rather than mankind be lost. It is his will too.

So too will it be at the end of time.

God may one day be in the position where man has destroyed all ways of escape from destruction, but it will only be when God permits it to be so. Time and time again God has seen fit to intervene in history, fulfilling his ancient promise that he will never utterly destroy disobedient mankind, that he will never leave himself without a witness. Only when mankind has committed the unforgivable sin will the end be at hand.

The unforgivable sin? What is it but 'blasphemy against the Holy Spirit'?

That most certainly does not mean using the words 'Holy Spirit' in a blasphemous way. The misuse of these English, Greek or Hebrew words can certainly be ugly and even hurtful, but not fatal. But there is a line of behaviour which is. It is when men take all those God-given attributes whereby they can discern and follow the way to God and wilfully destroy or pervert them and reverse their meaning and direction. It is when they call good 'evil' and evil 'good'! When they deliberately eradicate the means of moral and spiritual perception men commit spiritual suicide. It is when men and women become completely desensitised to love, forgiveness, beauty, peace, goodness, and all the ways whereby the Spirit of God can enter human hearts that they move outside the reach of God's redeeming love. This is the unforgivable sin, to strip ourselves deliberately of the means of grace and enthrone the evil as good – the devil as God.

Down through the ages progress has been made in discerning God's intention for mankind. The great religions, which are after all the repositories of this process, have reached some notable areas of consensus. The moral laws which reach their fullest expression in the teaching of Jesus are not arbitrary or open to compromise or negotiation. They are at least as eternal as the laws governing the structure of the atom, and the consequences of violating their integrity are infinitely more devastating. In reversing such God-given signposts so as to send men and nations on false paths, those responsible are in danger of committing the unforgivable sin, jeopardising men's eternal souls. But it is the good news of the gospel of Christ that, as long as man is able to discern the truth, to know right from wrong, as long as he can see and recognise goodness, honesty, purity, love and the rest as being fundamental to the right way, then he can yet come to see and accept God's redemption.

Jesus taught that this world will not simply go on and on in this way for all eternity. Here science and religion support each other fully. This globe had a beginning, the human race has a starting point, gradual or sudden, and earth and the human race will just as surely have an ending. Make no mistake about that. Time is not a roundabout but a road running from beginning to end. It has direction. This too is an integral part of the gospel of Christ. It is a vital part of our faith that we have this sense of end or goal for all history.

When Christ died on the cross he cried out in his agony, 'It is finished!' That was the turning point in the cosmic battle of human history. Now despite all setbacks, all the pain and loneliness and temptation to quit, Christ fought on in perfect obedience to God's voice in his heart to confront the last and greatest force that evil could put into the field against him. He faced utter desolation in his death, virtually a complete failure by every human standard, and he did it unflinchingly in his faith that this was what God required. So he died, and was buried.

Then the bombshell burst. The apparently victorious power of evil was suddenly destroyed by a series of mighty events. The dreadful finality, the silence of death was shattered by the incredible, triumphant shout, 'He is risen!'

Not just one or two close friends, or even a few hundred disciples, but soon millions, every colour and class, were proclaiming as their living conviction: 'On the third day he rose again from the dead, he ascended into heaven and sitteth on the right hand of God the Father Almighty, from THENCE HE SHALL COME . . .'

There IS a 'goal', an end; a final victory ahead of us. We are creatures of time; and time, as we have seen, has a beginning and an ending. When that end will be is not for us to foreknow. Certainly we must never treat this glorious hope as a funkhole into which we can withdraw from the battle to await the end. There is a job still to be done, and each of us has a part. Each must find the quiet certainty of God's commission, our part in his victorious master plan. Humble or exalted, that plan is the best possible way for each of us. Through it all it is the tremendous hope of the coming of Christ in his final victory which buoys us up and carries us into battle with new fire and fight.

This language of battle and warfare recurs throughout our journey, but thus far we have not defined the enemy. If the forces of religion are ranged on the one side, how do we best describe the opposition? It would not be greatly helpful to say they are the legions of the irreligious, for this is far from an adequate description. They are far, far more effective and purposeful than that.

In discussing God we have used such terms as personal, personality, love, grace, goodness and so forth – knowing that they are inadequate, but being devoid of concepts which go beyond them. Even in saying that God is absolute we have possibly ventured beyond human grasp, at least in some aspects of that word, especially of absolute love or absolute purity. In another way however we believe we can and must grasp something of ultimate reality in this way.

To take a scientific analogy. I hold in my hand a bar of copper. It is as pure a piece of copper as man can make it. I am aware of the degree of its purity. I know that it consists of atoms wherein each nucleus contains twenty-nine protons, and this means that under normal conditions there are twenty-nine electrons in its structure. I can test its reaction with other substances and check and recheck my experiments. In the end I can say with certainty that all copper, wherever it may occur in the universe is a metal which has twenty-nine protons in its atomic nucleus, and under stated conditions it will behave in certain ways.

So too with my knowledge of God. In Jesus of Nazareth mankind has been given a pure and perfect 'laboratory sample' as it were, so that Jesus could assure his disciples, 'He who has seen me has seen the Father'. God is far, far beyond our grasp or comprehension; but as to those attributes and qualities which affect and impinge upon our human lives, our loves, fears, feelings and individual persons, we can say with complete certainty: 'This is what God is like, this is how he acts', and point to Jesus.

But what of the enemy of all this?

If God is personal, is there an anti-person, for example?

Once again science can help us grasp a possible line of thought about God's traditional arch-opponent: the Devil. When I go out on a winter night and the frost and snow rise up to hit me with a blow that takes my breath away, I say that cold is very real and very evident. If there is no moon and the night is cloudy and I venture into the woodland, the darkness closes in on me and it too is real and tangible. Yet science tells me that there are no such things as cold and darkness. Cold is the absence of heat, darkness the absence of light. Heat and light are primary things, they are forms of energy, of activity. Cold and darkness are negative states, having no substance of their own.

Yet to feel the cold creeping in through every crack and chink in windows, under doors, and wherever a gap can be found, it seems to assume an almost animal cunning and determination.

Can it be the same with evil?

May it be that there is a negative personality, an active purposeful penetration of human life and affairs wherever the slightest gap or opening occurs in our moral and spiritual armour?

Whatever the explanation, for most ordinary purposes it is an highly accurate and adequate description of cold and darkness to treat them as tangible and real things. So with evil. The activities of evil are so structured, so purposeful, so persistent and so personal that the older I get, that is, the more I experience them, the more I find it impossible to describe them better than to say that there is a personal devil as the architect of their power and purpose.

In political terms one may at times tend to equate the devil with one's opponents! This is made especially easy when the opposition is avowedly atheist and dedicated to the overthrow of the concepts of God and religion.

When a leading Marxist philosopher like Max Horkheimer of the Frankfurt school, which nurtured Marcuse, speaks of the evil let loose in the world it is a sobering experience to listen. 'We too belong to the devils – we too', he writes. 'Radical evil is asserting its mastery over all creatures all over the world. Whatever comes, we cannot complain. We sit peacefully and comfortably in our arm-chairs, we dine and we discuss, although we know that all hell is let loose.'[1]

This sounds as though Horkheimer, like Pandora, is aghast at the prospect of the demonism he has helped to let loose in the world by an activity even he has not adequately understood. When the old moral standards and values discerned over the ages are deliberately negated or reversed, not just the destruction of bourgeois society and capitalist structures is found to be possible but the destruction of man himself.

The strategy which emerges from the adopting of such a philosophy is so cunning and apparently integrated that many people tend to ascribe its programme to a single ideological plot or some similarly contrived mechanism. That there are deliberate and purposeful strategies on the part of the Communist powers, for example, cannot be denied. But the magnitude and effectiveness of the processes which even these strategies evince go far beyond the capacity of any political machine to devise.

I have no doubt, for example, that Chou En-lai saw the use of narcotics as a valuable weapon to undermine the west and to reduce his opponents to impotence. This Communist purpose, which Chou once described as using the same weapons to destroy the capitalists as they had used a century earlier to try to destroy China, proved valuable to him in Vietnam where drugs gravely affected the strength of the United States Army. To pretend that the whole massive structure of drug abuse today is a communist plot however is a ridiculous oversimplification.

We have earlier recalled that it was Lenin who said, 'When the time comes to hang the capitalists they will be found competing with each other for the contract for the rope!' So too with regard to drugs. It is easy to move a huge boulder down a steep hillside. Only a little energy is needed to start it rolling. Other forces take over very quickly. Ideology may initiate some things which are anti-moral and destructive, but greed, self-indulgence and callousness soon add to developments which lead to exploitation of other people without concern for their enslavement, suffering or death.

The common denominator of it all is, of course, materialism. It is here that the forces of right and left interact to accelerate the processes of destruction. Materialism is the way of the jungle, the way away from God.

So too in other channels – for example in the peddling of pornography and violence through the media and the arts. There can be little doubt that films and stories of certain kinds stimulate the worst that is in our nature. Nor can there be any question that such appetites are being stimulated and whetted by deliberate intent. Ideological forces set about the publication of materials designed for that very purpose. Their intention is to undermine the moral fibre, and thereby the capacity to resist, of a society or nation which is under attack.

It only takes one or two persons in a television network who are dedicated to their task for ideological reasons to start a chain reaction which quickly enlists motives and incentives far wider than their political or ideological ones. If it is found that the ratings or sales figures increase by providing this emphasis on sex and sadism, and that they contribute to a trend in contemporary society, then they have it made. Parsons and academics will always be found to lavish praise on the most sordid themes as being realist or great art. The socially insecure find that they have to keep up with the trendies or risk that appalling punishment of being regarded as dull and outdated. So the factors pile up which lead to the wider and wider demand for filth and fury. Mounting profits soon quieten the consciences of those who ought to call a halt to the process and thus the objectives of the destroyers are fulfilled. The rope has been bought. The free and open society hardly pauses to note that such processes are rigidly excluded from the closed and imprisoned communities.

What is the answer to this catalogue of evil, to this inter-weaving pattern of negative motives which in our day have so proliferated as to threaten civilisation?

There are, once again, two vital ingredients to the answer.

The first is the acceptance of the pole star of absolute moral standards. Only ethical standards which are really absolute can cut like a knife through the cancers in modern behaviour. Comparative and situational ethics soon mean no moral challenge, and result in no ethics at all.

I was once talking to a high government official in a certain country which was deeply concerned with the inroads which communism was making into international affairs. The only answer this gentlemen could propose was anti-communism. He had devised an elaborate structure to proliferate such literature and had arranged conventions and conceived many other ways of conveying an anti-communist message to the masses. He grew more and more impatient when I insisted that this alone would eventually prove ineffectual or even counter-productive. Communism, which depends on the promotion of division and clash, would thrive on anti-communist vehemence.

When I told him story after story of Communists who had actually been won to a bigger and more constructive revolution, he smiled cynically and warned me that they were infinitely cunning, and capable of dissembling, in order to penetrate non-communist structures. How could one be sure?

So I told him two true stories. First there was the communist who was a sub-editor of a large national daily paper in Australia, which is no longer in circulation. I well remember his telling a group of us, after he had left the Party, that his assignment in his job had been to see that every opportunity was taken to overstate the anti-communist aspect of political and industrial reporting. He had to add adjectives and implications which meant that otherwise accurate reports would be seen as too extreme, exaggerated and thus unreliable. At the same time he was to attach the label of 'right wing' to all sound, centre-of-the-road trade-union and political figures. Every moderate must be made to seem an extremist. Anti-communism itself was a liability rather than an asset.

The second incident was even nearer the bone. I told him of one of his own country's ambassadors who had started to live his life in the light of Christ's moral standards. A secretary was appointed to his mission who at first seemed highly pleasant and efficient. He worked long hours and there seemed no reason to doubt his loyalty. The Ambassador however felt an inexplicable sense of disquiet about him. Then one day this official made a suggestion as to a course of action which would possibly prove highly advantageous to their purposes but which was morally unsound. This further aroused the Ambassador's suspicions. He decided to watch him carefully, and in a few days surprised him in the act of extracting classified information from files to which he ought to have had no access. The Ambassador told me that if he had not had the clarity which came from his decision to test his living by absolute standards he would in all probability never have suspected the traitor, as he proved to be.

St Paul said: 'Put on the whole armour of God that you may be able to stand against the wiles of the devil; for we wrestle not against flesh and blood but against principalities, against powers, against the rulers of darkness of this world, against spiritual wickedness in high places. . . . stand therefore having your loins girt with truth, and having on the breastplate of righteousness . . .'.

The structures of world society will crack and decay without such a foundation. The future urgently awaits the leadership of men and women who not only know this to be true but make a start in the only place such renaissance can begin, by applying the criteria of immovable morality and simple faith in their own lives.

The second part of the equipment which is available in the battle against evil is the plus of God's super-strategy: 'above all take the shield of faith'. Something more than merely human wisdom is available to us. It is essential of course that we use every scrap of wit and wisdom of which we are capable. We must be 'as wise as serpents as well as harmless as doves'. Having done our best however, all too often we can ordinarily only play the part of reacting to the initiatives of others, and it takes a large peace-keeping force to contain the activities of a very few violent men, becuse they have the weapon of surprise. In the battle against evil it is the same – with a major exception. There is available to those prepared to accept it the plus of a super-strategy. The kind of strategy which means that totally unexpected and unplannable things can happen, new doors open, perspectives change, and the most unlikely people suddenly emerge as vital keys to new advances.

There can be little doubt that evil forces were at work in trying to frustrate Francis and Edith Schaeffer's plans to set up a teaching centre in Switzerland. But who could have planned the counter-strategy so as to bring them into contact with the very men who could most help them except the God from whose hand they had long since known to expect an astonishing chain of 'coincidences'.

Sometimes these 'coincidences' can affect the destiny of nations. To take an example, when a fuller account of these days in Rhodesia comes to be written it will be seen that vitally important changes have been taking place in the past decade which confront us all with choices which could well determine our own future. In a remarkable way some of the leaders of both black and white groups inside Rhodesia have been drawn into processes of profound moral and spiritual change. Others, who have not been there to experience this virtual revolution of the spirit, have been drawn towards the communist way of change based on hatred, terror and war.

The story goes a long way back. The work of thousands of faithful Christians both black and white has laid sound foundations, but it is within the last decade that a significant development has come. Perhaps one of the keys to these new factors has been the 'conversion' while attending a charismatic meeting, of Mr Alec Smith, the son of the Prime Minister. Young Smith was a dropout. He had been expelled from his university because of his refusal to study or co-operate. He was hooked on drugs and was eventually arrested for drug-peddling at the international airport.

The experience of Christian change completely transformed his life. It brought him into contact with other Christians who were dedicated to bringing God's solution to his country's problems. He began to see his own part in the mess and felt deeply sorry for his own arrogance and indifference to the black people. He set out to try to put these things right. An early development was a visit to a black medical doctor to whom he made a costly and sincere apology. That man has since played an important role in the talks which led up to attempts at an internal settlement.

A little later a meeting was held in the university at which he and the doctor spoke. One of the white professors was deeply moved, and saw how he was treating a black colleague as an intellectual lightweight solely on the grounds of his colour. Honest apology led to real friendship and this to a dinner party in the professor's home to which leaders of both the black and white extremist groups were invited.

A Methodist minister who was treasurer of the African National Congress and who had worked closely with the guerillas felt he had good reason to hate and avoid all whites, but he too was won. His church in the heart of the crowded African township of Harare became the scene of amazing multi-national gatherings each Sunday night when blacks and whites met and prayed and shared feelings and experiences which deeply moved the many hundreds who attended.

One of the great privileges of my life was to be asked to attend an Easter houseparty in 1976 when young leaders of both black and white groups came to live and plan together. I've never heard such costly and stark honesty anywhere. There were moments of tension when the icy silence could have been broken by an explosion of violence as apologies were made which revealed former treachery, for example. But it all ended in deeper friendship and basic changes in human nature.

In 1978 hopes for the internal settlement faded as fear mounted. The Methodist minister, Arthur Kanodereka, was rejected politically because he spoke out against broken promises. He continued seeing the leadership of all parties however, even to dangerous visits to Mozambique and Lusaka. He was assassinated on December 18 just as he was about to launch a plan 'to enable sincere men on all sides to unite to search for what is right for our country'. Faced with many death-threats he told friends, 'I am not afraid to die . . . what matters is what we are living for when death meets us'.

Meanwhile the global ideological battle has intensified. Russia's military and naval might has grown, and with it her increasing incursion into African affairs. The Communists said after their victory in Vietnam that next in line was to be Southern Africa. Nobody denies the need for profound change there, as elsewhere, but more and more people are beginning to question the forces which can so distort perspectives as to allow a bloodbath of terror and repression to go largely unchallenged in Cambodia or Uganda yet direct world spleen against Rhodesia, which is immeasurably more democratic and benign.

The stark truth is that both Britain and America are aware that they face a force within their own borders as well as in Africa which has opted for the communist 'solution'. Even within our churches there are those who want to see a victory by way of the gun rather than by way of the cross. An orchestrated chorus of hatred tries to lampoon and drown out any chorus which points towards 'peace on earth to men of goodwill'.

The possibility exists, nevertheless, of a workable multiracial society in Africa. This is exactly the opposite to what the men of violence want, of course, and from Rabaul to Namibia, from Korea to Cairo, one can see the ruthless hand of forces which murder any leaders who promise peace and goodwill, based on justice and fair play. Evil is riding high in our day. We need the superior wisdom and power of God.

It is not enough to expose the truth, relying on decent people to see, agree and act.

I often long for a White Paper which will fearlessly lay bare the facts behind terrorism, strategic strikes aimed at crippling national and international economies, the real source and purpose of policies which are aimed at deepening the depression and the hollow cynicism of stagnation.

When the iron hand of Russia ground out the last resistance in Hungary, and later in Czechoslovakia, many in the West felt 'it can't happen here'. Today the potential power to paralyse the lives of tens of millions, of vast nations, is in very few hands, in many sectors – in the post office, in power industries, in transport, in banks and so forth. The framework of control now exists in our democracies which will soon mean a few can take over, with the masses reduced to impotence.

Surely, in these days of super-computers and global intelligence networks, it would be possible to expose the plots and purposes of those who play the ordinary man and woman for suckers, expendable pawns in a chess game where only one king can remain on the board?

Yet even as I think that way I know it is not enough. Without ideological training our leaders still see each phenomenon through the tired old eyes of economic cause and effect, or fail to see other and deeper strategies because they have no yardstick, no absolute standards by which to judge. Even were they to do so, little could be achieved without a widely-based demand for new and abiding values to replace expediency. The only armour against the attacks of evil, the strategies of the demonism of our day, is the whole armour of God.

Human wisdom has failed; few will admit it but most know it.

It is in danger now not of committing mere indiscretions and displaying ineptitude, but of carrying humanity into a final holocaust. The road of countering hatred with hatred, blame with blame, and violence with violence is no longer a viable option. In our hearts we know it. The time has come for a call to all decent human beings to rise above self, sectional and national interest, and to adopt such simple philosophies as 'there is enough in the world for everyone's need but not for everyone's greed: if everyone cared enough and shared enough, everyone would have enough.'

In my life, cluttered as it has been with fears for security, anxiety over assets, thronged with *things*, it is I who must begin by putting first the kingdom of God and his righteousness. All must be available for his use for his kingdom. The revolution we need begins with me.

CHAPTER 16

In our present situation, therefore, we have this ground of hope: that over and above all the ostensible factors at work there is an over-ruling factor which is the creative goodwill of God; and to this we cannot assign any necessary limits. When we survey the imminent possibilities of the situation, we must confess that the outlook is not promising. Much is said about the 'new world' for which we must plan, but the genuinely new factors upon which any plan must depend are not obvious. The more clear-sighted speak with a notable lack of assurance about what lies ahead. But we are not confined to the imminent possibilities of the situation. There is a further possibility; that creative energies from beyond history may enter into it and alter the whole prospect. God creates His Word, 'calling the things that are not as if they were.' In our present crisis, it may be, He is calling to something which does not exist in us, but will come into existence at His Word.

Roger Hicks, *The Endless Adventure*

CHAPTER SIXTEEN

Leadership and the Future

We have begun to find answers for many of the questions which have been posed during our search, but there is one which still requires a more exact reply. We have asked, 'What kind of leadership is able to avoid tyranny and yet provide an adequate global unity of values and purpose?'[1] The unity of values and the purposes have been discerned, at least as to their basic nature and source, but there still remain essential aspects regarding the matter of leadership.

If everyone was living in the light of such values, if everyone was a well-integrated, committed and intelligent follower of the voice of God, placing high value on the unity of the fellowship, then it might be different. But this world is not like that, nor will it be within our lifetime. So we must look further, especially into the matter of structures.

Taking the history of the Christian Church as a case study it would seem that a broad principle emerges in that the structure of the fellowship, as it expands and becomes a significant factor in society, takes on much of the shape of the contemporary political structures of the state. The Church of England reflects the tiered structures of English society in the formative centuries of its early development: so the Lord Bishop, the Church's parliament, the local squires and the rest all find easy identification. So too the fierce individualism of the Scots is reflected in the strenuous democracy of Presbyterianism. The Church of Rome and the Eastern Churches still reflect much of the tradition and structures of the days when they first assumed significant proportions in the then contemporary societies into which they were born.

There can be little doubt that the forms and constitution of society have been undergoing enormous changes in the twentieth century, and it is only to be expected that many of these have left the form and structures of the Churches open to equally great change. The entire nature of leadership in the world today can be readily divided into two groups: the reactionary societies where only lip service is paid to democracy and individual freedom, and where power and leadership have been taken and held by very few hands; and those still optimistically progressive cultures where there remains a hope for freedom. Within these latter nations however the traditional structures, even to the place and power of parliament, are under challenge. The whole scene is bedevilled by the fact that cells of revolutionaries are at work seeking to exploit the mood for change in the interests of their own group or closed society. Leadership in the main is therefore shrinking to leadership by reaction, a response to challenge and crisis rather than a primary thing.

So too within the company of believers. There was a time when the whole community needed to gather in central places, not only in order to pray and enjoy each other's fellowship, but to hear and study the scriptures and discern a sense of direction which was relevant to that day. Newspapers were a rarity, radio and TV were unknown, education was elementary and books were few and expensive. The exposition of scripture and the application of its principles to necessarily restricted horizons of living was managed by the clergy from these large central meetings week by week.

Their buildings are still to be seen, but seldom the crowds. Even within the buildings still in use changes are taking place which reflect the larger interests of our day. Leadership within the fellowship is itself in tension. On the one hand there is the task of maintaining and guarding those things which are eternal and unchangeable from the precocious and precipitate hands of new enthusiasms. On the other there is the plain fact that education, information, communication and travel have so enlarged the minds and hearts of the great majority of believers that they are frequently as well, if not better, informed and prepared for decision-making than the traditional leadership, the clergy.

One of the joys of our age has been the way old and largely irrelevant structures of bygone ages have been questioned and transmuted so once significant barriers to unity are disappearing. This is certainly increasingly true between Christian Churches. It is going wider than that. God-seekers are approving more and more the wisdom of Mukerjee the Hindu who referred to the basic division in mankind as being between the 'spirit-seekers and the matter-mongers'.

Nevertheless two very different streams of development are discernible. On the one hand there are entirely new structures or sects emerging which make a deliberate break with the more traditional bodies and they become entities in themselves. On the other hand there are those 'inter-denominational' or 'supra-ecclesiastical' bodies which continue within the broad structures of existing religious activity, making no attempt to replace or discard their fundamental differences in terms of the sacraments, clerical order and so forth, but forming a more deeply integrated and far-reaching *koinonia* within and across the boundaries of larger groupings. To oversimplify, the former see themselves as ends, the latter as means. The sects become self-sufficient, tend to an arrogance and exclusiveness which are all too often the breeding ground for fanaticism. Unrestricted by the traditional safeguards, discerned and developed over the centuries by the more established bodies, their leadership is able to assume roles in the lives of the membership which have brought suffering, tyranny and eventual disruption and disaster: 'By their fruits ye shall know them.'

An unfailing test of the health or otherwise of any sect or movement is whether it is becoming an end in itself, increasingly exclusive and arrogant, or whether it is contributing more and more selflessly to the needs of seeking humanity, to the great body of believers everywhere.

In a word, is it a valid part of the onward march of the God-seekers of the world or a reactionary regression? The truly revolutionary call of the last part of the twentieth century is 'believers of the world, unite'.

Unity, of course, does not mean necessarily unity of structure. Indeed one of the great dangers besetting the ecumenical movement is that we see the road to unity as a structural matter and fail to see that structures are only the crutches of a patient who should be improving and getting beyond the need of them. In any case structures have, in almost every instance, been a later development consequent upon the growth of a fellowship of believers in certain defined situations. The ecumenical tinkerers and mechanics who peer at existing structures with 'ingrowing eyeballs' are a menace to the future of God's conquest of mankind.

True unity is found in discerning the new tasks, the God-given strategy, the overwhelming urgency of human needs which brings us all into one fighting force, the true *koinonia*. Using the traditions and inherited wisdom of the past, which are invaluable to our common purposes, we move not inwards, to boost our numbers, increase our resources of money and streamline our bureaucracy, but outwards to the great tasks, on rapidly converging paths.

Some of this can be done from above – that is from the top level of leadership downwards – but very little, and then only if other more important things have taken place elsewhere. It is at the level of the tasks themselves that the true impetus to fellowship emerges, whose activities will make evident what is needed and what is irrelevant in structural change.

Yet there *is* an 'above'. There is a discernible leadership. In order to function in a co-ordinated way the body of God's people must have integrity and purpose directed towards the challenges and opportunities of the day. In a highly democratic system like the Presbyterian one, the Moderator, who is technically the Chairman or Speaker of the Church's Parliament, tends to be more and more regarded as the Prime Minister or spokesman of the Church's Government. The media, the establishment, the community at large all want someone to speak for the Church in innumerable situations, and so they ask the Moderator. The rest of the clergy, who recognise him as no more than the first of a band of brothers of equal status, often resent his personal opinions, however sage and weighty, being taken for the considered and deliberate voice of the whole.

There is, in short, a tension between leadership and the rank and file in Church as in State matters. The more educated, informed and capable the members of society the less kindly do they take to autocracy of any kind. Is it then simply a case of the breakdown of the ideal state as seen by Plato in *The Republic*, where he saw a cycle of transition from democracy to chaos to despotism to oligarchy and back to democracy and so on, over and over? Capitalism, or the rule of the money-makers, decayed, said Plato, because of 'the insatiable appetite for money-making to the neglect of everything else'.

Similarly, in a democracy he held that the passion for liberty would bring a corresponding decay:

> A democratic state may fall under the influence of unprincipled leaders, ready to minister to its thirst for liberty with too deep draughts of this heady wine; and then, if its rulers are not complaisant enough to give it unstinted freedom, they will be arraigned as accursed oligarchs and punished. Law-abiding citizens will be insulted as nonentities who hug their chains; and all praise and honour will be bestowed, both publicly and in private, on rulers who behave like subjects and subjects who behave like rulers . . . the parent falls into the habit of behaving like a child, and the child like the parent . . . the schoolmaster timidly flatters his pupils and the pupils make light of their masters . . . the old, anxious not to be thought disagreeable tyrants, imitate the young and condescend to enter into their jokes and amusements . . . and I had almost forgotten to mention the spirit of freedom and equality in the mutual relations of men and women . . .
>
> Putting all these items together you can see the result; the citizens become so sensitive that they resent the slightest application of control as intolerable tyranny, and in their resolve to have no master they end by disregarding even the law, written or unwritten . . .
>
> The same disease that destroyed oligarchy breaks out again here, with all the more force because of prevailing licence, and enslaves democracy . . . so the only outcome of too much freedom is like to be excessive subjugation.[2]

In the field of religious development similar dangers emerge. 'The glorious liberty of the sons of God', as St Paul described it, can readily degenerate into licence. Very early in the life of the Christian Church, as we have seen, a phenomenon arose which became known as Montanism which has had numerous parallels down to this present day.

Latourette says: 'The founder, Montanus, . . . believed that he had direct messages from the Spirit, that the age of the Spirit foretold in the *Gospel of*

John had returned, and that the second coming of Christ was at hand. In him and his followers, the early Christians with their emphasis on continuing revelation through prophecy seemed to have returned. The Montanists, too, protested against what they deemed the growing laxity of the majority of Christians . . . while not forbidding matrimony, they prized celibacy, and frowned on second marriage . . . They inculcated respect for their prophets rather than for the regularly established clergy . . . they spread widely . . . after more or less hesitation, the majority branded them as heretics.'[3]

Principal Rainy observes:

> One can understand the spread, here and there, in the Christian Churches of a feeling of dissatisfaction and distrust. (As a result of growing secularism etc). This would aim at having room made and effect given to impulses and convictions which the Spirit of God inspires in Christian hearts, as against secularity and worldly conformity – as against set methods that turn Christianity into a mechanical system going on itself, as against worldly wisdom and philosophy; finally as against the hierarchy and the centralised ecclesiastical authority which seemed to leave no room for the free upburst of the Christian heart to assert its desires and make good the result it longed for.
>
> There might be a great deal of prejudice and short-sightedness at the bottom of all this; probably there was also a great deal that was worthy and sincere. Dangers did lie before the Church against which it would have been well to guard. But the dissatisfied section were too apt to assert as the true marks of real Christianity – of the Spirit's presence and power – certain approved forms of self-denial and methods of work-righteousness; and they were apt to drive at these by what seemed to them the readiest means; as if when they got these things to be required and to be complied with, they would then have real and satisfactory Christianity. Thus, they too went astray with their own forms of externalism. And they deprived themselves by so doing of all durable influence; for it could with perfect truth and fairness be maintained against them that no such yoke as they would impose had been laid by the Lord upon His Church.[4]

On the same subject he says:

> Here, men said, is a new era and a new power. Now we see the secret of our vexations and disappointments. The era of the Paraclete had not come, and so things could not be set right. But now He has come. Now at last, not through Bishops and Synods, but by the Spirit Himself, the Church will become a society worthy of its calling; and Christians, shaking themselves free of entanglements and compromise, will be raised to the stature that becomes them, as disciples waiting the coming of the Lord.
>
> This seems thoroughly to explain the various phenomena of Montanism. It explains how Montanism kept clear of new doctrine – excepting the modifica-

> tion of the idea of the Paraclete; and how its whole energy was directed to disciplinary preparation for the coming of the Lord. It explains how ecclesiastical authorities in the neighbourhood of its first appearance saw in it a dangerously subversive movement that required to be instantly checked; and also how it came to pass that large-minded Bishops in regions farther off, seeing in it what it had in common with the feelings of many good Christians everywhere, feelings which they respected, and perhaps partly shared, were slow to commit themselves to a collision with it, and were anxious to treat it in a tolerant spirit as long as they could. That plainly implies that they saw mixed up with it Christian aspirations which deserved to be regarded.
>
> From the human point of view, it must be regarded as a calamity that the assertion of the Church's dependence upon the Spirit, in those ministrations of His which are not limited to clerical character, or standing arrangements, but belong to all believers, was made in a form so indefensible and fanatical.[5]

In the terms in which we have already described sects, Montanism became an end in itself for many of its followers, even though they believed their élitism was related to the imminent second coming of Christ. They made their rigid codes. They interpreted the moral standards for themselves, adding once more to the burden of regulations and rules which Jesus and the apostles had fought against. They built a blind alley. So too through every age the danger is the takeover of the sensitive and developing area of man's capacity for growth and experiences of God by some leader or group, thus usurping his decision-making responsibilities and confronting him with the way *they* choose to interpret moral and spiritual truth, even as conditions of fellowship. When a man or woman has come to know the joy and heart-filling unity which true *koinonia* affords it can be an enormous pressure to make such fellowship dependent on his or her toeing the party line. All the valid disciplines of one person's life can be transferred to another's life as binding obligations, and become quite invalid burdens in this way. A man may feel it wrong to take any alcohol, or to eat meat, a woman may choose to give up the use of cosmetics or wear long hair, another may feel led to equally peripheral disciplines in other fields. Woe betide the fellowship which makes such things into universal and essential requirements however, for they will thereby not only endanger their own integrity by substituting rules for the freedom of the Spirit, but place burdens on others they have no right to impose – burdens which can break backs.

Jesus was very definite about all this. He certainly saw and urged the need for discipline and for periods of abstinence and fasting on the part of his followers. St Paul even declared that this could extend, by mutual consent, to a period of abstinence from normal sexual communion between husband and wife, if both believed such self-denial to be the will of God and undertook it for special spiritual purposes on their part. But the whole tenor of New Testament morality and the teaching of Jesus and the apostles utterly repudiate the attitude that any of these things is in any way obligatory on anyone else.

Neither Jesus nor St Paul practised or preached total abstinence, while both utterly denounced drunkenness. They both gave wine to others on certain occasions, both ate meat and Jesus prepared a fish meal for his friends. While both were bachelors, both not only approved but blessed the estate of matrimony. Even the Sabbath, strictest of all Jewish religious obligations was 'made for man, not man for the Sabbath', Jesus taught.

Self-discipline is one thing. Conditional rules are another, especially if they are rather esoteric, and are demanded as the condition of full acceptance into spiritual fellowship. Such a development defies the express teaching of Jesus. For example, he said 'When you fast or abstain from something, don't blow your trumpet about it in public, but do it secretly. Indeed you should go out of your way to hide the fact from others by looking especially cheerful.'

Discipline within the fellowship then is primarily a personal thing between the individual and God, not an imposed requirement.

There is an ancient story of Jesus coming across a man working in the fields on the Sabbath. Jesus said to him, 'Man, if you know what you are doing, blessed are you; but if you do not know then you are accursed as a law-breaker.'

What Jesus came to offer men was not indifference to laws and customs, not licence and carelessness about obligations and behaviour, but a way of life which was beyond the petty and peripheral, and went right to the heart of the matter. He came to claim the commitment of all life to his discipleship. No mere record of points kept could meet his requirements. It was a case of 'your money and your life'. Not less discipline, but total discipleship. The little rules pale into insignificance before the overarching requirement of the laying down of self. Such is the basic consideration of Christian discipline and Christian order.

At the same time few sincere seekers-after-God have found it possible to do without the help of their own freely-chosen and hopefully secret self-disciplines. The season of Lent for Christians, or Passover for Jews and Ramadan for the Muslim are examples.

Fasting, as the teaching of these three great religious would demonstrate, is essential for all of us and for several reasons. Professor William Barclay puts one major reason for such discipline in these words:

> If there was nothing in us to which temptation could appeal then it would be helpless to defeat us. In every one of us there is a weak spot; and at that

> weak spot temptation launches its attack. The point of vulnerability differs in all of us. What is a violent temptation to one leaves another quite unmoved . . . what is a pleasure to someone else can be a menace to us.[6]

There is another reason for caution in our freedom too, and that is the weakness in modern society, in our environment, indeed in our brother's armoury. We are our 'brother's keeper' in the sense that we must so live that our freedom is not a cause of stumbling to another. The same principle applies to every aspect of living. St Paul in his first letter to Corinth discusses the question in detail, giving his personal opinions as well as what he believes to be the instructions of the Holy Spirit. In a word he offers his conclusion that he would rather abstain from anything, the use of which may be of little or no spiritual impediment to him, if his use of it could cause his brother to stumble. He adds that, like an athlete in training, he finds the need to bring his own body into subjection, and discipline is essential for that too.

But what of the role of leadership, and the issuing of restrictions or other directions where these are felt to be essential? We have already seen that a necessary principle is that 'leadership goes to the spiritually fit'. Nevertheless experience and developed skills are also obviously part of the process. Jesus chose and trained twelve disciples to be leaders in this special sense. They were given, and on occasion sternly used, the power of discipline.

It would be a grave mistake to imagine that no structural edifice ought to exist, that Christian freedom implies that no organisation or established framework of rule is needed. There is no necessity to discuss here the nature and growth of the visible Church or of rule and order within it, for that is a huge topic in itself, but for our purposes we will simply return to the highly relevant and important observation that any such structures, once in existence, are already obsolescent. They have grown out of yesterday's circumstances, out of past needs and experiences. Within their ranks there must always be the dynamic fellowship, the front-line troops of the Spirit, the creative, even revolutionary, minority. Priest and prophet, conservative and liberal, old and young, all types and emphases will properly co-exist and only the grace and power of God and his humility and love can enable this to happen with enhanced prospects for progress and growth rather than internal strife, division and frustration.

Spiritual leadership then is a product of the whole body under the unifying guidance of the Holy Spirit, who alone brings the diversity of pieces into a marvellous unity, the mosaic of the divine architect. The greatest leaders are often men or women whose spiritual maturity and commonsense enable them to be catalysts rather than initiators; discerning, sensitive and encouraging rather than authoritarian. They must always become lesser in order that others may become greater. 'Whoever would be great among you, must be the servant of all', Jesus said, taking a towel and commencing to wash his disciples' feet.

CHAPTER 17

I carry my ideas about me for a long time, often a very long time, before I commit them to writing. My memory is so good that I never forget a theme that has once come to me even if it is a matter of years. I alter much, reject, try again until I am satisfied. Then, in my head, the thing develops in all directions, and since I know precisely what I want, the original idea never eludes me. It rises before me, grows, I hear it, see it in all its size and extension, standing before me like a cast, and it only remains for me to write it down, which is soon done when I can find time, for sometimes I take up other work, though I never confuse that with the other. You will ask where I find my ideas; – I hardly know. They come uninvited, directly or indirectly. I can almost grasp them with my hands, in the open air, in the woods, while walking in the stillness of the night, early in the morning, called up by moods which the poet translates into words, I into musical tones. They sing and roar and swirl around me until I write them down in notes.

Ludwig van Beethoven, 1770–1827

The sound of a Voice coming from something not ourselves, in the existence of which we cannot disbelieve. Without it we are no more capable of saving the world than we were capable of creating it in the first place.

F N D Buchman

The world that you want to transform in a just manner will not be transformed because you yourselves are not transformed. And so long as you refuse to change yourselves, the world will not change. But the world can change if you change.

How do you change? By listening to God; because, as the sun is always shining, so God is constantly speaking. How do you listen to God? The best time is in the morning, before all distractions and activities intervene. How can you listen to God, you ask me? This is the answer; you write. Write, so that you may better hear the Word that is in you and keep His instructions.

Père Alphonse Gratry, 1805–72
Order of the Oratory, Member of the French Academy

CHAPTER SEVENTEEN

Into Battle

The last chapter in a chronicle such as this must try to answer the direct question of the reader, 'Well, tell us now what *you* really think about the outcome of it all! What are the chances for peace? What are the hopes for the victory of the God-ward forces as against those who want to destroy him?'

Let me therefore be as honest and straight as I can, in return.

First of all I see a world where what I believe to be evil is massing on every frontier in seemingly impregnable and irresistible array. In military terms the capacity of Russia is enormous and growing continually – far beyond the needs of defence. It is hardly questionable that, were it not for the deterrent capacity of the USA, the Soviets could call the tune to the rest of the world.

But that is not all. Vietnam showed how a technological giant can be defeated by ideas and subversion within its own borders. The battle-line does not run between nations any longer, but between forces within nations. The capacity of the anti-God forces to enlist the citizens of their opponent nations in multifarious fronts and specialist causes is a well proven fact. 'Uranium' is a word which has replaced 'Vietnam' in Australia, for example, as a focal point for protest and mob unrest. Its strategic and economic importance is obvious, as well as its dangers of misuse. There are dozens of these movements, all with a lot of good points to make them palatable, which are serving quite different objectives from those of their more genuine protagonists.

The plain fact is that today the seeds of violent revolution are being sown deliberately and skilfully at every level, from Baader Meinhof, PLO or IRA extremists through to school children. Flying pickets congregate at strikes, mobs turn into wreckers at football matches, protesters march on this, that and the other issue, all of which fits into a pattern which TV and films make commonplace today. You can see the red of the blood in your lounge even if you cannot yet feel the adrenalin. The road of anti-law-and-order, of defiance of authority, or demand for 'my own way or else' – this road is deliberately being forced and fomented within our society.

It is perhaps time that some government decided to get the evidence for this skilled and purposeful corruption plain and clear and show the millions who don't want violence the truth about such developments as the seduction of our schoolchildren who no longer fight with fists but want boots and blood.

Then too there is the deliberate fostering of sexual depravity and pornography. Highly suggestive slogans decorate T-shirts in our city stores, the patter of punk rock means a lot more to its devotees than the squares like to think, and those who think that sexual intercourse is for the physical consummation of married love get fewer and fewer. The fact that this permissive road is a tried and proven way to national impotence and decay apparently means little to the leaders of the 'free' world, for it is such a dreadful charge to be accused of being a 'wowser'* or a 'straight' man! They are terrified of the media's ridicule.

There was a time when one could feel that most people on earth would respond in some way to kindness, to real caring, to the innocence of small children, the appeal of a good woman, or the selfless bravery of a man. Today more and more people are being trained to revel in brutalising these things and are being roused to fury by love, peace, unselfishness, innocence and beauty. They lust to destroy, and exult in the destruction.

Again there is the economic factor. Into the laws of supply and demand, the market balances of capitalist society, have come other huge forces who do not operate for profit but for ideological purposes. Lenin made it absolutely clear that his followers would destroy the entire basis of western economics.

We are living in the twilight-days of free enterprise, because greed, organised graft and international banditry on the right are unwitting allies of those of the left who have set the bait and laid the traps for their destruction. The fragility of international exchange rates and the artificial nature of many of the remedies increasingly remind one of a chess game where the rules are remade even as you move.

Technology itself has withdrawn to laugh in the wings as the stage fills with scriptless actors. Mechanisation came in the late eighteenth century and began to raise standards of living while increasing unemployment and lowering the wages of craftsmen. Today the computer takes hold of unbelievably clever and capable machines which are hindered by man rather than helped. A modern warship goes into action with computers in control, for no human brain can react quickly enough to detect, identify and deploy defences against an incoming 'sea-skimmer' missile. More and more ships can be fought with all the controls handled from a central point. Before long it will be possible to send ships on patrol and have them fight each other without any human crew on board at all. The same goes for tanks, aircraft and submarines. Men are getting less and less necessary – and fewer but cleverer men are needed.

So too for industry and for primary production and mining.

* A term used in Australia of a sanctimonious person. [Ed].

But the world's population is leaping ahead as we lower the death-rate and fail to control the birth-rate. So some speak of euthanasia at one end and abortion at the other. Others want zero population growth, but fail to see the pattern its piecemeal imposition will produce. Unemployment figures soar, and the prospects for employment in the old-style economies become fewer.

The prices do not decrease however, because the methods of production are so costly. Modern farming methods, for example, call for massive capital equipment outlay, and need fewer and fewer men and women to work on the land.

So the ranks of the idle increase alarmingly, and who can expect much other than vandalism, violence, drunkenness and worse when the dole often pays better than work even if it were available? Frustration is the foster-mother of untold misery and destruction.

Have I gone on long enough?

These are, quite honestly, only a very few of the living nightmares which can and do project onto the screen of my mind in unguarded hours.

BUT . . . that is far from the whole story.

That is the Goliath side.

Now let me turn to David.

In my heart of hearts I believe that this world is standing on the threshold of one of the most momentous moral and spiritual advances in the history of mankind.

The prophet Isaiah, who had seen more than his share of national and international mayhem and decay, looked ahead to the coming of the Christ and cried to the suffering people of Israel: 'In the wilderness prepare ye the way of the Lord!'

In the wilderness, while the sky is yet dark, prepare for the dawn! That is exactly how I feel about this present time.

Why?

Well, I have looked into the lives of ordinary men and women as well as leaders in many countries and continents and have found unmistakable evidence of the hand of the living God at work. I have seen miracles which defy any appellation of coincidence or chance. I have talked with those who have talked with God. I have seen old barriers smashed into nothingness by a new birth of love, honesty, purity, selflessness and humility. I have seen despair fade before the thrill of hope. I have seen ancient prejudices and hatreds disappear as each has heard the call to tasks requiring their conjoint commitment and has found the other to be a person very like themselves.

There is more courage, more commitment, more adventurous launching out into the unknown today on the part of millions than ever before in history.

There will be and is a fury of opposition. A fanatical response from evil is inevitable. There will be persecution, suffering. The cross once again will be centre stage, but now that persecution, suffering and crucifixion will have the fact and fire of the resurrection experience as part of them.

I am betting my life and lives I cherish far more than my own on this victory. I'm glad I've got children and I have an answer to fear for their future if they hold to the faith.

Human wisdom has failed.

The world they will know will scarcely resemble the world I have known. It will be an increasingly apparent battleground between those who declare the answer to man's problems is to put him in man-made bonds and those who have the secret of liberating him into the glorious freedom of the sons of God.

I have found that God has a plan for every life and for each one of the teeming millions of his earth. I believe that implicitly. I have never found an exception to it. There is not a man alive today who could not be my beloved brother, not a woman who could not win my heart as a sister.

So we go into action.

We fight two wars.

One is personal, we must fight the deadly cancer of self in our own person.

The other is global, for this is our Father's world, and he has handed to us the responsibility to win and hold it for him.

We are told to be as wise as serpents and as harmless as doves. We must be aware of the strategies of those who seek to prepare mankind for slavery. The time may not be far off in many countries where the ideologically committed forces could shut down any newspaper (or cripple it anyway), subvert any TV channel, prevent communications, silence any leader or reduce him to an object of ridicule, stop any kind of production and undermine any currency. They can readily spawn corruption in the churches, mosques and synagogues, produce vast masses of programmeless unemployed. Hatred, fear, guilt and confusion can be sown in the highest places, and the age of silence and submission bred of fear is near at hand.

Human wisdom cannot cope with all this, for it is far more than the product of any one source of ideological initiative. Nothing explains such a canvas to my mind other than the proposition that evil is orchestrated on a global scale in a way inversely similar to that employed by the Spirit of God. I believe evil is at work in a personal and spiritual way.

Only God can defeat the genius of evil strategically and at each point on the battlefront. So we go into action on the one side or the other. There is no possibility of neutrality. 'Those who are not for me are against me', Jesus said. To be a significant individual today we need to discipline ourselves, to fight and live as approaching the end of time, for there will be no Shangri-La or haven of rest until this victory is won.

The plan begins for each one of us with basic change.

It is, as we have seen, a matter of a deliberate experiment – of daring to take successive steps on a wholly new path, in faith. Either we stay forever within the confines of those things which we ourselves can manage, explain and control – that is, within the limits of mere humanity – or we dare to adventure into another kind of living, the realm where evidences of the spirit become as real and necessary as sight, sound, and sense in the material world.

Where do we begin? With our feelings? Do we look for sensation, for excitement, for a sense of awe or some other emotional experience? Hardly. We are not out for a mere spiritual 'trip', much as some people today seem to think that is the hallmark of spirituality. The feelings are most unreliable guides, emotional disturbances and even synthetic developments divorced from reality are a very real danger. Feelings have their place, but only as a by-product.

Then what about the intellect? Well, by very definition, we must go beyond that. We will often not be able to explain or comprehend the new experiences, but at the same time the intellect is a valuable part of our equipment. Nothing which violates our intelligence should be allowed to pass unchallenged, even if we know at times that we must be prepared to pass beyond the usual, the provable and the predictable because of other and deeper imperatives which we have learned to trust.

That leaves the will.

Jesus said, 'If any man would be my disciple he must deny himself and follow after me.'

Deny himself!

That means the whole self. Even to crossing our own will.

'Not my will but thine be done', Jesus prayed in Gethsemane as he faced the hideous prospect of execution.

I can only outline what I have found personally at this point, both for myself, and in trying to help others to discover solid rock beneath their feet as they step out of the old sinking boat and begin to wade to the welcoming shore.

Suppose you, the reader, are now at the place where you quite seriously wish to give the way of the spirit a bigger and wider role, the primary place in your life. What do you do? The great question for each of us as we face the heavens is this, 'Is there someone there or not? If so, how do I meet him?'

Well, first we must find time to be alone.

A N Whitehead once described religion as what man does in his solitariness. It is an inadequate but interesting definition. Jesus advised his friends to go into their private room to pray. You need to be alone, with your real self. Quiet. Unhurried. A constant problem in many a crowded life. Jesus went off alone into lonely places: a mountain, the desert. The 'desert' can even come to us in crowded places as we learn the secret of quietude. It can be behind a newspaper in a busy railway carriage or bus. The quietness before God is what really matters.

Then, if you don't find it immediately apparent who and what you really are, if you can't focus on yourself clearly enough to be able to take your whole 'self' to God, then you may find it helpful to make a conscientious appraisal, to take an unhurried look at yourself in the light of all that you already know of God's hopes and dreams for your life. Forget anyone else and what they think or do at this point. The crucial thing is that you are here and now deliberately entering into the presence of your Creator and you are saying to him, 'I am far from the person you intended me to be' (and all of us have some knowledge of this, bury it though we will). 'I've made a mess of much of my life and I need your help. I need a total overhaul, not just a grease and oil-change. I want renovation, all the defects removed. I need renewal. In human terms I need to be able to begin again as though from the moment of birth.' That's how Jesus described it – as being born again.

If that act of self-realisation and self-surrender to the Recreator is done honestly, evading or rationalising or excusing nothing, then you will soon find unmistakable evidence that God is alive, speaking to you and actively proceeding with you. For example, you may be prepared to be honest enough to commit new insights into yourself to paper, and to note also the new glimpses into the future which follow upon the prospect of renewal, the restitutions, the first steps of the new life which are revealed to you.

Christ asserted, with every ounce of the great authority he possessed,

'Seek and you *shall* find; knock and it *shall* be opened to you . . . *Everyone* who asks will receive . . .'

That is the promise.

For most of us one thing speedily becomes more than apparent, there is at first more often than not a hollow feeling inside at the realisation of steps that must be taken. That is only natural. These are our very first steps outside our old self, with its securities, its conventions, its experiences and its pride.

If the thoughts which enter our minds in this time however, can stand the scrutiny of the highest standards of morality we know, then we should treat them as from God himself. If they square with Christ's standards like honesty, unselfishness, purity and love then they can't lead away from God.

You may feel they ask the impossible. Even that it feels like suicide.

Fine!

That's how it should be. This is miracle territory, you see, and the old self has to die. So the next step is not to discard your new concepts but to ask for help, to ask for the power to do it – thoroughly. You will get it, and later when you look back, you will jump for joy because you will discern the first clear set of footprints tracking beside your own in the dust of the way you have come.

In addition you will soon find several other things have begun to happen:

You will be seeing people and circumstances through different eyes.

You will begin to see possibilities of change and hope where none was likely before.

Fear will begin to shrink.

New friends will emerge who share your new adventure – often people you have never really noticed before.

All *that* can now begin.

The next phase of activity has to do with the development of an inner sense of direction, by learning increasing reliance on the 'still small voice' through daily discipline and practice. Often this is a matter of 'mind over mattress' in order to have time alone with God, to get the course for the day set and the priorities established each morning before other voices intrude. Nothing can take the place of those times of quiet personal encounter which lead to a new and transforming friendship with the living God.

This growing experience is what Jesus came and died and rose again to make possible in all of our lives. The meaning of those mighty events of the risen Christ may always be beyond our comprehension, but one available and vital truth is found in the way Jesus paved the way for his friends to know that he was to be always there, always available, 'nearer than hands or feet'. He was proving that he would always come to them in ways which transcended the 'I and thou' distinctions, the 'self and not-self' limitations of experiences through the physical senses. Spiritual communion is 'closer than breathing' only the actual experience can describe it better.

Thomas was a slow learner in terms of this resurrection experience but when he met Jesus in this new way, not now in the old way of touch, see and hold, but within the pervasive wonder of the new and glorified presence of the risen Christ, he lost all desire to use his hands and used his heart and soul instead. He fell on his knees saying, 'My Lord and my God'. Jesus said, 'Have you believed because you have seen me? Blessed are those who have not seen and yet believe.' Blessed are those who, without the evidence of physical senses, find certainty and transcendent reality in their hearts and spirits. They are alive indeed.

So the new era of eternal life begins. It soon erupts into new and deeper friendships than were ever known before. The desire to propagate this vital experience grows. They are not inward-looking, self-satisfying relationships which emerge, but are more like the comradeship of a fighting unit. The binding force is the unity found in a common commander and a common task, in sharing a vision for a transformed home, industry, community, church, city, nation, world. New cells for effective and revolutionary change emerge as men listen and obey, and find this Friend. A whole new strategy begins to take shape. Soon you too are really in business, so busy that every day and hour is important and precious. There are things in his plan that God can do and disclose to you and only to you. You are at home in your heritage. You have discovered that the Lord of the whole earth is *your* Father, and your eyes open to your true inheritance. What began as merest 'coincidence' has become the daily expectation of a new dimension of living.

Table of References

Chapter 1

1. *The Courier*, No 45, Sept/Oct, 1977, p 10.
2. *Reshaping the International Order*, Hutchison, London, 1976, p 25.
3. ibid, p 26.
4. Dag Hammarskjold Report *What Now*, 1975, p 32.
5. *Reshaping the International Order*, pp 44, 45.
6. op cit p 61.

Chapter 2

1. Dr Berkeley Vaughan, *Doctor in Papua* (The Saint Andrew Press, 1979), p 126.
2. ibid, p 127.
3. ibid, p 132.
4. ibid, pp 132–136.
5. ibid, p 136.
6. ibid, p 139.
7. *The Courier*, No 45, p 10.
8. See pp 15–16
9. I M M Macphail, *A History of Scotland*, Book II, p 85.
10. ibid, p 85.
11. Dr Berkeley Vaughan, *Doctor in Papua*, p 122.
12. ibid, p 124.

Chapter 5

1. See also Leonid Ilyichev in speech to Central Committee of CPSU, 18th June, 1963.

Chapter 7

1. *The Listener*, 25th March, 1976, p 359.
2. *On the Correct Handling of Contradictions . . .*, Feb 27th, 1957, p 18.

Chapter 8

1. Mao Tse-tung, 'Problems of War and Strategy', *Selected Works*, vol III, p 224.
2. ibid, p 219.
3. ibid, p 225.
4. Mao Tse-tung, *Selected Works*, vol III, p 257.
5. op cit vol II, p 198.
6. op cit vol III, p 119.
7. op cit vol IV, pp 424 ff.
8. Dr Ross Terrill, *800 Millions—the Real China*, p 28. Penguin, 1972.
9. Mao Tse-tung, *Selected Works*, vol III, p 322.
10. Quoted in Premier Chou En-lai's Report, Dec 1964.
11. op cit vol II, p 33.

12. Report to Central Committee of CPSU, 1972.
13. Report to 25th Congress of CPSU, 1976.

Chapter 9

1. *The Bulletin*, Sydney, Nov 12th, 1977.

Chapter 10

1. *Brother or Lord?*, Fount paperback, 1977, pp 42–44.

Chapter 11

1. *Soviet Marxism*, (Columbia University Press, 1958), p 232.
2. The Saint Andrew Press published part of this story under the title *Doctor in Papua* by Berkeley Vaughan in 1979.
3. Davidson, A B, *Old Testament Prophecy*, (T & T Clark, Edinburgh), p 2.
4. E F Schumacher, *Small is Beautiful*, (Abacus Press, 1978), pp 30–31. See also Schumacher's *The Age of Plenty*, (The Saint Andrew Press, 1974).

Chapter 12

1. Extract from article in *Free China Weekly Supplement*, Nov 7th, 1976.
2. J A Denton Jr, *When Hell was in Session*, (Reader's Digest Press, New York, 1976), pp 187–189.
3. *The Bulletin*, Sydney, Nov 12th, 1977.

Chapter 13

1. Edith Schaeffer, *L'Abri*, (Norfolk Press, 1969), pp 96–98.
2. op cit pp 112–115.

Chapter 15

1. *Notizen 1950–69 und Dämmerung*, Fischer Verlag Frankfurt, 1974.

Chapter 16

1. See above, p 130.
2. Plato, *The Republic*, Book VIII, p 562 (Cornford).
3. Latourette, *A History of the Expansion of Christianity*, vol I, pp 346–7.
4. Rainy, *The Ancient Catholic Church*, pp 136 ff.
5. ibid.
6. *Commentary on the Gospel of Matthew*, vol I, p 230.